Walter Baier, Cornelia Hildebrandt,
Franz Kronreif, Luisa Sello (Eds.)

Europe as a Common

Europe as a Common

Exploring Transversal Social Ethics

With contributions from:
W. Baier, J. Baquero Maldonado, L. Bekemans,
M. Brie, B. Callebaut, L. Castellina, P. Coda,
Pope Francis, C. Hildebrandt, F. Kronreif, A. Lo Presti,
M. Löwy, A. Mokrani, J. M. Pureza,
P. Steinmair-Pösel, T. Stuke, S. Syropoulos,
P. Tóth, A.V. Zani

Volume I

edited by

Walter Baier, Cornelia Hildebrandt,
Franz Kronreif and Luisa Sello

LIT

Cover photo: INTIME sports&news photo agency, www.intime.gr

This book is printed on acid-free paper.

Bibliographic information published by the Deutsche Nationalbibliothek
The Deutsche Nationalbibliothek lists this publication in the Deutsche Nationalbibliografie; detailed bibliographic data are available in the Internet at http://dnb.dnb.de.

ISBN 978-3-643-91298-5 (pb)
ISBN 978-3-643-96298-0 (PDF)

A catalogue record for this book is available from the British Library.

Flössergasse 10
CH-8001 Zürich
Tel. +41 (0) 76-632 84 35
E-Mail: zuerich@lit-verlag.ch http://www.lit-verlag.ch
Distribution:
In the UK: Global Book Marketing, e-mail: mo@centralbooks.com
In North America: Independent Publishers Group, e-mail: orders@ipgbook.com
In Germany: LIT Verlag Fresnostr. 2, D-48159 Münster
Tel. +49 (0) 2 51-620 32 22, Fax +49 (0) 2 51-922 60 99, e-mail: vertrieb@lit-verlag.de

Content

Preface

This book is dedicated to the dialogue between Christianity and socialism, two movements with very different characteristics, which though long at loggerheads with each other nevertheless together shaped world history in past centuries.

What has changed since the days of intransigent atheism and militant anti-clericalism on the one side and excommunication under the banner of an irreconcilable anti-Marxism on the other side?

One way of answering this would be to pull together positive examples of changed attitudes on both sides and emphasise them. But if we want to be honest we would have to acknowledge that it has always been minorities within each of the two communities that were open to a dialogue, which is why it was always a precarious project.

But dialogue always became significant and possible in the face of misery, deprivation, colonialism, and wars in the 1960s and 70s, opposition to the destruction of the planet through nuclear confrontation at the end of the 1970s and beginning of the 1980s, the devastating consequences of globalisation as discussed in the Social Forums at the beginning of the 2000s especially in Latin America, and today in the struggles for a humane approach to refugees or to the world's limited resources in the face of climate change.

And there was always need of concrete, credible proposals and of partners ready for such a dialogue, in order to tackle the fundamental problems of a changing world. From the beginning of his pontificate Pope Francis has been describing the dangers of catastrophic escalations that have become even more evident in 2020 under the burning glass of the Corona crisis, resulting from an economy that kills, a globalisation of profit and indifference, and, with climate change, the destruction of Creation.

In his Encyclical *Laudato Si'* Francis urgently appeals 'for a new dialogue about how we are shaping the future of our planet. We need a conversation which includes everyone, since the environmental challenge we are undergoing, and its human roots, concern and affect us all.' (LS 14)[1]

Laudato Si' can be understood as a large-scale and urgent invitation to a dialogue, an invitation that Francis explicitly directs at all people, Petra Steinmair-Pösel writes in her recently published essay on the significance of dialogue and social ethics in Pope Francis's theology.[2]

In his efforts to foster a dialogue among all people of good will, the Pontiff recalls the spirit of the Second Vatican Council in the very beginning of his Encyclical: 'More than fifty years ago, with the world teetering on the brink of nuclear crisis, Pope Saint John XXIII wrote an Encyclical which not only rejected war but offered a proposal for peace. He addressed his message *Pacem in Terris* to the entire 'Catholic world' and indeed 'to all men and women of good will'.' (LS 3)

The issue is as burning today as it ever was: an acute danger threatening humanity understood as a community, but which ought not to throw us into panic and fatalism, instead challenging us to make a great and common effort to shape the world for the better.

During the September 2014 private audience that Pope Francis granted to the two left politicians Alexis Tsipras and Walter Baier as well as Franz Kronreif of the Focolare Movement he presented freshly printed copies of *Evangelii Gaudium*, and so the more than 30-minute conversation focused, among other things, on the environmental crisis and the worldwide social crisis; it ended with Francis's call to us to launch a transversal dialogue capable of involving the broadest strata of society and above all of the youth. This was the moment in which the idea of the initiative arose, which we called 'RESET – transversal social ethics'.

It is this dialogue about which we would like to give an account in this book.

That Christianity not only provides an ethical orientation but gives meaning to the life of believers through belief in a Trinitarian God does not need to be demonstrated here. What is more difficult to understand is that

---

1 Encyclical Letter *Laudato Si'* of Pope Francis on Care for Our Common Home.

2 Petra Steinmair-Pösel, 'Ein Wort, das wir bis zur Erschöpfung wiederholen müssen' in: Klissenbauer, I. et al. (eds.), (2020), p. 143.

socialism, although it is not a substitute religion, certainly has the 'quality of a conviction' whose intensity the Protestant theologian Paul Tillich described as a 'condition of being gripped by an imperative concern that makes all others merely preliminary'.[3]

The road to dialogue was a long one on the Marxist side as well. The theory founded by Marx, as it was represented by the social democratic and later communist parties, at first positioned itself in an apparently unbridgeable antagonism to the Christian churches. For the working classes toiling in the misery of industrialisation it was hard to recognise the salvific dimension of the Gospel because they perceived the ecclesiastical hierarchies as allies of the rulers. But the leaders of the socialist and communist parties who invoked Karl Marx, on their part, overlooked the most important aspect of his critique of religion, that is, that it 'ends with the teaching that *man is the highest being for man,* hence, with the *categorical imperative to overthrow all relations* in which man is a debased, enslaved, forsaken, despicable thing.'(Marx K. 1975, p. 182)

While the mainstream of the social democratic wing of the labour movement moved away from the original radical critique of capitalist society and sought to realise its goals in the framework of capitalist societies, the communist wing counted on overcoming capitalism through the seizure of power by revolutionary means. The establishment of one-party regimes under state socialism and the intolerance this brought with it could not be acceptable to the churches.

Seen from a historical distance, it is safe to say that the battle for people's souls expressed by this antagonism did not bring out the most positive traits of either side, and it certainly was not suited to motivate them to mutually respectful cooperation in the project of liberating the oppressed and exploited.

We have spoken of the changes occurring, for some time now, within the Catholic Church for some time. The extent to which the situation changed in the course of the twentieth century on the Marxist side as well can be gauged by the fact that in the encyclopaedic *Historisch-Kritisches Wörterbuch des Marxismus* (Historical-Critical Dictionary of Marxism) edited by Wolfgang Fritz and Frigga Haug along with 500 scholars there

[3] Tillich, P. (1964); quoted here from Kroll T. (2007), p. 10.

are no less than four entries on the Christianity/Marxism relationship, one of them entitled 'Christian-Marxist dialogue'.[4]

Politically, the attitude of the communist-dominated mainstream of Marxists began to shift with Stalin's death and the thaw ushered in by the CPSU's Twentieth Party Congress. In the face of the threat to civilisation represented by nuclear war, Marxist theorists – Ernst Bloch, Roger Garaudy, Lucio Lombardo Radice, and others – used the possibilities opened up by the Second Vatican Council.

After the crushing of the Prague Spring by the Warsaw Pact countries the ideological conflict hardened again. Paradoxically, the military and political détente of East-West relations in the 1970s did not lead to an intensification of the dialogue but to its dormancy. The common resistance to the stationing of medium-range missiles in Europe at the beginning of the 1980s indeed united leftists and Christians through common action but generated no new dialogue.

With the fall of the Communist dictatorships in Eastern Europe, Communists were obliged to face up to the collapse of their projects and measure the reality they had created against the ideal for which they originally joined the struggle. Christians had to recognise how much the worldwide triumphal march of neoliberal capitalism itself threatened human rights and the natural environment. In his Encyclical *Centesimus Annus*, on the centenary of the first social Encyclical *Rerum novarum*, Pope John Paul II thus warned of the 'risk that a radical capitalistic ideology could spread which refuses even to consider these problems [i.e., the situations of great material and moral immiseration], in the *a priori* belief that any attempt to solve them is doomed to failure, and which blindly entrusts their solution to the free development of market forces'. (CA 42)

A broader and international dialogue emerged in the framework of the World Social Forums, the first of which, in Porto Alegre (Brazil) took place

---

4 The articles are 'Christen für den Sozialismus', 'Christentum und Sozialismus', 'Christlicher Sozialismus' und 'christlich-marxistischer Dialog', in: Haug W. F., Haug F. et al. (Eds.) (1995). pp. 487 – 504. Moreover, references are found in several other entries, among them 'Menschenwürde' (human dignity) and 'Menschlichkeit' (humaneness). By contrast, the 'canonic' *Marxistisch-Leninistische Wörterbuch der Philosophie* (edited by Georg Klaus and Manfred Buhr), first published in 1964 in the GDR and then in 1972 in the West, had no entry for 'Christentum', which naturally made unnecessary one on a Christian-Marxist dialogue.

in the Pontifícia Universidade Católica do Rio Grande do Sul, in which alternatives to neoliberal globalisation were sought.

At this point we need to remark that the predominantly European authors of this volume are aware what importance the non-European impulses, especially those from Latin America, have for the revival of the dialogue in Europe, something that is embodied in the person of Pope Francis.

We are carrying on this dialogue not with the purpose of mutual conversion, or of producing a syncretism, but in respect for diverse outlooks. A serious dialogue is not a simple or formal exercise but a process of searching for what is common while being aware of fundamental differences. This is seen in the discussion on the role of women where we come up against institutional barriers and fundamental questions. Here we are challenged to listen to our partners in dialogue even if they speak something which is unutterable from one's own standpoint. Thus Christians insist on extending the protection of life to the embryo in the mother's womb, while Marxists insist that the right of women to self-determination takes precedence here.

Under changed circumstances – both for the churches as well as for the left – a small band of steadfast people are attempting to take up the threads of this conversation. On the left side there is the think tank connected to the Party of the European Left, transform!, whose statues read: 'The purpose of the Association is the promotion of alternative thinking and political dialogue aimed at transforming the current societies to develop a common social, feminist, ecological, democratic and peaceful Europe and global solidarity.'[5]

On the Christian side, Pope Francis, during the meeting with Tsipras and Baier on September 2014, stressed that in the face of the current difficulties and dangers in the world, all people of good will must unite, independent of their philosophies, their religions and their practical and theoretical approaches, to find ways out of the crisis.[6] Both transversality and a dialogue across the traditional dividing lines are requested.

This book is a report on questions which we have been discussing in the Christian Marxist symposia and a one-week summer school (2018) since the historic encounter with Pope Francis. We intend it for all people who are

---

5 https://www.transform-network.net/fileadmin/user_upload/articles_of_association_mm17.pdf

6 See also the Pope Francis's Apostolic Exhortation *Evangelii Gaudium (EG)*, 236.

interested in the complex problems of contemporary globalisation and in how these can be understood from different perspectives. The book brings together authors from Austria, Belgium, France, Greece, Hungary, Italy, Portugal, Tunisia, and the Vatican.

A feature of this dialogue is that it is especially aimed at young people. The texts constitute a first provisional basis for a university curriculum whose development has up to now been supported by four universities – in Portugal (Coimbra), Spain (UNED), Austria (Innsbruck), and Italy (Sophia/Florence). Franz Kronreif provides more details in his contribution to the first part of this volume.

The book in detail

The essays are grouped in four chapters:

The first part presents the participants' diverse points of departure or entry. Franz Kronreif suggests how a dialogue not limited to method and techniques of communication, but having to do with styles of thinking and living, becomes transformative and can lead to a 'differentiated consensus' in questions that have up to now tended to separate people.

He is followed by Walter Baier who in a tour d'horizon through the world of Marxist concepts attempts to trace affinities with Pope Francis's theology.

This section closes with a contribution by archbishop Angelo Vincenzo Zani, Secretary of the Congregation for Catholic Education. In his message to the participants of the 2018 Syros Summer School he emphasised that all people constitute a single community of fate with one another and with the earth.

The second section contains theoretical reflections on the methodology of performative-transformative dialogue.

In his contribution, the Founding Rector of Sophia University, Piero Coda, sees Christ as not having redeemed only the human individual but also his or her social relations. On this he bases his appeal for non-violent thinking.

Bernhard Callebaut indicates how the road already travelled by the current project has already left its traces in Sophia University and demonstrates that 'unity' – not uniformity – can be achieved precisely within 'plurality'.

Thomas Stuke treats the theoretical framework of the dialogue between 'others' and distils attitudinal features as well as methodologies of this specific form of communication, situating them within the matrix 'debate – decision – discussion – dialogue'.

With their jointly authored essay 'Naming the World in Order to Change It', a Marxist and a Christian, Cornelia Hildebrandt and Pál Tóth, engage in dialogue and formulate the demand that instead of being conducted as 'l'art pour l'art' the dialogue be aimed at common practice as the goal.

The 2007/2008 financial crisis and the arrival of the refugees have changed Europe. It is true that Europe is not identical with the European Union. But the EU is at the core of many European problems and therefore also of its possible solutions. The urgent need to rethink Europe and the EU was again highlighted by the Covid-19 crisis and its social and ecological effects.

The European Union as a community of values founded after the Second World War is in crisis, Léonce Bekemans shows. If Europe wants to respond adequately to the global challenges and to the newly emerging world order, it needs a strengthened, open-ended vision and a new forward-looking storyline.

If Greece is rightly regarded as the prototype of democracy, although it was built on the basis of a slave-holding society, Spyros Siropoulos presents the empire of Alexander the Great as the prototype of all succeeding empires. Alexander's most progressive idea was to have realised that there needed to be social and national integration of numerous cultures. It is clear that this model of rule was applied by the great empires of Rome, the United States of American, and Europe, in that order.

Michael Löwy assumes a relationship of tension between capitalism and liberal, parliamentary democracy. The decline of democracy is particularly visible in the oligarchic functioning of the European Union, where the European Parliament has very little influence, while power is firmly in the hands of non-elected bodies such as the European Commission or the European Central Bank.

Luciana Castellina, from the perspective of a passionate Europeanist, confirms Löwy's criticism of the present state of the integration process and calls for political initiatives to change its course.

Adnane Mokrani opens a window onto Islamic theology and spirituality, which constitutes a part of Europe, and makes clear the different tasks of religion and politics.

The question of democracy from a Christian perspective is taken up by Alberto Lo Presti who points to the new challenges to democracy, such as pluralism and globalisation.

The fourth and last section of the book consists of essays on the future and the dialogue participants' shared values. It opens with an essay by Walter Baier who, from a Marxist socialist perspective, attempts a balance sheet of the current global and European crisis, from which he derives an orientation for an alternative.

He is followed by Petra Steinmair-Pösel and Michael Brie in their joint article on the concept 'commons' and its meaning from a socialist and Christian perspective.

The text 'How to Transform Problems Into Solutions' was written jointly by all participants in the summer school in Ermoupoli (Syros).

The volume is rounded off by José Manuel Pureza's article 'Three Challenges to Deepen the Dialogue'. Starting with Francis's statement, Pureza names three obstacles to the necessary individual and collective liberation: 'alienation, individualism, and deficient spirituality' – and the answers to them – critical thinking, solidarity and liberating spirituality – are as undeniable challenges to the new steps of dialogue between Marxists and Christians.

The RESET university course

And, finally, we would like to outline the basic features of the RESET university course, which can provide a general outlook.

RESET's innovative methodology based on transversal and critical examination of two opposite traditions (Socialism and Christianity) aims to pull people out of their bubbles in order to find common ground. More than ever now the EU needs a strong Community-building foundation whose core is a shared social ethics. Grounded in social philosophy and state and economic theory, transversal social ethics needs to be reflected in the goals of the social behaviour, that is, in the relationship of individuals to community and society as well as the structures of coexistence.

Marxism and Christianity will be addressed with their long histories of social theory and social ethics. Their dialogue is particularly exciting in view of the long historical period in which they faced each other as fundamentally antagonistic.

Our ambition is therefore to achieve a critical reading of the social ethics inherent in the traditions of Christianity and socialism both of them, embracing feminist and ecological views with a window on Islam and other cultures and traditions.

In fact the crisis of the ecologic system as well as Covid-19 demonstrate the necessity of rebalancing the relationship between economics and ethics in the different ideological traditions. Any agreement on new social ethics must be transversal in the sense that it embraces different cultures and philosophical and religious traditions. This requires more knowledge of the different ethical systems as well as appropriate techniques of dialogue, especially relevant for the young generation who will have to cope with unprecedented challenges. Still today, Christianity and socialism are two of the most important cultural trends – having spread globally and contributed to the shaping of the contemporary world. We will revisit these cultural trends, taking critical stock of their achievements and failures. We do not conceive this as an exercise for its own sake but as an attempt to get the two traditions to 'talk' to each other. The goal is to identify a set of notions in a common language of social ethics, which would enable communication between the different philosophical and cultural communities in order to design common strategies. We call the method 'differentiated consensus'; it can only work through a 'kenotic dialogue', which means the opposite of either ruthlessness or intellectual backscratching. In this framework young people play a key role. Young people generally endorse inter-European cooperation. However, this positive attitude must be nurtured and developed so that it grows alongside a higher level of civic knowledge, as the lack of clear ethics undermines the future of Europe and the world.

The main goal of RESET is to pave the way to a pan-European social-ethics system based on an innovative transversal approach, looking at critically examined diverse traditions of thought and establishing a widely accepted common ground.

At this point we would like to thank all our friends at transform! europe, the Congregation for Catholic Education at the Vatican, the former rector of the University Sophia, our friends at Sophia and every expert, scholar, or interested person who have been accompanying the project since its very inception with great energy and personal dedication. A special mention goes to Javier Baquero Maldonado, a young Columbian professor of political science at Sophia University who coordinated the data and the collection of the single essays for this first publication.

8 May 2020 – 75th anniversary of the end of the Second World War

the editors:

Walter Baier

Cornelia Hildebrandt

Franz Kronreif

Luisa Sello

PICTURES OF

DIALOP

TRANSVERSAL DIALOGUE PROJECT

Roots of the DIALOP – transversal dialogue project:
The chairman of the Austrian Communist Party Walter Baier meets the founder of the Focolare Movement Chiara Lubich in Vienna in November 2001.

Walter Baier and Marga Ferré (Izquierda Unida) at a joint event of transform!europe and the Focolare Movement in January 2011 as part of the World Social Forum in Dakar / Senegal.

After the memorable meeting between Alexis Tsipras, Walter Baier and Pope Francis on September 18th, 2014, the then launched DIALOP initiative held **four symposia** with Christian and socialist experts at the Sophia University Institute near Florence, Castelgandolfo near Rome and in Vienna.

Impressions of the **Syros Summer School** in September 2018

DIALOP
truth equality social-justice human-dignity
dialogue
summer-school
challenge Greece
politics
civilization
Europe´s wealth:
opportunity and challenge
democracy
transversality
respect
Europe
DIALOP
DIALOP

contexte
background
cefndir
fundal
bakgrund
taust
tle
hintergrund
sfondo
háttér
pozadinu

BACKGROUNDS
AND
STARTING POINTS

Towards a 'Differentiated Consensus'

Border Crossing to Unexpected Alliances

Franz Kronreif[7]

Human we were counted once, perhaps,
Or one far-off day we may be so
When we've found an answer to these traps;
But, here and now, to call us human? No.

We're just a name that's written on a pass,
A dumb reflection in a looking glass,
The echo of what once was finely said,
The rumour of a rumour that's long dead.

What was human long ago stamped out –
Why should we up the empty show?
In our faceless cities swirled about
Shall we still pretend we're human? No.

We are the dust that's blown from lamp to lamp,
The queue that waits for the official stamp,
The number in a bureaucratic file,
And our own shadows could not be more vile.

A poor half-finished sketch is all we are
A glimpse of humans in their finished state,
A tune suggested by the opening bar –
You call us wretches human being? Wait!

Song of the human

Poem by Jura Soyfer, translated by John Lehmann

---

7 Austrian architect and theologian. He started in the late nineties a structured Marxist-Christian dialogue together with Walter Baier and other comrades in Vienna. He is part of the coordination team of DIALOP and a member of the international Focolare Movement.

By 1998, several years had already passed since Karl Rahner's dialogue took place with Marxists such as Roger Garaudy. When there did not appear to be sufficient grounds for Christians to engage with Marxism and communism after the end of the Soviet Union, regular dialogue between the Austrian Communist Party (KPOe) and the Focolare Movement started in Vienna on common themes: the beginning of a journey to an unknown destination.

Nine years later in the spring of 2007, the former leader of the Austrian Communist Party (KPOe), now the coordinator of Transform! Europe – the think tank of the Party of the European Left – summed up his experience in these words, 'We have built a stable foundation of trust. We are open to each other without illusions. [. . .] An active humanism must always be accompanied by discussing the motivations. Love is undoubtedly the peculiar contribution of Christianity to human coexistence. [. . .] I, therefore, propose an initiative aspiring to redefine the relationship between Christianity and Marxism. It should focus on answering the question of what we, people gifted with ethics and morality, have in common; we start with a dialogue of life to ensure proximity to reality'[8]. The founder of the Focolare movement, Chiara Lubich, immediately replied calling for 'a redefinition of the relationship between Christianity and Marxism'[9].

On September 18, 2014, I witnessed the conversation between Pope Francis, the future Greek Prime Minister, Alexis Tsipras and Walter Baier. The pontiff declared that war, poverty, the environmental crisis and the resultant migratory flows were issues too serious to be resolved by a single force, including the Catholic Church. He considered transversal dialogue among people of goodwill as the only way forward, crossing the fences of their respective visions of the world.

A joint project was thus launched: DIALOP – a transversal dialogue project. While Baier is the coordinator of transform!europe, the Secretary of the Congregation for Catholic Education, Archbishop Vincenzo Zani, was appointed interlocutor by the Vatican. In 2016, the guidelines to regulate the dialogue's conduct were drafted together, followed by three symposia of experts, that culminated in a Christian-Marxist Summer School, 'Europe as a Common – let's think about it', on the Greek island of Sy-

8 F. Kronreif et al., Personal communication with C. Lubich, 6. April 2007

9 C. Lubich, Personal communication with F. Kronreif et al., 27. April 2007

ros in September 2018. Fifty-four professionals and students from nineteen countries, mostly Europeans, spent a fruitful week together, working successfully towards building bridges among generations, cultures and world views. Rigorous self-criticism of some weak points did not discourage the steering team from considering the possibility of further study and extension of their experience, however.

RESET – an experiment of transversal social ethics

The project is represented by the acronym RESET – which is 'tRansvErsal Social Ethics'. Social ethics has become the obvious focal point of the project. Together with some universities from different European countries as partners, it has been decided to continue addressing the relevant themes with a double approach: the Catholic social doctrine's viewpoint guided by Laudato Sí and the neo-Marxist critical social theory of the School of Frankfurt. It should be mentioned that it is not difficult to reach a basic consensus considering the topics; the summary of the 'Compendium of the Social Doctrine of the Church' is widely shared by the Left. And yet, those in the know come across significant conflicting issues when analyzing the texts.

Nevertheless, the project is gradually beginning to emerge and take shape. In a propaedeutic phase, the Marxist experts will introduce the basic ideas of today's Marxism while Catholic theologians will unveil some basic knowledge of Christianity to non-Christians, followed by a presentation on the specific path of dialogue, which is the soul of the whole project. The question, 'What is man?' will form the prelude to real social ethics. It will not only be addressed during the conferences and discussions by the socialist and Christian experts, but the students are also invited to reflect on it throughout the future two-week summer school. The result will be presented to the European Parliament and published in a new series in English, edited by a German publisher. There will be two approaches to social ethics: the ecological encyclical of Pope Francis, *Laudato Si* ', and Walter Benjamin's thesis, 'On the Concept of History'.

We believe that this dialogue is likely to open unexplored horizons. Drawing inspiration from the *Differentiated Consensus* which formed the basis for the rapprochement of the Catholic Church and the Lutheran World Federation, making possible the formulation of the *Joint Declaration on*

Justification, signed in Augsburg in 1999, social ethics is also expected to undergo an analogous experiment to achieve a shared transversal social ethics despite completely different conditions. Although we are exploring a completely new realm, the experience made so far gives us reason for hope.

Through dialogue toward 'differentiated consensus'

The fundamental declarations on 'humanity, society, world', formulated unequivocally through the Differentiated Consensus Method, must form a solid basis to allow the partners to speak and act together, at the service of men and women in society. The common fundamental assertions must refer explicitly to authoritative texts in order to be compatible with the respective traditions of the Catholic Church and that of the Left of transform!europe.

How is the project arranged for this experiment?

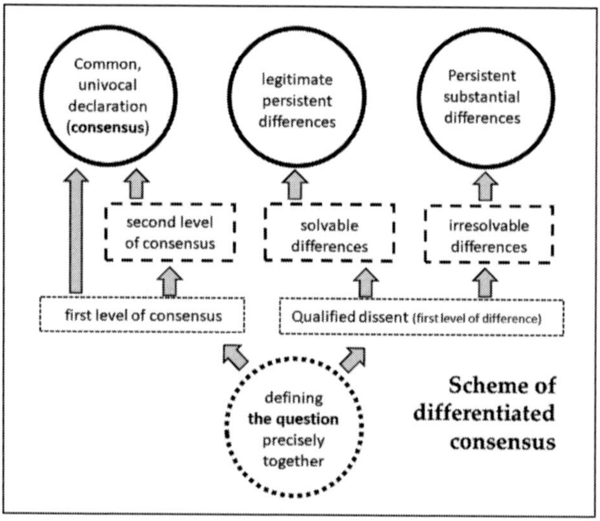

First of all, it focuses on defining the question with precision. In a dialogical process moreover, the interlocutors' respective approaches and positions are presented to other partners and received by them with maximum openness. All participants try to see reality through the eyes of the 'different' interlocutors. At this point, a process for clarification follows which lasts until each participant understands the vision of the other in depth and can reproduce it with his or her own words. The search for a common univocal declaration can be initiated from here, reflecting one's own tradition, while being enriched by the other party.

Certainly, there are going to be various types of differences. If significant differences undermine a coherent fundamental declaration they must be clarified until they can fall into a second category, the legitimate divergent interpretations of the joint declaration. These do not endanger the common core, but rather enrich it. Even these *legitimate persistent differences* will be formulated and accepted by both parties.

Furthermore, the points on which a differentiated consensus has not (yet) been possible, will not be hidden. Persistent and substantial differences – the third category – must neither be erased nor simply maintained, in the sense of leaving them unaltered. Instead, these fundamental differences will remain open and considered to be valuable.

Why does RESET apply differentiated consensus?

Truth and reality are both complex and complementary. This has been recognized not only by the discovery of the wave-particle property of quantum physics but also ever since Nicholas of Cusa wrote the *Coincidentia Oppositorum*.

There is a hierarchy of truths; beyond that, there is also a fundamental difficulty in phrasing any expression of truth.

Language – as the house of being (Heidegger) – is a limited human experience therefore, since a linguistic expression rarely portrays reality in its entirety. Mankind looks at the world as though through a window. The position and extent of the view may vary from observer to observer. In addition, the reality can be seen from different angles, and there is finally the background horizon that influences perception. Joseph Ratzinger/Benedict XVI expresses this phenomenon, 'If a man's mind acquires something as it is, then man has found the truth. But only a small part of what is real – not the truth in all its dimensions and as a whole.' (Ratzinger, 2011, p. 215).

The differentiated consensus is meant to connect one's personal horizon with that of others, resulting in its expansion. It yearns to experience unknown perspectives and to integrate the limited vision of a personal linguistic perception of reality with that of others. To arrive at a common statement of the facts in their essence – in which one's own knowledge does not succumb to an imposition, but is dissolved into a greater knowledge – the explicit will of both the sides is necessary – the will to engage in a dialogue that is kenotic in attitude and transformative in its result.

An in-depth dialogue is kenotic and transformative

Over the years a common path of dialogue has emerged, which has the strength to change people, perceptions and facts. This form of dialogue is not only an instrument but a constant encounter therefore, a journey of common intellectual and spiritual experience in which the peculiarity of the respective partners does not vanish but becomes clearer; it unfolds and develops. In this sense, opposites become complementary. Recognizing this does not necessarily lead to trivial pluralism or indifferent tolerance but to treating the position of the other so that polarity occurs without polarization.

Dialogue thus turns into an existential process in which the participants put their humanity into play. It can be applied to what Jacques Derrida describes with the concept of hospitality. 'So it is indeed the master, the one who invites, the inviting host, who becomes the hostage – and who really always has been. And the guest, the invited hostage, becomes the one who invites the one who invites, the master of the house. The guest becomes the host's host. The guest (*hôte*) becomes the host (*hôte*) of the host (*hôte*). These substitutions make everyone into everyone else's hostage.' (Derrida, 2011, p. 123). Hospitality, therefore, means losing one's house. Paul pushes this loss to the extreme in the hymn of the letter to the Philippians: Christ 'loses' divinity in his kenosis in order to be a man among men.

In earthly conditions therefore, Jesus of Nazareth explains losing and finding in these words, 'A new commandment I give to you, that you love one another: just as I have loved you, you also are to love one another.' (John 13: 34) and 'This is my commandment, that you love one another as I have loved you. Greater love has no one than this, that someone lay down his life for his friends. You are my friends if you do what I command you.' (John 15: 12-14). There is no surprise for Christians as far as this goes.

Who would think though that a piece of Karl Marx's early writings could be similar to this? In his Parisian manuscripts of 1844, he writes, 'Assuming human beings as human beings and their relationship to the world as human beings, you can only exchange love for love, trust only for trust etc. [...] If you love without provoking mutual love, that is, if your loving does not produce Love, if you – by expressing your life as a loving person – do not make yourself a loved one, then your love is powerless, a misfortune' (Marx, 1953, p. 301). Also, in his essay for the school-leaving examination in 1835 Marx writes, 'History calls those men the greatest who have ennobled themselves by working for the common good; experience acclaims as happiest the man who has made the greatest number of people happy. Religion itself teaches us that the ideal being whom all strive to copy sacrificed himself for the sake of mankind, and who would dare to set at nought such judgments?' (Marx, 1953, p. 301).

These words of Jesus and Marx to this point converge in the same direction. John's Gospel indicates the goal to which mutual love leads according to the standard set by Jesus. Addressing the Father, Jesus says, 'The glory that you have given me I have given to them, that they may be one even as we are one, I in them and you in me, that they may become perfectly one, ... ' (John 17: 22f).

This can be linked to what Matthew 18:20 proclaims, 'For where two or three are gathered in my name, there am I among them.' In this verse, the verb '*symphonein*' suggests an agreement – the unity mentioned in the Gospel of John, unity based on mutual love without any conditions. Bishop Klaus Hemmerle writes, 'the communion, unity with one another [rises from here], which creates space for the living Lord to manifest himself and to communicate' (Hemmerle, n.d). The communion created by mutual love is the widest possible access to a vital and palpable encounter with the Risen Lord. But a question arises here: Are even those who do not profess Christ entitled to such a tangible encounter with him? St John Paul II says, 'By dialogue we let God be present in our midst; for as we open ourselves in dialogue to one another, we also open ourselves to God.'[10] For Chiara Lubich, this presence of 'the Risen" opens the possibility for Christ to emerge from the tabernacle and enter the mundane everyday world in a certain sense, as the sacrament of the laity (Lubich, 2019, p. 145). The community becomes a divine place where the mystical presence of the Lord can be experienced therefore. (John Paul II, 1996 quoted by Francis 2018, p. 142)

[10] With reference to his speech to the members of other religions, Madras, 5 February 1986, n. 4: Incisivo IX/1, 1986, S. 322f. English: http://www.vatican.va/content/john-paul-ii/en/audiences/1998/documents/hf_jp-ii_aud_09091998.html

It is a fact that in this atmosphere of encounter with Christ, ample common space is discovered for real or presumed extremes. A *'communio oppositorum'* comes about unexpectedly. The participants are no longer themselves in this dialogue. The presence of Christ brings with him the gifts of the Spirit which renews the face of the earth. From this we hope that the resultant social ethics could draw a temporary, perhaps 'half-finished sketch' (see Jura Soyfer's poem) of the Kingdom for which Christians pray in the Lord's Prayer. At this point the dialogue becomes transformative and performative.

What kind of transformation?

One question still remains unanswered. Why did DIALOP – transversal dialogue project – start as a Christian-Marxian dialogue? I will try to answer this from the Christian point of view.

Marxism is not only one of the various expressions of secularity, but it is also one of the most studied and consistent; it has strongly marked the course of recent history. This is true in spite of its contradictions, deviations and even the atrocities with which it is associated. Similar discrepancies can be attributed to Christianity as well nevertheless. Communism has been one of the most avid opponents to the Catholic Church for more than a century, at least in certain regions of the world. If these two approaches, which seem so divergent, enter into dialogue now, they will open up a vast realm where other approaches will be able to enter afterwards. The need to bridge the – sometimes great – distance between different starting points promotes critical and even self-critical thinking to be able to accept different thoughts without prejudice and precaution.

This transversal social ethic approach is meant to produce a radical transformation that goes to the root of the problems. It does not look for scapegoats on which to load one's fears. Instead of diversionary manoeuvres, this dialogue seeks real solutions, which is why the project also includes (Critical) Service Learning, which overcomes monolithic solutions and starts reflection processes taking the political context into account.

RESET welcomes Pope Francis's message of 12 September 2019, when he launched the educational pact extending an invitation to 'boldly undertake processes of change and look to the future with hope.' We need to find 'other ways of envisioning economics, politics, growth and progress.

In the development of integral ecology, a central place must be given to the value proper to each creature in its relationship to the people and realities surrounding it, as well as a lifestyle that rejects the throw-away culture.' It is hoped that this project will contribute to that educational path which is a precondition for every transformation and underlines what is referred to as universities' third mission: In addition to research and teaching this also includes a commitment to build – with dialogue and with the strength of goodwill – a more just, supportive, fraternal and welcoming society.

Socialism and Community

From a Socialist Perspective

Walter Baier

I.

The social and cultural rise of the European working class is a chapter in the progress of humanity. It is inseparable from the growth of the socialist movement.

The shortening of the working day, the prohibition of child labour, the protection of workers in old age and in the event of unemployment, illness, or accident, and the right to paid vacations – all this, far from being voluntarily granted by the owners of the means of production, had to be wrested from them against their fierce resistance.

The Encyclical *Rerum Novarum* issued in 1891 by Pope Leo XIII has to be understood in the context of the broad class struggles extending to the entire capitalist world of that time. True, the Pope's message was far from being a declaration of love for socialism; however, and this is important, it embraced the dignity of workers, thus becoming – perhaps even unintentionally – the starting point of a dialogue between socialism and the church.

Considering the progress, the labour movement brought about, it is interesting that the welfare state, its major achievement in the twentieth century, was not its ultimate goal from the outset; its goal was socialism. Thus, it came into being as a compromise between the revolution advocated by socialists and the existing capitalism, defended by the conservatives, among them most of the official church.

The fact that such a compromise was possible is the result of the second great victory won by the socialist movement – universal, equal suffrage through secret ballot, first covering all men, and then only at the end of the First World War, won by women.

It is well to keep in mind the nexus between welfare state and democracy, since with neoliberalism's dismantling of the former the foundations of the latter are being undermined.

Socialism's encounter with power has brought to light its dark side – a tendency towards authoritarian, even terrorist, rule. It is useless to argue about how many millions of people were unlawfully convicted or died in the gulags, and how many victims of famines and civil wars were attributable to one side or the other.

I cite the case of the Communist Party of Austria (KPÖ) as an example, because I am personally close to it and also because belated knowledge of the fate of Austrian victims of Stalinism has permanently altered my understanding of socialism. As the archives of NKVD were opened in the wake of perestroika, a reality that had burdened and indeed compromised this small party for decades became an empirical fact: 320 Austrians, this is a third of the anti-fascist émigrés to the Soviet Union, former Social Democrats, Communists, ordinary members as well as party leaders, fell victim to the Stalinist terror. Not more than a 'tear in the ocean' (Manes Sperber 1988).

Although we cannot say that most of the victims of Stalinism were communists, it is important to realise that the most deadly persecution communists ever suffered in a history full of persecutions took place under Stalin's dictatorship in the Soviet Union. (Baier W.; Muhri F. 2001, p. 9)

Therefore in the preface to a short book in which the names and brief biographies of the victims of our Party were collectively published I asked how one could remain a socialist or communist in light of these facts, unless one e radically and auto-critically rethought both, theory and practice . . .

II.

The centenary of the encyclical *Rerum Novarum* coincided with the collapse of the actually existing socialist states in Eastern Europe and the end of the Soviet Union. Pope John Paul II undertook to interpret this world-historical upheaval in the Encyclical *Centesimus Annus* . . .

Although the keynote of the Encyclical is the fundamental rejection of Marxism, in it the Pope raises a concern that in effect points to the relevance of Marx's critique of political economy:

Can it perhaps be said that, after the failure of Communism, capitalism is the victorious social system, and that capitalism should be the goal of the countries now making efforts to rebuild their economy and society?

[...]

The answer is obviously complex. If by 'capitalism' is meant a system in which freedom in the economic sector is not circumscribed within a strong juridical framework which places it at the service of human freedom in its totality, and which sees it as a particular aspect of that freedom, the core of which is ethical and religious, then the reply is certainly negative. (CA 42)

What can Marxian socialists learn from this ambiguity?

John Paul II, draws advisedly on the 'condemnation' of class struggle in *Rerum novarum*, that is, the rejection of 'the idea that conflict is not restrained by ethical or juridical considerations, or by respect for the dignity of others (and consequently of oneself); a reasonable compromise is thus excluded, and what is pursued is not the general good of society, but a partisan interest which replaces the common good and sets out to destroy whatever stands in its way'. (CA 14)

No enlightened socialist could identify with this description. Is this a misunderstanding or is the Pope holding up a mirror to one of the political tendencies that invoke Marx?

How did Marx himself come up with the idea of class struggle? His 'Introduction' to the *Crtitique of Hegel's Philosphy of Right* documents the evolution of his thought in this regard. The most famous passage from this text is:

To be radical is to grasp the root of the matter. But for man the root is man himself [...] The criticism of religion ends with the teaching that *man is the highest being for man,* hence, with the *categorical imperative to overthrow all relations* in which man is a debased, enslaved, forsaken, despicable thing. (Marx K. 1975, p. 182)

However, this categorical imperative raises a question which Marx explicitly asked:

Where, then, is the positive possibility of [a German] emancipation?

Answer: In the formation of a class with radical chains, a class of civil society which is not a class of civil society, an estate which is the dissolution of all estates [...] which does not stand in any onesided antithesis to the consequences but in an all-round antithesis to the premises of the German state; a sphere, finally, which cannot emancipate itself without emancipating itself from all other spheres of society and thereby emancipating all other spheres of society […] (Marx K. 1975, p. 186)

This is of course great literature, and obviously times have changed; through trade unions, parties, and cultural associations created in the course of its social rise the working class has transformed itself from being an outsider of civil society to a part of it.

However, it is noteworthy that even from Marx's emphatic standpoint class interest does not appear as collective egoism, as portrayed in *Rerum Novarum* and invoked in *Centesimus Annus* by Pope John Paul II but with the goal of liberation of the entire society.

What is the new point of view?

In emphasising class interests as crucial to the emancipation of society as a whole, Marx places the poorest and least educated class at the centre, declaring it to be the chosen subject of human progress.

This, I think, is one of our meeting points: the centre-staging of the most neglected members of society, an engagement, which, as Pope Francis says in the Encyclical *Evangelii Gaudium*, is based in faith in Christ who himself has become poor.

Class in the sociological sense denotes groups of human beings whose positions in society are commensurate in relation to the production process.

As the material standards of each group depend on their position in production, any change in the production process will favour one or the other. The group whose material interests would be affected negatively will try to resist, and other groups whose situation is improved by the change will demand and promote it. Expressing this kind of opposition, which we can call *class opposition*, seems not unchristian. Even in *Evangelii Gaudium*, Pope Francis, arguing against uncritical expectations of a spontaneous trickle-down of economic growth, explicitly warns of 'a crude and naïve trust in the goodness of those wielding economic power and in the sacralized workings of the prevailing economic system'. (EG 54)

So much for the distance marked by Marx and the Encyclicals from a corporatist outlook. But this does not exhaust the Marxian theory.

If I understand it correctly, Christian social philosophy considers society to be a personal relationship of individuals. This is not the individualism of liberal provenance à la Margaret Thatcher – *'there's no such thing as society'* – because in the Christian view individuals are bound to a strong desire for Community, understood as an affirmative, personal relationship, because of their relationship to God.

In the mainstream of Marxist theory this viewpoint received too little attention. However, there were some tendencies that did share this outlook: here I will only mention Max Adler, the Austrian socialist who represented the left wing of Austro-Marxism and made an ambitious attempt at grounding socialism ethically.

In modern society, whose existence is characterised by objectified, institutionalised, impersonal relations, it is not easy to create a community in terms of human relationships.

On this point the teachings of Jesus are swimming against the current of time.

III.

Is a scientific interpretation of social facts possible in modern civilisation, such that we are able to judge the extent to which our social organisation fulfils the criteria of a community?

Enlighted Marxism would never neglect the social and ethical dimension of human community. However, they also think that whatever else stands in the way of realising a community, it is the conditions of material existence that must be taken into account. Its thesis is, that the immediate obstacle to the realisation of communion in the present phase of human history is the historically specific way of organising production, that is, the way in which people organise their relation with nature and the conditions in which they relate to themselves in doing so.

In order to demonstrate this, the Hungarian-Austrian social philosopher, Karl Polanyi, in his article 'Christianity and Economic Life', explains the basic categories of Marx' social analysis: production, labour, use-value, exchange-value, the fetish character of commodities[11] and capital.

[11] In Karl Marx's critique of political economy, commodity fetishism is the perception of certain relationships (especially production and exchange) not as relationships among people, but as material relationships among things (the money and commodities exchanged in market trade). As a form of reification, commodity fetishism perceives economic value as something that arises from commodity goods themselves, and not from the interpersonal relations that produce them.

Following Ricardo, Marx understands the value of a commodity as determined by the quantity of labour contained in it. What appears to us to be value or price is nothing other than the reflection of the reciprocal relationship that individuals, working independently of one another, produce in the production of the goods necessary for their survival. But, instead of being controlled by their producers, the products of their labour control *them*, 'behind their backs' as Marx writes.

Moreover, once the social relation of value production is transformed into the production of capital, that is, once labour power becomes a commodity which is bought by the owners of the means of production, the fair exchange of equal quantities of embodied labour turns into the appropriation of unpaid labour by those who buy the capacity to labour.

From the Marxist and Christian point of view, the concept of equality of capital and labour is an incredible misperception, writes Polanyi. It means equating humanity with an objectified fetish.

In the *Economic and Philosophical Manuscripts of 1844* Marx writes:

The worker becomes an ever cheaper commodity the more commodities he creates. The devaluation of the world of men is in direct proportion to the increasing value of the world of things. Labour produces not only commodities: it produces itself and the worker as a commodity – and this at the same rate at which it produces commodities in general. (Marx, K. 1844-1932, p. 272)[12].

This sounds familiar because it points to the same phenomenon about which Pope Francis writes: 'Human beings are themselves considered consumer goods to be used and then discarded.' (EG 53)

Socialists / communists have created the impression that they value class struggle in its own right, as something good in itself, which provides them with the universal key to understanding human history. If they do so, they are wrong.

Polanyi warned against this:

Thus, the limits of the theory of class struggle in Marx are the following: Class struggle is not a last reality. The ultimate reality is the interest of society as a whole. […] Class interest only represents a moving force

12 Karl Marx, *Economic and Philosophical Manuscripts of 1844*, p. 272, https://archive.org/details/economicphilosophicmanuscripts1844/page/n63/mode/2up

in society insofar as it represents the interests of society as a whole in an objective situation. (Polanyi, K. 1934, p. 128f).

Thus, Marx's critique of political economy is a critique because it deals with the limits which capitalist economics set on the human possibilities it has created.

About the capitalist mode of production and consumption, Polanyi says that it lacks a sense organ for the spontaneous recognition of the social. (Polanyi, K. 1934)

The missing sensorium for perceiving the whole, the full dimension of our reality has by now become also obvious in the destruction of the natural environment through a profit-driven growth logic. In the 1844 Paris manuscripts, Marx spontaneously discovered the very important link between patriarchy and humanity's alienation of nature:

'In the relationship to woman as the spoil and handmaid of communal lust is expressed the infinite degradation in which man exists for himself, for the secret of this relationship has its *unambiguous*, decisive, *plain*, demasked expression in the relationships of *man* to *woman* and in the way in which the *direct* and *natural* species-relationship is conceived. The direct, natural, and necessary relation of person to person is the *relation* of *man* to *woman*. In this *natural* species-relationship [man's relation to nature is immediately his relation to man, just as his relation to man is immediately his relation to nature – his own *natural* destination. In this relationship, therefore,] is *sensuously manifested*, reduced to an observable *fact*, the extent to which the human essence has become nature to man, or to which nature to him has become the human essence of man. From this relationship one can therefore judge man's whole level of development.' (Marx, K. 1844, p. 295f).[13]

The failings of a social analysis reduced to economy and sociology characteristically for both big currents of the labour movement, social democrats and communists became politically devastating with the rise of fascism in the first third of the last century. After Antonio Gramsci who saw a moral revolution as an integral part of social transformation it were particularly the theoreticians of the Marxist-oriented Institute for Social Research, Theodor W. Adorno, Max Horkheimer, and Erich Fromm, who,

13 translation adapted.

drawing on psychoanalytic methods, brought cultural and psychological issues into the analysis of the victory of fascism in Europe.

In 1968, by hindsight, Paul Felix Lazarsfeld commented ironically on this shift in theoretical interest, at least in the part of a group of Marxist intellectuals, to the hitherto neglected field of psychic facts: 'An incipient revolution must have economic conditions on its side (Marx); a victorious revolution needs the engineers (Lenin), and an unsuccessful revolution needs psychology (Vienna).' (Lazarsfeld, P. F. 2008, p. 21)

In his book *The Mass Psychology of Fascism*, Wilhelm Reich makes an interesting observation:

[. . .] the political ideology of the European Marxist parties operated with purely economic conditions characteristic of a span of about two hundred years of mechanical development from the end of the 17th to the 19th century. Fascism of the 20th century, on the other hand, threw into focus the basic questions of the *human character, of mysticism and the craving for authority,* problems pertaining to a span of *4-6000 years*. (Reich, W. 1946, p. xxiii).

Little can be said here about Reich's particular psychological method; however, the important point is that the susceptibility to fascism was due not only to the economic crisis but also the psychic structure of the individual members of whole societies and that this is rooted in social conditions which go far beyond capitalism.

Earlier than other movements did, socialism embraced the social and political equality of women as one of its core goals. However, throughout most of its history it failed to understand that there will be no human emancipation without overcoming the culture of patriarchal domination.

After Antonio Gramsci who saw a moral revolution as an integral part of social transformation it were particularly the theoreticians of the Marxist-oriented Institute for Social Research, Theodor W. Adorno, Max Horkheimer, and Erich Fromm, who, drawing on psychoanalytic methods, brought cultural and psychological issues into the analysis of the victory of fascism in Europe.

IV.

For Polanyi, socialism is almost synonymous with the idea of social freedom. (Polanyi, K. 1944a, p. 143)

In his essay *On Freedom*, we read:

> For the socialist, 'acting freely' means acting while conscious of the responsibility we bear for our part in mutual human relationships – outside of which there is no social reality – *and realizing that we have to bear this responsibility*. Being free therefore no longer means, as in the typical ideology of the bourgeois, to be free *of* duty and responsibility but rather to be free *through* duty and responsibility. (Polanyi, K. 2018, p. 304).

Surprisingly at first glance, his thoughts revolve around the seemingly apolitical term 'accounting'.

In 1922, in the discussion on socialisation he writes, 'Humanity will only be free if it knows what its ideals are costing it. Only then, it will realize that it depends solely on itself for their realization.' (Polanyi, K. 2018, p. 109).

He emphatically rejects the idea that socialism is nothing more than a *bread-and-butter question*, at best embodying a claim to justice. He argues:

> It is not only an unjust order which should be overcome, in favour of a just one; rather, through the way in which it is overcome, humanity ought to reach a new, unprecedented level of freedom. It is true that equality is an indispensable prerequisite for a society founded on humans. […] But there can also be dictatorial justice; and if justice is realized through democracy, in fact it is not the essence of justice, but the value of democracy, which represents moral progress, and this is inseparable from the responsibility, however small, of the individual person. (Polanyi, K. 2018, p. 109).

But why is it so difficult to leap from the realm of necessity to the realm of freedom?

Obviously, the young Marx was over-optimistic when he noted in the *Economic Philosophical Manuscripts*:

> *Communism* as the *positive* transcendence of *private property* as *human self-estrangement,* and therefore as the real *appropriation* of the *human* essence by and for man; communism therefore as the complete return of man to himself as a *social* (i.e., human) being – a return accomplished consciously and embracing the entire wealth of previous development. This communism, as fully developed naturalism, equals humanism, and as fully developed humanism equals naturalism; it is the *genuine* resolution of the conflict between man and nature and between man and man – the true resolution of the strife between existence and essence, between objectification and self-confirmation, between freedom and necessity, between the individual and the species. Communism

> is the riddle of history solved, and it knows itself to be this solution. (Marx, K. 1844, p. 296)

No, it was not, nor can it be, because what can be said of human beings is not exhausted in their empirically describable social being and economic existence!

I like Lazarsfeld's bon mot so much because it describes well the intellectual development many of us have undergone since the collapse of state socialism. But there is also something disconcerting about it. Does intellectual progress in social science require dividing society into ever finer units, each to be studied by different disciplines: from economy to sociology, from sociology to political science, to ideology, and finally to psychology? And if so, what would the unity of the result guarantee?

Christians, it seems to me, endure the imperfect unity in the here and now better then Marxists do. They are better equipped to accept mystery, because they see unity in the transcendent as assured. I, as a non-believer, can only recognise the hypothetical value of this capacity.

I can even say, I envy you the optimistic realism it provides. Nonetheless I have to walk in my own way. But since we are going to walk a long stretch of the path side by side, I am looking forward to learning from you how to positively deal with the necessary imperfection of any human endeavour.

Europe's Common Destiny

A Vatican Perspective

Angelo Vincenzo Zani[14]

From Vatican City, September 2nd, 2018 to
Dr. Walter Baier, Coordinator of Transform-Europe,
and to the Summer School participants:

Esteemed Dr. Walter Baier, coordinator of Transform Europe, distinguished authorities,

I am very sorry that I could not participate in the important event of the Summer School for youth, because of commitments I could not postpone. In fact, I had already assured my participation in the Summer School some time ago.

I would like to thank all the organizers who promoted the initiative. It is the result of an interesting series of meetings which have produced a line of work leading to an interesting proposal oriented to young people in particular.

I offer my cordial greetings to you young people, together with the hope that the meeting in these days will sustain your ideals of justice, fraternity and solidarity, so that you can develop your personal choices and commitment to building the common good in Europe and the world.

We are questioning in these years what skills will be required of young people to be mature citizens in the 21st century. It is evident that the current educational systems are often inadequate to deal with a completely changed

[14] Archbishop, theologian and sociologist, Secretary of the Vatican Congregation for Catholic Education, contact person for DIALOP in the Vatican.

frame of reference, marked by an explosion of scientific requirements and knowledge and by increasingly complex social issues.

Understanding our time means understanding the globalization that burdens the human adventure, which has become interdependent throughout the world. It is constituted by actions and reactions particularly in the political, economic, demographic, mythological and religious spheres. It means questioning mankind's outcome which is being pushed by the engines of science, technology and economics toward becoming a 'larger man', although this larger man is not at all better. These engines generate a society governed by algorithms guided by artificial intelligence thereby reducing us to trivial machines at the same time.

These same engines simultaneously lead to interdependent catastrophes: degradation of the biosphere and climatic warming, leading to massive migrations; the multiplication of deadly threats as nuclear and chemical weapons are further developed, along with the emergence of cyber weapons which can disintegrate societies. All this causes anguish, introspection, closure and nightmares. On one hand therefore, the inhumanity of the 'Best of the Worlds' is loathed; on the other hand, there is the barbarism stemming from a mega-catastrophe on a global scale.

In this constantly changing context, the challenge of the human adventure, poses a question: What does it mean to be human? However, the nature of our own identity is not taught in our schools and universities at all, and therefore it is not recognized by our minds. All the elements which can be used to recognize this human identity are dispersed and fragmented in countless sciences and in literature as well, where human complexities are revealed by its masterpieces.

Pope Francis reminded us in the encyclical, Laudato Sí, that the issue of human identity encompasses the problem of nature. This problem is present in a vital way not only in the environment, but also within the human identity itself, which leads to the problem of the physical and cosmic temporal dimensions of nature. The human being is not only a singular element in the cosmos, but it brings the cosmos into its interior dimension. In life, a human being is not only a singular being; it carries life within itself. So the question is amplified and rendered complex as we proceed from one step to the next. It requires transdisciplinary knowledge which can extract, assimilate and integrate the knowledge which is still separated, compartmentalized and fragmented. A new approach and complex thinking are needed to connect and articulate what we know, not merely juxtapose notions.

In this framework it is necessary to understand human complexity which is to be situated in its cosmic, physical, biological, social and cultural contexts together with the worldwide community's common destiny. To situate human complexity is not to isolate what is human.

What some philosophers and social scientists propose as a response to the challenge of complexity is interesting. They draw attention to anthropological and cultural change. They delineate an anthropological perspective where human identity emerges as an evolving and irreducibly diverse identity, through the interweaving of many histories. They show how our time makes thinking about identity and diversity together unavoidable, in contrast with opposing them to each other. This makes it urgent to reform thought and education, thereby enhancing individual and cultural diversity, while simultaneously integrating fragmented knowledge. What emerges basically is that humanity is constitutively unfinished, even as a species. And what is constitutively unfinished and manifold is its individual and cultural manifestations.

So the challenge for Mankind's perilous future is to develop the awareness of the 'Community of destiny' of all the earth's peoples, of all humanity with the earth itself. In this framework we must draw out a new worldwide humanism that can only be born from the encounter among the world's different cultures, from the ability to think unity and multiplicity together, from a solid culture of dialogue. It is a demanding but possible prospect, because the universe of what is possible is recursively regenerated to coincide with the turns and the discontinuity of evolutionary processes. One must not surrender to those visceral impulses therefore. They not only cloud the vision, but they conceal an overwhelming disintegrating 'will to power'.

What direction should you take? I would like to offer some considerations for your reflection in these days. These thoughts were suggested to me as I read the OECD 2030 Learning Framework in which a fundamental question is posed: What should countries do to prepare people to understand a changing world, to engage in it and to shape it? 2030 is the year in which those attending primary school will graduate from secondary school and university to enter a world with an environment in danger, with a constantly increasing population while resources diminish, with climate change. All these are factors requiring everyone to face their responsibility – that of sustainably developing our planet, with an eye on the needs of future generations. New challenges will be manifested at the same time, as a result of the interaction between technology and globalisation.

As a body the OECD is particularly attentive to cooperation and economic development. It highlights the issues from this specific viewpoint. But we know that economic problems have strong social and cultural implications and always pose questions that demand confrontation with anthropological, ethical and even religious values. All these dimensions cross through what it is to be human. If on one hand the global economy shows evident signs of crisis with vulnerability in many industries as a result of attacks by industrial organizations and the increasing disruption of professions because of automation, on the other hand, the newly emerging economies have unleashed new growth, but at the expense of growing inequality.

In a world marked by glaring inequalities where people move and migrate either by personal choice or because they are forced to move by war or poverty, investment in the formation of young generations is needed so that they do not think of solving the great problems of mankind by accentuating conflicts and erecting walls. Instead they would come to know how to reconcile the interests and needs of individuals, communities and nations within a common framework of mutual fairness. To achieve this objective, we need to have open borders, clear arrangements for trade and a sustainable future, within a framework of values and laws that can 'hold' the differences together.

Young people must be helped in this context, through conceptual models, open and dynamic frameworks of values and an articulated system of knowledge. They would thereby acquire a compass to be innovative, accountable and aware making it possible to navigate their lives and their own world.

In other words, we need to develop more creativity and have the courage to think in an innovative way in order to transform current social, political and cultural models, through transformative processes strengthened by imagination, curiosity, commitment, collaboration and self-discipline.

Within this complex reality moreover, we need to be able to cope with tensions, dilemmas and negotiations. Solutions to problems in this society must also be complex and young people will have to acquire skills to manage conflicts and seek balances between equity and freedom, autonomy and solidarity, innovation and continuity, efficiency and respect for democratic rules. Very competent people will be needed; they will know how to include empathy (i.e. the ability to understand others' views); adaptability (i.e. the ability to change one's perceptions in the light of new experiences and new information); and trust in others and in the future (i.e. the theme of hope).

And the third element to be developed is responsibility. It is the transformative competence that leads individuals to 'think for themselves and to share'. Young people should be prepared to consider their actions' consequences, to have a sense of responsibility, and the moral and intellectual maturity to reflect on their actions and assess them on the basis of what is right and what is wrong. And this ability to judge is related to ethics. It implies the ability to respond to issues based on norms, values, meanings and limits.

Imagining that a meeting of a few people can affect the great problems and challenges that characterize the world today may seem utopian to some. But history teaches that the most significant turning points always sprang from the firm convictions of few who have been able to interpret the signs of the times and decisively invest themselves to bring about change. This Summer School is a seed of something new which must be cast into the soil of our time to bear abundant fruit.

And in this regard, I would like to point out two elements for reflection which could be useful in the work during these days. I draw them from Pope Francis's teachings: the need to develop the culture of dialogue and to relaunch the great heritage of Europe.

Concerning dialogue, the pope has been inspired by a fundamental principle of Vatican II: 'Man [...] is not confined to the temporal horizon alone, but, living in human history, it retains in its entirety its eternal vocation' (GS 76). In the formation of the new generations therefore it is necessary to educate young people to appreciate all human values, introducing them into all of reality; and one dimension of human reality is transcendence (Pope Francis).

This vertical dimension crosses the horizontal one and together they lead along the paths of the true encounter, of the dialogue that goes in depth, of building bridges with everyone with respect, esteem, and reciprocal acceptance. Dialogue is an indispensable element for the construction of the common good in a multicultural, multi-religious, and in many ways confused and disoriented, society. Dialogue helps to orient humanity towards its common destiny.

In addition to this theme, the main speeches that Pope Francis addressed to Europe in different circumstances are particularly rich in strategic cues. They reveal that for the Pope, Europe is called to rediscover itself, its soul, that humanistic spirit which also loves and defends. Faced with a widespread individualistic idea of man, a conception of a human person detached from any social and anthropological context, almost like a monad, the pope proposes a relational vision of the person, incorporated in a community, precisely a 'community of destiny', as the experts of social phenomena express it. This is the antidote to the widespread tendency in the West today to conceive and to live in solitude, to think of freedom as the duty to repudiate any bond, thereby generating a rootless society devoid of a sense of belonging and inheritance. The Pope denounces such a vision which opens the way to that globalization of indifference arising from selfishness, resulting from a conception of man incapable of accepting the truth and living a true social dimension. Pope Francis appeals instead to a responsible freedom, rooted in the truth and able to give life to solidarity in fact.

As a non-European from this perspective, Pope Francis insists above all on what Europe represents in the eyes of the rest of the world. 'The only continent that can bring a certain unity to the world, it is Europe', he confided to a French delegation received on March 1, 2016[15]; 'China has perhaps a more ancient, deeper culture, but only Europe has a vocation of universality and service.' His speech to the European Parliament concluded with a wish in this respect: 'The time has come to abandon the idea of a Europe that is afraid and bent on itself in order to arouse and promote Europe as the protagonist, bearer of science, art, music, human values and also of faith. The Europe that contemplates the heavens and pursues ideals;

15 Pope Francis to the French movement 'Poissons roses', March 2nd, 2016

The Europe that looks and defends and protects man; The Europe that walks on the safe and firm Earth, a precious point of reference for all mankind".[16]

Dear friends, as I offer you these considerations I renew the most sincere wishes for all of you – speakers and students – so that the experience of these Summer School days may constitute the beginning of a journey full of reflection, friendship and commitments contributing to the realisation of the common good and of a world of fraternity and peace.

---

[16] Pope Francis: Address to the European Parliament, November 25th, 2014: http://w2.vatican.va/content/francesco/it/speeches/2014/november/documents/papa-francesco_20141125_strasburgo-parlamento-europeo.html

ference
vers
dia
logue
dif
trans
form
ativ
per

A PERFORMATIVE TRANSFORMATIVE DIALOGUE

Toward a Culture of Encounter

A New Paradigm

Piero Coda[17]

Christian Inspiration and Todays Challenge

1. Just as we need bread for our survival, today we face the urgent need for a new 'cultural paradigm'; indeed, Pope Francis affirms that we require a real 'cultural revolution' to interpret and transform our world. Therefore, we need 'a different and higher perspective'.

As the disciples of Jesus, we have been called to this purpose – walking alongside all those who strive to follow this vision.

This leads to the question that I would like to address briefly: What does the Christian inspiration – which Jesus had and that is ignited from time to time by his Spirit in the conscience and actions of his followers – say and offer to the dialogue and common work in which we are all involved?

2. Let me begin with the proclamation of Jesus – his 'glad tidings', his 'Gospel'. The words, gestures, actions and style of the Nazarene – everything revolves around one fact: the advent of the 'kingdom of God' (cf. Mk 1, 14-15).

But what does it mean? Jesus takes up an Old Testament metaphor, assigns it a new meaning and expresses it like this: the event of events is the 'discovery' (combining the unexpected gift and concrete experience of his presence, though still requiring the risky leap of faith) that God is Abbà, Father. Therefore, not an impenetrable Mystery, an absolute master or the

[17] Italian philosopher and theologian; founding President of Sophia University Institute, Florence, Italy; former professor at the Pontifical Lateran University, Rome; member of the Vatican's International Theological Commission.

vertex of a social and political pyramidal order: on the contrary, He's the source of freedom of the Son and of all his children as well as of brotherhood and sisterhood among all – a framework that implies freedom, justice, sharing.

In one word, Jesus once and for all disambiguates the face of the Sacred and of God that can no longer be made into a tool to guarantee any kind of status quo that is not fraternal, just, free or solidary.

It implies that the advent of the kingdom of God is manifested and fulfilled in the fabric of social life as this proclamation and commitment is received and embraced by Jesus himself, in his words and actions. In doing so he completely redirects the minds and the hearts of people. Consequently, He gives a new form to relationships among men and women, starting with the poor and the excluded.

The novelty generated by Jesus is not expressed with the perspective of a definite ultimate social organization, but rather in the relationship among people capable of entering into the social and hence political sphere, becoming the yeast that ferments the dough from within.

The community gathered by the message of Jesus and those convened around the risen Jesus after the Easter event, constitute living places where ferments of this particular social dimension germinate. One only needs to read the texts, which are idealized in fact, from the Acts of the Apostles: 'No one among them was destitute' (see 2,42ff; 4,32ff).

The experience of Jesus, where God – who is One – says: 'We are'; 'I and the Father are One' (see John 10,30); is 'the declaration of consistency and significance of history and sociality'.

Since the other is already constitutively in God (the Father and the Son and the Holy Spirit), the other, also generated by God, is true and good and beautiful. The imperative which God himself freely obeys is: 'it is good that the other exists! Because the other is "another myself", distinct and different from me'. Thus man and woman, moulded 'in the image and likeness of God', (see Gen 1:26) are called to rediscover themselves – as Gaudium et Spes writes (cf. n. 24) – 'in the sincere gift of oneself', that is in a reciprocal and reciprocating, free-willed and gratuitous relationship.

The social current set in motion by Jesus, therefore, aims at changing the 'social project' by changing the conditions that make it work.

Participation in the community of disciples changes the underlying conditions of social action. The form and style of building relationships based on fraternity, is the 'social treasure' of the community of Jesus. It is a social culture, which has, as its 'fixed structural part', the ethos of the two-fold commandment of love: love for God/Abbà, in response to his love and love for each other, including every single human being – starting with the poor – as brothers and sisters. The Sermon on the Mount describes the horizon of this specific social ethos which is dialectical with respect to the 'spirit of the world', Mammon, as Jesus calls it, the idol of power and money.

This social culture tends to transform the 'incentive structure' of thought and practice so that individualistic and utilitarian action is replaced by a commitment to just and supportive social construction as the decisive operational strategy.

It is not the individual perspective that rises to maximum ethical achievement but it is the pre-constitution of a specific space of social relationship that enables and supports a conscious, critical and transformative praxis. The 'text' of social action becomes comprehensible only against the background of the 'con-text' represented by a space for social experience, which is the ekklesia, the assembly of disciples, or better – the convocation of disciples who walk together (they are sýnodoi, they make a 'synod'). The apostle Paul writes, it is where, 'there is no longer Jew or Greek, there is no longer slave nor free, there is no longer man nor woman' (Gal 3:28), in the sense that enmity and inequalities are abolished.

3. In this regard, a phenomenological, rather than an axiological, observation is required.

Every religious experience and tradition generates, preserves, and nourishes – as the history of civilizations testifies – a relatively autonomous social space. But this occurs in an explicit and singular manner starting with the event of Jesus.

H. Bergson notes that every religion lives on the intrinsic dialectic between being 'closed' and 'open', between being 'conservative' and 'prophetic' precisely because it is embodied in the historical process. On one hand, this dialectic often makes religion integral with the status quo, where it can become an ideological justification. On the other hand, it pushes the status quo, especially in the moments of change, to evoke ever new and unexpected energy for innovation and social transformation.

When the Christian inspiration is experienced only as a religion, it lives on this dialectic. When it is transmitted as inspiration and faith, it becomes completely and uniquely a prophecy, even if it is committed to incarnating social forms. Otherwise, it contradicts itself; it is dead.

4. Over the centuries in the western world – marked by Christianity as its religion and held together by consensus around a compact constellation of values derived from tradition – a specific inspirational force for social life emerged from the social culture that passed down from one generation to another in the practices of the Church.

The establishment of truce in time of war, community kitchens for the poor in cities, free education provided to the less fortunate classes, care for the marginalized, the struggle against usury and the abolition of slavery, for example, are some of the social achievements that arose from the most genuine Christian inspiration.

A paradigm of social ethics has remained predominant however. It aims at changing the project of the individual life, without seeking to change the basic social conditions. In fact, the structures of society are perceived as indisputable, pre-established by tradition – the legacy of the relationship between the sacred and the profane that not only precedes Christianity but also continued within it, attaining its own religious configuration.

Only 'utopias' like those of Tommaso Campanella and Thomas More bear traces of a vision for change in the social design by altering the basic conditions of life in society.

5. The dawn of modernity created a rift in the cultural and social history of Western civilization, not only because our complex society (based on the division of labour and differentiation of functions) is subject to principles that radically transform the structure of traditional society. But it was also because the cultural and social project that it imposes, especially starting with the Enlightenment, tends to deny and marginalize the role of Jesus Christ's approach toward God as the generator of both consistency and social innovation at one and the same time.

It's a complex subject and this is not the place to discuss the relationship between Christianity, secularization and secularism. I would just like to make a general comment however, which seems fundamental to me. In the process of the critical marginalization of the Christian event from the social dynamics that led to the modern world, we can actually distinguish two dimensions.

On one hand, there is an undervaluation of the cultural and social contribution offered by Jesus Christ's approach toward God, (the Trinitarian God of freedom, as defined by Hegel as well) to the point of keeping the Church from offering protection and providing support to the integral human person and social relationships. This became tragically evident during the Twentieth Century which was engulfed by totalitarian ideology (Nazism for example).

On the other hand, there is an irreversible thrust to liberate that emancipating and innovative energy that spreads its roots back to, though not immediately, the Christian event itself. The contradiction lies in not being able to seize (on both the sides: modern and Christian cultures) the possibility of synergy between this energy and the evangelical inspiration, which is present in the history of the ecclesial community, going beyond it.

6. Vatican II, just like the prior development of the Church's social doctrine starting with Rerum Novarum by Leo XIII, represents a fact that is extremely significant in the maturation of Christian self-awareness.

The Council lays the foundation for the restoration of the original dynamism of the ecclesial presence based on the design engraved by Jesus and testified by the New Testament. We have a largely new and unexplored model before us to configure the presence of Christian inspiration in society.

Vatican II stresses Jesus' teaching linking access to God with social action as its consequence, today as at the beginning. It does not invite us to return to the 'old order'. Instead, it tends to introduce a new order of relationships that invites people to become critical and proactive leaven for transformation. One can read Gaudium et Spes [GS] and Dignitatis Humanae [DH] from this perspective.

Now that we have begun to perceive it more clearly and think about it critically, this dynamic has not been definitively concretely established. Rather, it has been entrusted to the work of cultural elaboration and social praxis emerging from the life of societies and different cultures throughout history.

In this process, the charismatic impulses (the Spirit of Jesus in action!) not only generate a new vision of the God of Jesus but as a result, they also activate the leaven for cultural and social renewal, becoming prophetic indicators of the future.

I look at past history and reflect, starting from Benedict of Nursia at the end of ancient history, to Francis of Assisi and Dominic of Guzman in the Middle-Ages, to Ignatius of Loyola at the dawn of modern history, until arriving at the ferment of renewal in our time. A principle appears so clearly only today in the wake of Vatican II which can be recognized at a level of reflection (even if not entirely). It is the principle of co-essentiality of institution and charism, of tradition and prophetic openness. Christian inspiration tends to be credited as a religion of the future in this sense, also with regard to its presence in civil society.

The Council's definition of the world as 'space of true fraternity' (GS 37) converges toward this point; it is full of significance. The theologian, Enrico Chiavacci, wrote years ago: the Council takes seriously the supreme commandment of love; it is just as much about the liberation of an individual as it is about the liberation of human activity in history, and ultimately of history itself. Pope Francis wrote these striking words in Evangelii Gaudium: Jesus not only saved the individual but also the social relationship (see EG 178). As John Paul II had emphasized earlier as well, this implies combatting the 'structures of sin' and imagining the 'structures of freedom and communion'.

A decisive step is being taken here, where I believe, an essential role has been played by the critical analysis of Marxist society, contributing to a deeper understanding of Christian revelation.

7. The turning point propitiated by Vatican II has not been fully understood yet: the proposed interpretations too often maintain an outdated framework, both in the terms of history and the Gospel itself.

At least two stimulating points in the panorama of contemporary Christianity must be noted, however. Both of these testify to the critical and transforming value of Christian inspiration today.

First is the prophetic message of Pope Francis. He has put back into circulation – facing rejection and resistance – the breakthrough brought about by Vatican II and made at least two things evident, expressing them with two slogans.

The first defines the Church as a 'Church that goes forth', in the radical sense that the Church is born and lives always and only 'outside itself'. This means that the Church is a sign and an instrument of the advent of the Kingdom of God (as Vatican II writes) inasmuch as it shares and promotes itself with and for everyone. The path that leads from Vatican II to Pope Francis, therefore, concentrates the attention of the Church not so much on what the Gospel of the Kingdom is, but on how the Gospel of the Kingdom unfolds itself in history.

His second slogan focuses on the epochal sign of the times: humanity, today, does not simply live in an epoch of change but in an epochal change. This change demands a paradigm shift in the performative interpretation of reality, a paradigm called to uproot the creeping omnivorous dictatorship of the technocratic paradigm and to respond effectively to the situation that mankind faces today: a Third World war in pieces.

Consequently, this leads to the challenge that Pope Francis describes with a third slogan: crossing the threshold of the 'culture of encounter'. I would say that the quid (the what?) of the Gospel – since it is proclaimed and given in the Spirit of freedom, justice and love –, is the quo, the 'means by which' different cultures in their interactions proclaim and offer words and actions to each other, building the human experience together.

8. While the fabric of ecclesial communities has experienced an erosion of its consistency and effectiveness in the West in recent decades on the other hand, it has silently been traversed and nourished by innovative thrusts and experience in Latin America, Africa, Asia, and even in old Europe.

Even if these practices are most often limited to an experimental level, they tend to awaken the kind of social dynamic that originally belongs to the Christian event which is capable of intercepting today's needs: cohesion, dialogue and innovation.

The crucial goal here is to explicitly and actively refer to the experience in which access to the God/Abbà of Jesus is made tangible, by activating (at the social, economic, and political level) the sphere of interpersonal communication based on freedom, justice, reciprocity and solidarity – beginning with the last, those who are excluded and rejected – which implies the transformation of the structures that mediate social relations at all levels.

For all this not to remain a dream and utopia – especially when ideologies of closed identity and unrestrained profit overwhelmingly seem to prevail – it is clear that training and research institutions play a crucial role just as meetings and discussions held between those who nurture analogous inspirations play such a role.

Pope Francis writes in Veritatis Gaudium[18] (the Constitution on the academic institutions of the Church) that today, we need to foster the vital experience 'of a true evangelical hermeneutics in order to understand life, the world and men better, not a synthesis, but in a spiritual atmosphere of research and certainty based on the truths of reason and faith' (VG 3). This is, 'a great cultural, spiritual and educational challenge that will involve long processes of regeneration' (VG 6).

It is a great and magnificent challenge that at Sophia, with joy, conviction and tenacity, we want to live together with you too!

For a Nonviolent Way of Thinking

In the brief reflections offered here I am prompted by a provocative idea of the philosopher Emmanuel Lévinas and by an approach enunciated by Pope Francis.

1. Lévinas writes in Otherwise Than Being, the true problem for us Westerners is not so much refusing violence as to question ourselves about a struggle against violence, which without blanching in non-resistance to evil could avoid the institution of violence out of this very struggle (Lévinas, E. p. 177).

Directly addressing the depths of violence into which twentieth-century Europe fell, Lévinas laid bare the structural (to be precise, metaphysical) connection between a certain form of thinking and violence.

Indeed, thinking is never neutral and does not function independently of the liberty of the person doing the thinking, in the recognition or non-recognition of the dignity of the other qua other. And, Lévinas stresses that, even when thought wants to defuse the violence that destroys relationships where liberty flourishes, the subtle danger – which is no less destructive for being insidious – is wanting to vanquish violence with violence, that is, by waging war against violence, by means of coercion or even by eliminating the alterity of the one practicing the violence.

The history of religions as well as political thought has had ample experience with the consequences of succumbing to this tragic tendency. The exercise of thinking needs to be brought back to its roots and educated with

[18] http://w2.vatican.va/content/francesco/en/apost_constitutions/documents/papa-francesco_costituzione-ap_20171208_veritatis-gaudium.html

extreme attention and constant vigilance to exorcise the temptation to violence, even when it is devious and vestigial.

It is a fact that the dominant mode of thought today, which is Western in form, has characteristics that (even when its points of departure are quite positive) have become unilateral and violent. It even destroys the free and creative flourishing of the individual and society, beginning with the weakest and most rejected, in their diverse human, cultural, social, and ecological expressions.

I will briefly list what I think are the most important of these characteristics:

- individualism: thought exercised with a view of wielding absolute individual ownership in which otherness is not considered, let alone seen as constituting identity;
- possessiveness: thought exercised to capture the thing that it contemplates, which is thus reduced to a mere object to be dominated;
- instrumentalisation: thought exercised as a tool to pursue what is individually useful for oneself, with tragic consequences on the level of economic and political practice and in the exploitation of Creation;
- ideologism: thought exercised as the dictation of law to reality, which is imposed on it and bends it to the (explicit or concealed) aims of the person exercising it;
- male chauvinism: thought exercised in the form assumed in fact in the context of a society dominated by a certain masculine model and, in any case, with disregard for the experience of the relationship of symmetrical-asymmetrical reciprocity between the masculine and the feminine;
- uniformism: thinking that is exercised as something univocal and standardising, aimed not only at reducing all diversity to a lowest common denominator, but at ignoring, as a matter of principle, the value and richness of diversity;
- immanentism: thinking that is exercised without taking account of, or intentionally disregarding, any reference – not an external and accidental reference but an internal and qualifying one – to the transcendence of the other.

The need for a 'new way of thinking' – as was incipiently defined by Franz Rosenzweig and of which we find an example not only in Lévinas but also in some exponents of the Frankfurt School, in Jacques Derrida, and in others – comprises a radical metanoia of thinking at each of these levels.

A significant if small convergence of many voices and many accents is taking place around this, often with a prophetic flavour, though, to be sure, with tensions and the obstinate resistance of the political, economic, and technocratic establishment. This offers a crucial advantage: the determination to travel the road of a kind of thinking that defuses the temptation and the practice of violence through a radically nonviolent way of thinking; to express it positively, it is precisely a way of thinking inspired by reconciliation and the construction of peace.

2. Now as to the impulse given by Pope Francis: His testimony – in words and deeds – is motivated by an inspiration that has the gospel of Jesus, or, better still, the Gospel that is Jesus at its centre, as symbolised by the Cross – as we read in his message for the World Day of Peace: 'Nonviolence: A Style of Politics for Peace' (Pope Francis 2017, 6).The context evoked by Francis is that in which the concept of 'politics' is understood in its original and most complete sense since it involves 'cultivat[ing] nonviolence in our most personal thoughts and values.' (Ibidem)

Pope Francis gave the short and intensely inspired formula for nonviolence in the Regina Coeli address of Sunday, 23 April 2017. As Lévinas would have it, this challenges the way of thinking in order to impregnate everything with nonviolence – at the roots:

'Mercy in the light of Easter enables us to perceive it as a true form of awareness [. . .] [because it] opens the door of the mind in order to better understand the mystery of God and of our personal existence. Mercy enables us to understand that violence, rancour, vengefulness have no meaning,[19] and the first victim is whoever feels these sentiments, because he deprives himself of his own dignity.'[20]

I will confine myself to deriving some suggestions from this.

- First: mercy 'opens the door of the mind'. That is, it lets it exit from the closed space of the 'ego', understood in the individualistic sense, tending to possess and be ideological, in order to open it up to the freedom of relating to the other. This involves more than opening oneself up to the

19 Translator's note: that is, 'are senseless'.

20 http://w2.vatican.va/content/francesco/en/angelus/2017/documents/papa-francesco_regina-coeli_20170423.html

other because space is given to him; he is respected; the merciful one puts herself in his shoes in order to understand what he is experiencing and thinking. Essentially one is taking care of the other. At bottom, what is involved is perceiving oneself and behaving like the 'misericordiati' (receivers and bearers of mercy), that is, people who live gratuitously through giving ('perdono') and through forgiveness ('di perdono').
This is what mercy really is: recognising the primacy of forgiveness (perdono) as the event from which life arises and is regenerated.

- It is thus that thinking – and this is the second suggestion – looks through the open door of mercy gazing on a new horizon and seeing in a new way. In other words, mercy is the ingredient – the style – of 'a true form of awareness'. This is not a matter of a passing superficial ornament for an inexpensive bland, apolitical 'good feeling'. Instead it opens up a horizon of light illuminating the landscape and making it possible to see the meaning and the justness of things and situations in greater depth.
  If giving in to the temptation of violence is to deprive oneself of one's own dignity while depriving another person of hers or his, forgiving recognises and rehabilitates the dignity of the other while affirming one's own. The dignity of a human being is recognised in forgiveness and is exercised through the capacity to forgive.
- This means reading and managing conflicts – and this is the third suggestion – according to the logic of reciprocal recognition in which each of the polarities at play (and in struggle) is in principle conscious of its own perspectivalness and incompleteness, of its own limitations and its own pain, and expressly searches out the true and good part of this in relation to that of the other in a broader and richer horizon. So it does not mean ignoring or removing conflicts according to the dialectical logic in which one term of the conflict is removed and reabsorbed into the other, which then ultimately prevails. According to Pope Francis, this implies, 'the willingness to face conflict head on, to resolve it and to make it a link in the chain of a new process' (EG 227). [. . .] 'Active nonviolence is a way of showing that unity is truly more powerful and more fruitful than conflict. Everything in the world is intimately interconnected' (Laudato Si, 16, 117, 138). Certainly differences can cause friction. But let us face them constructively and non-violently, so that 'tensions and oppositions can achieve a diversified and life-giving unity (preserving) what is valid

and useful on both sides'[21] (EG 228). (50th WDP 6).
This matter of the deep 'logic' of thinking that is manifested in (but not exhausted in) how conflicts are managed is a key issue because it expresses everything about the way of thinking. Hegel's intuition, brought back to earth by Marx, so to speak via Feuerbach, deserves credit for the effort to express the 'dialectic' of identity-alterity as a movement of life and thought. But it ends up reducing alterity to a negative factor that needs to be removed as such. We need to go to the roots of this intuition, which is the Trinity – in which one part is in front of the other, not to remove the other but rather to meet it again in what is new springing from the encounter, even if it is conflictual. This is the dialectic of 'per-dono', of forgiving/doing in order to give – the Trinitarian dialectic.

- Finally, I draw a fourth suggestion from Pope John Paul II whom Francis quotes and whose idea he develops in his Message for the World Day of Peace: 'This peaceful political transition was made possible in part "by the non-violent commitment of people who, while always refusing to yield to the force of power, succeeded time after time in finding effective ways of bearing witness to the truth"'. (50th WDP 4)

A nonviolent style of thinking is performative, individual, and even creates at once ever new, realistic, and prophetic solutions because it is able to look at the conflict and the problem not only with its own eyes but also through the eyes of the other in a sense.

+++

As we were told two years ago by Pierre, a Sophia student from the Congo, who was actively committed to the political struggle and therefore exiled far from his family and homeland – some things can certainly only be seen by 'eyes that have cried' – the eyes of the victims of violence and of the person who has united with them in mercy. Because in themselves, these eyes already radiate the light of the new world of peace that expresses justice. These are the eyes of Easter.

---

21 Translator's note: Literally, in Italian: '[preserving] the precious potentials of polarities in conflict'.

To the Roots of Transversal Dialogue

Reflections on a Domination-free Style of Dialogue

Bernhard Callebaut[22]

A few words to introduce myself: I'm Belgian; I was born in the fifties, only a few years after World War II and grew up in a Catholic environment, in the years of the economic boom, '*Les trente glorieuses*' (Fourastié, J. 1979). As a young man, I was proud to belong to Europe and its project of integration, benefiting from the Rhineland social model where economic success and social adjustment (the Welfare state) seemed a better solution to me than the North American capitalist version.

I was fifteen-years-old in 1968 and lived May, '68 with great awareness, also because my elder brothers were studying at the university at that very moment and they were involved in some of the student protests. I chose to study Sociology at one of the oldest universities of Northern Europe[23], and dreamed of doing something useful to change the situation of the so-called Third World, becoming more and more aware of the dark side of European history as well with respect to the rest of the world. Gandhi, Martin Luther

[22] Studied Law and Sociology. PhD in Social Sciences. Taught at the University of Antwerp, Rome, Lublin. Currently holds the Chair of Sociology at Sophia University Institute (Loppiano, Florence). Published in the field of the Sociology of Cultural and Religious Processes. Founding member of the international Research Group Social One, of the Interreligious Research Group Wings of Unity and the Research Group on Transversal Ethics DIALOP.

[23] See Lubich, C. (2007). Lubich is the foundress of the worldwide Focolare Movement. A sociological and historical analysis of Focolare was published in Italian as Callebaut, B. (2017). A presentation in English is Masters T. – Uelmen A. (2011).

King, but also Nyerere and Helder Camara were the interesting figures in my pantheon. Mao, Che Guevara and other Lumumba's were also there in the margin.

But in the search for the deeper meaning of life, I met Christians with a sound evangelical spirit, combined with a developed sense of social solidarity, and I personally adopted a way of life where the communion of goods was an integral part of my economic lifestyle.[24] After my studies, where I also met Marx of course and the world of leftist activists,[25] I was professionally engaged in the academic world, and continued in my personal life project of combining spirituality and social commitment. The Theology of Liberation[26] was one of the issues that interested me in the eighties, and the courageous choice of the Latin American Church for the preferential option for the poor, was one of these moments when I was proud of my faith community and my Christian identity.[27]

As a sociologist[28] I became more and more specialized in the field of the Sociology of Religion. In the last decades I also became increasingly

[24] A title like the following one was very representative for the spirit some engaged young christians of my generation had at the end of the sixties: R. Coste, *Pas de pauvre chez toi. La pensée sociale de l'Église,* Nouvelle Cité, Paris 1984. It cannot be a great surprise that the recent texts of pope Francis on economy and social justice (*Evangelii Gaudium*) and on the climate crisis (*Laudato sì*) were well received also by intellectuals of the European Left. See also Papa Francesco, *Terra, casa, lavoro. Discorsi ai movimenti popolari,* Il Manifesto – Ponte alle Grazie, Roma – Milano 2017.

[25] A synthesis of my relationship with this Latin American reality was published as *The reception of CST and the 'Movimenti' Phenomenon in the Latin American Context: A Critical View,* in «Journal of Catholic Social Thought», X, 2 (2013), pp. 413-419.

[26] My first interest in the early seventies was on the impact of technology on our global society, and *The One dimensional Man* of H. Marcuse, the legacy of the Frankfurter Schule and the first books of J. Habermas, but also the radical protestant French author J. Ellul with his *The Technological Society* were important and inspiring partners in the shaping of my intellectual horizon. From this last author I retained the idea that Marx if he would have lived in the twentieth century would have studied the overall impact of technique on our society. Even if I was never a leftist militant, my engagement as a young Christian had some elements of the journey a fellow and academic colleague described in his autobiography, in many ways representative for what my generation born in the fifties and children of May 68 experienced. See Baggio, A.M. (1980).

[27] See my *Economy of Communion. A Sociological inquiry on a Contemporary Charismatic Inspiration in Economic and Social Life,* in «Claritas», I, 1 (2012), pp. 71-82.

[28] I published mostly on the reality of the new ecclesial movements in the Catholic Church.

involved in interreligious dialogue with Jews and Muslims. This all seemed fitting when I participated ten years ago as a professor in the start of the Sophia University Institute, one of the founding academic partners of this Summer school. Sophia is a young university, a university that practices dialogue as one of its core values (De Beni, M. (Ed.) 2019); I felt prepared by my experience to be part of the challenge.

Sophia University Institute has its roots in the Catholic Church, a Church – at least in part – shaped by the orientations determined by the Second Vatican Council in the sixties.[29] There the Catholic Church chose the path of dialogue on all fronts. That is, dialogue within the Church, ecumenism with the other Christian confessions, dialogue with the believers of other religions, and with the variegated world of people of good will, the formula used to designate the non-believers open to dialogue with the Church. Obviously, this required a process of transformation that in the view of most observers is still an unfolding story; it is not yet clearly part of the profound, rooted attitude and moral vision of all Catholics worldwide.[30] But I can say today without fear of being corrected by the 'Holy Office', that you cannot be a Catholic if you do not feel that ecumenism, interreligious dialogue and dialogue with non-believers are an integral part of your identity. If you don't, in a certain way you're not in touch with the God of our times, as we understand Him now.

Partly Prepared, Partly Surprised by the Initial Dialogue

You understand that when we started the initiative we now call DIALOP in 2016 with the partners of Transform/Europe at our University, and when we organized the first seminar with the European Left, the Vatican and our own academic team, I was partly prepared and also partly surprised by one particular detail: my Leftist partners in the dialogue spoke much more about Pope Francis than we as Catholics. And in the more than three years of our

[29] From a sociological point of view, see M. J. Wilde, *Vatican II. A Sociological Analysis of Religious Change,* Princeton University Press, Princeton and Oxford 2007. In a more theological and pastoral perspective the recent P. Coda, *Il Concilio della Misericordia. Sui sentieri del Vaticano II,* Roma, Città Nuova 2015.

[30] From a sociological point of view, see Wilde, M. J. (2007). In a more theological and pastoral perspective the recent P. Coda, *Il Concilio della Misericordia. Sui sentieri del Vaticano II,* Roma, Città Nuova 2015.

collaboration they surprised me many times. I remember a spontaneous exclamation of one of our partners: but religion is not an obstacle between us anymore. And if I interpret correctly, that was not because religion became insignificant.

Over time, we experienced the solid foundation of our dialogue through the sincere appreciation of our partners and many strong affirmations by the Pope. The Pope's critique of the current situation of the world economy and his letter on the ecological crisis created not only the intellectual platform, but also the common ground for our transversal thinking. And the Pope's encouragement was obviously the direct cause for launching our dialogue before what he called 'the intolerability of a world order built on profit and greed'. (Baier, W.; Sello, L. (Eds.) 2018*)* .

After more than two years of ongoing conferences, two academic seminars (on ecology and on peace and violence) among specialists, we felt strong enough to make another step. We were also moved by the sense of urgency to broaden our experience to the next generation and transmit what we had experienced and thought together. The idea of giving more academic and institutional strength to our initiative came to life at a certain moment in a conversation between Walter Baier (European Left) and Franz Kronreif (Focolare). It resulted in the idea of launching a Masters in dialogue between the Left and the Christian world, where students of the Left and Christian students could converge, dialogue, live together and learn from each other in a common effort to think about the changes our present world needs!

We know that nothing changes without a great vision! So that was the first step to flesh out this vision. The 'Greek' week, the Summer school of September 2018, became our first attempt to realize this vision.

Truth: Variable, Subjective, a Social Construction or …

Within the organizing team we agreed that I should enucleate some thoughts about the spirit with which we hoped to live these days. Starting from the experience of launching a young international university grounded in the effort to give an intellectual backing to the lifestyle of dialogue I mentioned, I offer what I hope are three stimulating initial conclusions from our recent experience of dialogue.

1. Nobody possesses the absolute truth.

2. We must avoid subtle violence in our thinking in an individualistic context – the need for the virtues of diversity.

3. A dialogical dialectic relationship.

First of all, I think that the spirit underlying our Summer school had to do with a deep conviction that Pope Francis outlined in a conversation with Eugene Scalfari (Papa Francesco, Scalfari, E. 2013), the renowned Italian journalist of La Repubblica. Scalfari introduced himself to the Pope as a non-believer.

Francis affirmed in this interview that the 'truth makes us humble, because we know that rather than possessing the truth, it is the truth that embraces and possesses us, (...) An absolute truth would mean something without bounds, links, relationships'(ibidem). The Pope explained that his conviction is rooted in the concept that truth and the love of God that comes to us in Christ, are one and the same thing in the Christian faith. Truth so defined has everything to do with relationship. And I quote again: '... so each of us can make it bear fruit, and express it starting from him/herself, from his/her story and culture, the situation in which he/she lives, and so on'. And the Pope completes his thought as follows: 'That doesn't mean that the truth is variable and subjective, not at all. But it signifies that the truth gives itself to us always and only as a way to go, and as life' (ibidem). I guess this can help us. None of us will possess the absolute truth this week, but I assume that something of the truth will come to us, through our dialogue, through our life together. As men and women of good will in this journey together, we are equal partners.

A second element was suggested to me by the discussions we had in our second seminar in April 2017. It helped me at least, to better understand what I said about the truth. If none of us possesses the truth, we can say we try to cultivate a non-violent way of dialoguing with each other in our Summer school, in our journey rooted in the common conviction that we can contribute to a better understanding of our common task in this transversal dialogue to provoke change in Europe and the world.

In the seminar we spoke about the subtle violence that was very common in the past when there was the conviction that you had to convert the other to your point of view, especially when that other had his/her own strong convictions. And many means to convince the other were considered legitimate in the past, but we now feel they were a form of an imposition, of violence. The theologian, Piero Coda, President of Sophia University Institute analyzed the violence exercised by our thinking. (Coda, P. 2018, pp. 284-288). In a world where many elements promote an individualistic way of living and thinking, we strongly feel a subtle violence at work in much thinking, because when the thoughts become the absolute property of an individual, the other has nothing to say or add. That's my thought and that's it.

Our Summer school is meant to go in the other direction. In my opinion, as for example, private property is not absolute in the Church's tradition of social thinking, so also my thoughts can't be 'absolute', they need confrontation with the other. I cannot think if I do not listen to the other, if I am not able to be changed, modified by him or her. I experienced this so many times on occasions of sincere, open, authentic dialogue. I exposed strong convictions, but striving to offer them as a contribution, not as an imposition, and then I experienced inside, even while I spoke, that the quality of listening of my dialogue partners opened me up to new insights, moderating my convictions, deepening but also correcting and enriching them.

And so, I come to my third point. Recent articles hit me when they spoke about the ongoing culture wars in our contemporary world. An example given was the one between 'sovereignist' and 'europeanist'. We here today represent two traditions that fought more than one culture war in recent centuries. We here today still represent two traditions of thinking about the world. Are we condemned to arrive at a synthesis where one of the two eliminates the other? No. If we are here, it is because we share a strong belief, consciously or even unconsciously; we have a vision where we appreciate not the merits of a dialectic of opposition, but something that Coda in his contribution calls a dialogical dialectic relationship. [31]

What does this mean? I quote Coda again: 'It is the great merit of modern thinking and especially of Marxism to have introduced the dimension

---

[31] See P. Coda, *La trinità come pensiero. Un manifesto,* in «Sophia» IX (2017/1), pp. 9-17; also from the same author: *The Unity of reciprocal love: the charism of Chiara Lubich and the theology of Klaus Hemmerle,* in «International Journal of philosophy and Theology», Vol. 78 (2017/1-2), pp. 155-171; and *Trinitarisches Denken benötigt trinitarisch geteiltes Leben,* in M. Sellmann (Hg.), *Gedanken Gänge. Klaus Hemmerles Theologie als Project beweglichen Denkens,* Echter Verlag, Würzburg 2017, pp. 123-135.

of history and the relation with otherness into our philosophical tradition'[32]. In Christian thinking, he continues, and I summarize: the last decades saw a strong current that stresses again the idea that unity, God in other words, is not to be understood as marginalizing diversity: diversity is no longer seen as a dimension outside God, outside unity; that would mean that unity in God is uniformity. But it is part of the core of the Christian understanding of unity that unity has to be understood as unity in diversity, in the theological language as unity and distinction. Both in God are seen on the same level: unity calls for distinction; distinction calls for unity. Translated into more common language: the vertical-hierarchical line so characteristic of Christian thinking and acting is not more relevant than the line of the horizontal relationship among equals. They have equal dignity.

I read an exemplary story about this in these days. After hearing a talk during a retreat for priests and bishops in the eighties where the insights of recent theological research were exposed in an atmosphere of real brotherhood, also towards his own person, a very conservative Brazilian bishop, linked with the integralist French Bishop Lefebvre, took the floor at the end and told of the metanoia he had undergone. Everybody in the assembly knew of his arch-conservative perspective.

> 'I was a theology professor in the priests' seminary for many years, but I heard speak here for the first time about trinitarian relations – translated: relations that combine unity and distinction. I always imagined the Trinity as a platoon of soldiers where all obey the chief without the least resistance, because in front of the greatest mystery of our faith, you can only bow your head, be silent and obey. And that for me was perfection. Here for the first time I understood that Trinitarian relations make each Person equal and distinct and that divine unity comes forth from reciprocal love among the divine Persons' (Pepe, E. 2018 pp. 164-165).

Obviously, the language used here is theological, but you easily grasp the way we can translate it into more secular terms. Relationship, authentic, respectful, open inclusive relations where unity does not signify uniformity but always increasingly enriching diversity are the key for a dialogic dialectic relation, for the real possibility of transversal thinking.

---

32 Ibidem

Experiencing «Otherness»

On Dialogue between Christians and Marxists

Thomas Stuke

During a marvelous week on the Greek island of Syros (1.-8. 9. 2018) I had the pleasure of designing and leading a daily slot of 30 minutes after lunchtime in the plenary, where the theoretical topic 'Dialogue' was examined and transferred into practical experiences. All the students and professors of the summer-school participated in these *'Exercises in Dialogue'*. Of course, the setting of a summer school including international faculty and students with different ideological backgrounds is an invitation to not only think about or discuss the mutually challenging aspects of the other or to dispute with the other. Rather, the aim was to really *experience* the other, and as a result to become able to integrate different positions into a shared view. Dialogue was taught and practised as a way of experiencing the always biographically formed history and the always socio-economically formed legitimation of the 'others" positions. Instead of immediately misunderstanding these differences as signs of structural, irreducible obstacles, they should serve as resources for deeper understanding.

The following paragraphs [1] give a brief insight into some theoretical frameworks [2] present the didactic presuppositions and the exercises and [3] conclude with three considerations of Lacan's differentiation of the 'O/other', discerning four different types of communicative interaction, and exploring the sensible role of silence in real dialogue.

Some theoretical frameworks for exercises in dialogue

It is a performative paradox that speaking about dialogue necessarily presupposes clarification of some terms in advance. At least the following differentiations should be made without claiming to be exhaustive.

Three levels of communication can be distinguished using linguistic analysis: An *analogical level* that includes our body reflexes primarily, mimicry and gestures emphasising or diminishing certain aspects of meaning. A *performative level* uses volume, tempo, and accentuation in order to modulate the communication as an enactment of spoken grammar (questioning, hesitating, shouting, accusing, etc.), as Speech-Act-Theory has clearly demonstrated (Austin 1962, Searle 1969/ 1979, Alston 2000). On a *digital level* finally, the meaning of dialogue is determined to a certain extent by vocabulary, and by the semantical and grammatical rules of each language. The complexity is great enough to make misunderstandings quite probable even on this level (Watzlawick 1993/ 2014).

In addition, the well-known model of the floating iceberg illustrates that at first sight, only superficial understanding becomes visible in communication oftentimes, while emotional and intuitive meanings usually stay below the surface. Therefore, focusing only on the objective meaning of terms in dialogue and arguing about these is not necessarily helpful for understanding. Quite to the contrary, these might even contribute to more dissent. Processes of counselling and therapy show how working with these subtle dimensions can help. They bring to light how personal backgrounds contribute to a given situation, transferring meanings and evaluation of formerly historical-economic, social-cultural, and psychological-biographical experience.

Moreover, the theory and practice of dialogue require awareness of the differentiation of *function*, *role*, and *person*, and the interference among these dimensions. Processes of personal and team development must consider which of these dimensions should be in the foreground or background in a particular situation. These considerations not only raise complexity but they can also contribute to successful communication and add precious insight as has frequently been shown in value-based feed-back-processes (Luft, Ingham 1955) where talking about one's own resonance becomes a necessary resource for fruitful dialogue.

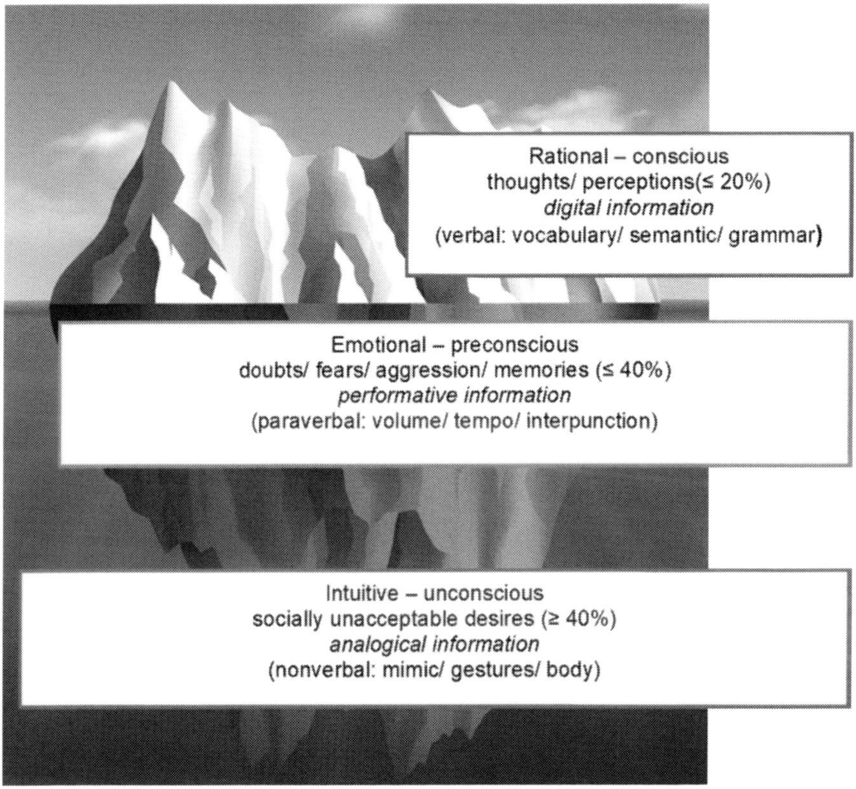

The arrangement of the exercises in dialogue during the summer school followed not only the daily topics (Dialogue, Commons, Democracy, Europe) within this theoretical framework, but also used analogical and digital communication, and patterns of organizational learning (forming, storming, norming, performing (Tuckman 1965/ 1977, Senge 1990/ idem et al. 2000) as a matrix to shape a 'communication circle' (Stuke 2015, p. 165):

To start the communication-circle, the most crucial factor is *accepting* the fundamental reality of *co-existence*, because the other might be disturbing, frightening and even threatening to one's own fundamental values and worldview. To continue the circle, it becomes important to *co-orientate oneself among others*, to understand their positions as others, and to widen the range of arguments. In a third phase, communication is *deepened* by the *co-ordination of mutual understanding*: We find common grounds and shared

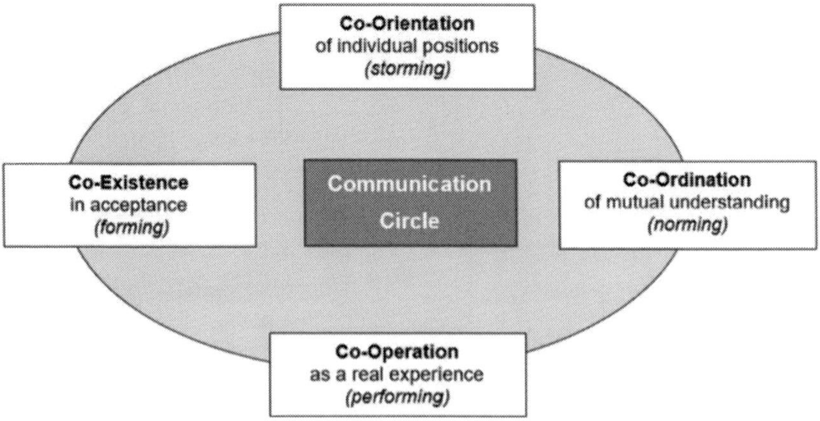

positions, we differentiate our own point of view and might even change it due to the arguments made by the other. The final phase in communicative interaction turns to *transferring communication into real co-operation*. Therefore, it is necessary to widen and de-contextualize the experiences made in the previous phases from the field of interaction in speech-acting, to action in the target field of socio-political cooperation.

Didactical presuppositions and a brief description of the exercises

As the difference between theory and practice is always larger in practice than in theory (Ferstl 2011) the approach of illustrating *theoretical* ideas by using *practical* exercises seems paradoxical. Concrete holistic experience can generate a deeper understanding, although it is less semantically language-based than explanation (Lind 2016, Fauser 1991/ 1996/ 2003). Therefore, I chose this 'inductive' and 'practical' approach to dialogue for the summer school.

On one hand, such exercises can open new, unknown possibilities for self-reflection and self-development. Under certain personal and situational circumstances on the other hand, they might also become a disturbing or even overwhelming experience for some. It was important therefore to make the participants aware of their personal responsibility to end or continue participation based on their feelings and thoughts.

'Three times twice' – Becoming Aware of One's Own Reactive Patterns in Different Roles

The first exercise was designed to enter the communication circle on the most profound level: accepting coexistence and preparing the ground for practically entering the topic of the day – dialogue. In an exercise in pairs, the participants were asked to stand in front of each other with hand contact (putting their palms together but not holding or gripping each other). In this position they were then invited to take turns playing the roles of leader and follower changing the position of their hands in accordance with three patterns: accepting (leader and obedient follower), resisting (wannabe-leader and adversary) and redirecting (wannabe-leader and creative counterpart). After the exercise, the participants were asked to assess their personal experiences in each role first individually in silence, then sharing with their partner, and finally with the whole group.

The aim of this exercise was to become aware of one's own reactive patterns through interaction (Cohn1997, Russell 2003), not by theoretical reflection alone, in order to prepare the ground for a more profound self-reflective attitude toward one's own dispositions and tendencies in communicative settings: Do I spontaneously prefer to lead or to follow? Do I feel better in a situation of cooperation or opposition? How do I feel about using the other's moves for my own intentions and how do I feel if the other redirects my interventions?

'The whole picture'

The second experience prepares the ground for the meaning of 'the common goods', that day's topic. To responsibly deal with the commons, it is not only necessary to see one's own interests, but 'he whole picture' as well. In this sense, the second exercise continues the communicative circle by exemplifying the reality of necessary co-orientation of oneself *among others*. It's mainly about accepting that the 'other' might use 'other' words and descriptions with the same intent because they have had different experiences beforehand; they may apply them as a framework for their interpretation. Moreover, the leap from the analogical to the digital level might introduce another obstacle to the mutual understanding of a shared reality. This obstacle consists in the codification of experiences in different digital terms, which might obstruct understanding as a consequence, instead of facilitating it.

In this exercise the participants were split into two groups, standing back-to-back with one another in pairs. Each group was shown one of these images for 30 seconds:

Then, *all* the participants were briefly (2 seconds) shown an image combining both the previous images:

After that, they were asked to *silently* draw the last picture they had just seen – without any spoken or written communication. The experience they had during the drawing process was then shared in small groups of 4-6 persons considering the individual and common reality in iterative communication (function, role, person, prejudices or biases, priming effects etc.) as well as the possible role of language/semantics (How do you name what you have seen?) in the whole process. The aim of this exercise was to become aware of how pre-experiences form our perception (Fauser 2003), and to experience how helpful and even necessary and indispensable the other's perspective can be to grasp 'the whole picture'.

'Drawing attention'

If we ask ourselves, what might be the most crucial source of communication in modern *democracy*, it becomes obvious that the digital revolution and the globalization of the internet have led to a new order of discourse

(Foucault 2003). The dilemma of this kind of discourse is that we are simultaneously confronted with too much information through structures that are not really suitable for the content, and without a profound understanding of the meaning of the words to which we listen. We still perceive others therefore, but through a kind of opaque veil that makes the digitally distanced others seem less real. They often serve as a kind of projection screen for our own strong emotions, rather than really coming into sight as who they are. This happens for example, when the refugees fleeing to Europe over the Mediterranean appear as undifferentiated alien masses threatening Europe's culture and wealth rather than becoming visible as individual persons – each with their own story and trauma.

How can we not only coexist and co-orient ourselves under such circumstances (maybe even against some scapegoat or common threat) but also *coordinate* our intentions and actions in a more constructive and sustainable way? As it is vital for democracies to articulate and aggregate interests in political processes (Coleman 1966, Kevenhörster 2008), the third exercise was designed to make participants experience aspects that are essential for this coordination between systems (Luhmann, Schorr 1986/ Luhmann 1984/ 2012a/b) and monadic spheres (Leibniz 1720, Sloterdijk1998), which otherwise stay opaque and irreducibly separated from each other (Pariser 2011).

Therefore, the participants were asked to divide in pairs and while looking at each other, both the partners had to simultaneously write a single word in their common language (English) with their index finger on an imaginary whiteboard in the air in front of their counterpart. The partner had to guess what the corresponding partner had written. It is almost impossible to simultaneously write and focus on the other's writing of course (especially since the partners were looking at each other, they also had to practice reverse reading). Nobody was able to guess what the other had written as a result. The pairs were advised to write one after the other in a second step, then guess again what the other had written. It seemed a little easier this time, as complexity was reduced by avoiding simultaneity. They were finally asked to write one after the other in a third step, and to adopt mirror writing. Almost all pairs were able to understand what the other had written at this point because of the 'translation' of the word into an image which the other could actually 'read' and understand from his/her perspective.

In the subsequent reflection in small groups, the participants were able to understand that it is necessary to stop and listen (against the overabundance of simultaneous information and the human tendency to already think about one's own reply while the other is still explaining his/her idea) in order to pass on and receive ideas and to take into account the other's perspective (ideal role taking: Kohlberg e.a. 1983/ Shaffer 2008). Thus, being silent and trying to temporarily empty oneself of one's own perspective in order to assume the role of the other became evident as an important aspect of *co-ordination.*

'Listen to what I didn't say, answer what you didn't hear'

The fourth exercise finally was chosen to illustrate the fragile complexity of *digital* communication thereby introducing the participants to Schulz von Thun's communication theory (Schulz v. Thun 1998, 2002, 2004/ idem e.a. 2018) (also known as the four-sides model or four-ears model). *Every* human utterance has four facets according to this model: (1) fact, (2) self-revelation (the speaker consciously or unintentionally reveals something about him/herself, his/her motives, values, emotions etc.), (3) relationship (the message states something about the relationship between sender and receiver), and (4) appeal (the message contains a desire, advice, instruction etc. the speaker is seeking) – and can be perceived accordingly on different levels. As sender and receiver might not put the same emphasis and attention on each of these facets, the multi-layered structure helps understand (and hence possibly avoid) another potential source of misunderstanding.

In order to experience their own biases in hearing, the participants were asked to choose one of a series of strong (positively and negatively connoted) judgments, maybe disturbing and annoying quotes about the topic of the day, *Europe*. Participants were then asked to read the chosen phrase alone two or three times and to pay attention to *their own reactions* (analogical body, emotional, situational memory). After that they were supposed to analyze these reactions using the four-ears model, asking themselves through which ear they had immediately heard more (the ear which tends to be overcrowded as a consequence) and with which ear they didn't hear anything at all (the ear which could be considered to be deaf). Being aware of one's own listening tendencies can at least facilitate mutual understanding, for example discovering the tendency to preferentially hear with the appeal-ear and not even recognize the self-revelatory message concealed behind this communicative wall.

In the next reflective phase, the participants were asked to consider how to enter into a dialogue related to one of the disturbing sentences: What could/should be my next sentence to shift communication from my established reaction patterns to my less developed ear and thereby activate more of my communicative resources and lead the interaction to a more constructive level?

Conclusions: From a Coincidental Project toward an Attitude of Transversal Mutual Understanding

Reflecting on our experiences in the transversal dialogue between Marxists and Christians during the summer school, I want to strengthen two theoretical implications and one personal annotation:

Differentiating the Small 'other' from the Big 'Other' in the Wake of Lacan

In each of the phases in communication (Co-existence, -orientation, -ordination, -operation) there have been certain patterns of interaction which demand certain forms of cognitive and emotional resources, of mental and behavioural mindsets. Each of the offered exercises is only one of many possible paths to strengthen these resources and to become more aware of their necessity for successful communication. While the participants experienced this along with the different phases, it also became obvious that there is a strong pattern characterizing all of them: When entering into dialogue, it is helpful to *be aware of how the counterpart is experienced*.

For this, Jacques Lacan (Lacan 1991/ Evans 1996) suggests differentiating between 'the little other' (l'autre: a) and 'the big Other' (l'Autre: A). While the small 'a' is not really other, but only a reflection and projection of the Ego, the big 'A' is characterized by a radical otherness, which transcends the illusion of assimilation through identification.

Based on Lacan's differentiation, I want to propose a four-field-matrix to systematize different ways of experiencing the dialogue partners and respective modes of relating to them. Basically, the other can be understood as good or bad and as superior or inferior to oneself:

IMAGINING THE OTHER AS	SUPERIOR	INFERIOR
GOOD	rivalry-circle	mourning (showing your wounds)
BAD	fear	hatred

Whenever the other is experienced as good and thus worth imitating, there is the danger that he/she not only serves as a model, but becomes a rival.[33] This is especially true if the other is relatively close to oneself and his/hers spheres of possibility are within one's own reach. In contrast, if the other is the transcendent divine other, chances are better that the 'Other' is seen in the radical and irreducible otherness precluding such rivalry from occurring. A second mode of perceiving the other in a communicative setting is as good and inferior. In this case, chances are high that emotions of empathy – mourning the other's wounds and showing one's own wounds – become possible. If the other is perceived as superior and bad, the main emotional reaction will be fear, while the emotional mixture of attributed inferiority and evil might end in hatred.

Differentiating Four Types of Communicative Interaction

I also want to propose another four-field-matrix, this time placing four types of communicative interaction along the axis of process-orientation vs. result-orientation, and person-orientation vs. topic-orientation. Each type has its own strengths and weaknesses and is appropriate to reach different goals. In order to constructively understand and practice dialogue, it seems

[33] I am very thankful for the inspiring discussions about Renê Girard's Mimetic Theory during the annual meeting of the Colloquium on Violence and Religion (COV&R) in Innsbruck in July 2019, namely Wolfgang Palaver, Roman Siebenrock, Jozef Niewiadomski and especially Petra Steinmair-Pösel.

helpful to distinguish dialogue from other forms of communicative interaction. Practically, it is necessary to clarify in a preceding discourse (Habermas 2015) 'to know where we are' (Chiara Lubich, quoted in Turin 2012, p. 49) in the sense of becoming aware of the communicative setting as well as the main aim pursued within the communicative circle (co-existence, co-orientation, co-ordination or co-operation).

Dialogue is neither a complicated technique nor a negligible factor in finding solutions for complex problems in a participatory and democratic way. Dialogue is a deeply based *attitude*, that can be learned and cultivated; therefore, it must be taught, rethought and renewed in ongoing dialogical processes. It is not a dialogue in the everyday use of the term therefore, but rather in the way coined by Martin Buber. Emphasizing the special quality of dialogue, he differentiated real dialogue from chit-chat (Buber 1973, p. 282). Although there is a strong natural tendency among human beings to *cooperate*, there is no such thing as a *naturally* continuing dialogue. Therefore, dialogue has to be *organized, institutionalized and protected* against any abusive forms of pretended 'dialogues' that actually try to reproduce paternalistic power-structures:

> 'In our time, in which the understanding of the nature of true conversation has become rare, its conditions from the false sense of openness have been so

> thoroughly misjudged that one supposes that such a conversation can be organised in front of an audience of interested listeners with fitting journalistic assistance. But an open debate of such a high 'level' can be neither spontaneous nor completely unreserved; an interview performed for a sound bite is completely divorced from a true conversation.'(Buber 1973, p. 297)

Although it's *practically* useless to enter into a never-ending discourse, it's *philosophically* unavoidable at the same time. Therefore, the order and extent of the four types and phases in communicative interaction have to be defined beforehand. As each of these forms has its weaknesses and strengths, to 'know where we are' (Lubich) means to know in which of these fields (and therefore with the support of which techniques and rules) the communication has to be organized *in a particular setting*. This knowledge cannot be found in the four-field-matrix, but has to be found in a *pragmatic discourse* (Habermas 2005/ 2014) about the question, where we begin this process. Entering into a dialogue *presupposes and presumes* – following the theoretical approach of Martin Buber (1973/ 1982)[34] – that the other might be right, and therefore that the concrete outcome and output of a dialogue isn't predictable. The 'third' position – the heteronomous, marginalized, alienated, excluded, unacceptable argument – has to be actively strengthened and thereby at least reconsidered as having the *potential to be integrated* by those who are already capable of joining the dialogue at a given moment. The productive side of a dialogue can be measured by the following *qualities and indicators:*

- widened mutual understanding among the participants
- higher awareness and reduced risks of unintended side-effects
- higher satisfaction with the process as well as with the results among the participants
- realistic, resource-oriented plans for coordinated ongoing practical subsequent steps.

[34] Many other theoretical approaches could be mentioned here. In particular I would like to mention Hannah Arendt: 'It is the companionship with others, calling me out of the dialogue of thought, make me one again.' (Arendt 2018, 546) and David Bohm's 'Vision of Dialogue' (Bohm 1996, p. 36ff.).

Silence as a Necessary Precondition for Real Dialogue

One final personal remark might be useful: Aside from all the experiences and differentiation of dialogical talking, speech and use of language, dialogue needs and therefore presupposes the dynamics of interaction *and* contemplation (Steinmair-Pösel 2019). In this respect, the particular understanding and practice of a 'kenotic dialogue' (Kronreif 2018) as practised within the Focolare Movement seems helpful. The term 'kenotic' here refers to an attitude of emptying oneself of all prejudices, presuppositions and ideas about the other in order to be able to perceive the 'other' as 'Other', i.e. as he/she 'really' is. This *being* silent as a way of pausing since exterior *and* interior silence is not only the precondition for active listening; it also opens the required space for the dialogue partner to articulate him/herself. It can be clearly differentiated from being passively silent or actively silencing someone.

Practically, not only the discourse about the four-field-matrix, but also their various phases must be punctuated by structurally protected silence as interruption of ongoing verbal communication. As experience on the Greek island has shown, the awareness of (inter- and intra-subjective) silence is a necessary basis for mutual understanding that has to be strengthened in any way possible.

Naming the World in order to Change It

Dialogue – a Nonviolent Strategy in a Pluralistic World[35]

Cornelia Hildebrandt[36] – Pál Tóth[37]

Key points for a new Marxist-Christian dialogue in the 21 st century

We are living in a rapidly changing world with new challenges on a global level. There is an epochal metamorphosis going on: new risks (challenges, problems) require new forms of thinking and acting (new frames of reference, new ways to collaborate).

The world has dramatically changed in the last few decades, and we are far away from the scenarios of the Marxist-Christian dialogue of the late

---

37 Lecture during the First International Summer School of Dialogue between Christians and Marxists: Europe as a common. September 1 – 8, 2018, Syros University of the Aegean – Ermoupoli, Greece.

37 Philosopher; Vice Director and Consultant for Parties and Social Movements at the Rosa Luxemburg Foundation in Berlin; Board Member of the European Left Foundation, Transform!Europe. She is part of the coordinating group of DIALOP.

37 Lecturer on the 'Theory of Communication' at the Sophia University Institute – Florence/ Italy. He was also named a professor for the course 'Global Dialogical Studies'. He is a member of the scientific board of the Focolare Movement

60s with emblematic figures like Milan Machovec[38] and Karl Rahner.[39] It was a dialogue about different world views and ideologies in the contexts of two opposite world systems. In the globalized world of our day we have to face a fundamentally different scenario: we should find common strategies for action in order to solve humanity's fundamental problems like poverty, climate change, the devastation of war and terror and organized crime. Dialogue is not an option today; it is necessary for survival.

I. The Dialogic Challenge

On Dialogue Itself

A Tentative Definition of Dialogue

We find the question of Global Justice first among the top ten philosophical issues of the 21st Century according to some Stanford philosophers. What new principles of justice will help us manage in a distinct way 21st Century problems like preserving the environment while allowing the poorer nations of the world to improve their living standards? The philosophy of the past has not produced real models to answer such questions. Philosophers of the 21st century urgently need to do so.

It is necessary then to find a new basis for common sensibilities and common values. The world is more economically interconnected than it ever was. But the unequal worldwide economic development, including Europe, is reflected in social inequality and social fragmentation. Can we find a new basis for shared values that will bring us together rather than tear us apart?

Finally: New models for collective decision-making and collective rationality are needed. Solving the problems of the 21st Century will require rational coordinated action on a massive scale. It is not rationality that characterizes international relations however, but rather increasing unpredictability, the renunciation of international treaties, so that the basis for

38 Milan Machovec was a Czech philosopher, professor of Marxism at the Charles University in Prague and mastermind of the Prague Spring.

39 Karl Rahner was an important Catholic theologian who worked on the preparation of the II. Vatican Council.

rational action becomes more limited, and at the same time, more necessary.[40]

The problem is that we really have no models for collective rationality to deal with the widespread problems in the globalized 21st century. The CSCE process (Collective Security System) was developed under the conditions of the systemic confrontation in the 20th century. We are not yet living in the time of collective reflection on the relationship between peace, justice and democracy today.

Dialogue is an excellent tool now for collective rational discourse, problem-solving and co-creation instead of other competitive forms. The recent findings of evolutionary anthropology on the essentially collaborative nature of the human mind open new possibilities for developing more collaborative cultural patterns. Homo sapiens has adapted, at an unprecedented level, to act and think cooperatively in cultural groups. In fact, all the most extraordinary human cognitive achievements – from complex technologies to linguistic and mathematical symbols to the most intricate social institutions – are the product of individuals who interact, not of individuals operating alone. In this framework dialogue is a collaborative and constructive form for communication, in contrast with more competitive and non-committal forms like debate. This definition represents a pure type; in real life situations you can find a merging of collaborative and competitive dynamics. Dialogic cultures tend to realize this pure form of communicative collaboration.

The Difference between Dialogue and Discussion

Dialogue processes are becoming increasingly widely used. But there is no consensus on the use of the terms 'discourse', 'dialogue', 'discussion', 'debate' and other similar expressions. We understand discussion to be a rather competitive, sometimes combative approach which seeks to be victorious; a participant in a discussion wants to express himself and say he is better than his counterpart. Discussion can be described as debate with a facade of being nice. Much like debate, it is oriented to advocating particular viewpoints and challenging others.[41]

---

40 Read the whole list here: https://www.philosophytalk.org/blog/move-over-letterman-philosophical-top-10-list-21st-century

41 Among the numerous conceptualizations of these difference see Edgar H. Schein: The

In positional or adversarial discussion, the conversation continues in the adversarial (I'm right and you are wrong) mode that conflicts typically take. In adversarial discussion disputants engage in positional bargaining (they focus on firm, usually mutually incompatible, positions in other words) and blame each other for the problem. But discussions are not necessarily combative; competing dynamics can help clarify positions.

On the other hand, dialogue is oriented to finding a shared connection. It is not concerned with winning or losing; rather it aspires to listen more deeply, understand more fully, and build a collective point of view. When diversity of personality and opinion present moments of conflict and tension, dialogue steps in to mediate the conversation and lead it back to a renewed sense of connection.

The first form of dialogue is dialogue in human relations. Pope Francis emphasizes the importance of the culture of encounter. Participants explore their feelings about their differences; they break down negative stereotypes and come to know members of the other side as persons, and even, sometimes, as 'friends'. They develop a sense of trust and understanding with the people involved in the process, though they may still disagree on some fundamental issues.

A second form of dialogue is activist dialogue. This type provides a foundation for action. Participants from opposite sides of a conflict get together to rebuild a war-torn city, form a bi-partisan school, or deliver health care to the sick and injured. The purpose of such dialogue is not just talk and understanding, but mutual cooperation and assistance.

A third type of dialogue involves the process of strategic problem solving. In such workshops, special attention is focused on the parties' fundamental human needs, the absence of which is seen to be a primary cause of most deep-rooted conflicts. An intense effort is made to jointly reframe the conflict in terms of needs, and then engage in joint problem solving to develop ways to meet those needs, and hence resolve the conflict. In several cases the starting point is not a conflict, but a common challenge and the dialogue is aimed at broadening options for joint action.

The principal elements of dialogic behaviour are: suspending judgment, listening carefully, inquiring and exploring assumptions.

---

process of dialogue: creating effective communication. https://thesystemsthinker.com/the-process-of-dialogue-creating-effective-communication/

When we suspend our judgment, we temporarily silence our thoughts and open our capacity to be engaged as listeners. Greater inquiry into others' viewpoints helps us better understand those with whom we work; it offers us the opportunity to adopt new ways of thinking. When we explore our assumptions, we encounter unchallenged ideas, unchecked biases, and patterns of thought that influence, and possibly inhibit our engagement in the collaborative effort.

A collaborative culture promotes dialogue and a diverse perspective as elements leading to richer thought, opportunities to act and new innovation.

Summing up the difference between dialogue and discussion as pure types:

Discussion	**Dialogue**
Hierarchical and competitive culture: competition, dependence, exclusion	Horizontal and cooperative culture: collaboration, partnership and inclusion
Convince each other of the own point of view	Investigate and learn together
Justify and defend your own reasons	Understand the statements of the parties
Confute the other's reasons	Accept and understand each other's position (values, interests)
Obtain the consent of the other	Share ideas, experiences, feelings
Select the best solution	Integrate the different perspectives
One-sided and often fragmented vision	Full vision, a synergy of different thoughts
Victory / defeat	Gain for all participants
Individual leadership	Shared leadership

Communities of Co-creation

According to Ulrich Beck, global challenges create new forms of communities which are oriented to managing global problems. The main identity-building factor in these groups is the common awareness of the challenges and a joint intention to collaborate with each other in order to find valid solutions. (Beck, U. 2016).

We are united by the shared analysis of this world. Pope Francis wrote, 'This economy kills.' (Naomi Klein explained in her book, 'Shock Doctrine,' the autonomy of the shock strategy and the rise of disaster capitalism (Klein, N. (2007). Gayatri Chakravorty Spivak speaks about postcolonialism and subaltern articulation (Spivak, G.C. 1990). Jean Ziegler makes the accusation: Every child who dies of hunger is murdered (Ziegler, J. 2009). Susan George, a famous intellectual, describes the secret capitalist cabal behind European austerity: 'Ordinary people in the [global] south from the late 1970s until today have had to pay for the crimes and the greed and the odious debts of the dictators of their own governments, of their own upper classes, and they know very well what this means for the population – it means deep cuts in housing, education, culture, health'[42].

These analyses and shared goals and resources are the foundation for a common commitment. Nationality, religion, world views and other identity building factors are put in second order. This is the case with DIALOP[43] as well in our view.

In these groups dialogic communication is co-creation first of all, a sharing of relevant capabilities and only in second order, confrontation of different views. Professional methods of co-creation like World Café, Open Space, Knowledge Gardening and others are the focus of interest.

Dialogue as Naming the World in order to Change It

Among the numerous excellent authors on dialogue we have chosen excerpts from the book by Paulo Freire, a Brazilian scholar of Marxist inspiration with a strong Christian eye: Pedagogy of the Oppressed.

> 'As we attempt to analyze dialogue as a human phenomenon, we discover something which is the essence of dialogue itself: the word. But the word is more than just an instrument which makes dialogue possible; accordingly, we must seek its constitutive elements. Within the word we find two dimensions, reflection and action, in such radical interaction that if one is sacrificed – even

42 https://www.theguardian.com/global-development/2013/dec/30/susan-george-secret-capitalist-cabal-behind-european-austerity

43 The ongoing project of marxist-christian dialogue

in part – the other immediately suffers. There is no true word that is not at the same time a praxis.[44] Thus, to speak a true word is to transform the world.[45]

An unauthentic word, one which is unable to transform reality, results when dichotomy is imposed upon its constitutive elements. When a word is deprived of its dimension of action, reflection automatically suffers as well; and the word is changed into idle chatter, into verbalism, into an alienated and alienating 'blah.' It becomes an empty word, one which cannot denounce the world, for denunciation is impossible without a commitment to transform, and there is no transformation without action.

On the other hand, if action is emphasized exclusively to the detriment of reflection, the word is converted into activism. The latter – action for action's sake – negates the true praxis and makes dialogue impossible. Either dichotomy, by creating unauthentic forms of existence, creates also unauthentic forms of thought which reinforce the original dichotomy.

Human existence cannot be silent, nor can it be nourished by false words, but only by true words, with which men and women transform the world. To exist humanly is to name the world, to change it. Once named, the world in its turn reappears to the namers as a problem and requires of them a new naming. Human beings are not built in silence[46], but in word, in work, in action-reflection.

But while to say the true word – which is work, which is praxis – is to transform the world, saying that word is not the privilege of some few persons, but the right of everyone. Consequently no one can say a true word alone – nor can she say it for another, in a prescriptive act which robs others of their words.

Dialogue is the encounter between men, mediated by the world, in order to name the world. Hence, dialogue cannot occur between those who want to name the world and those who do not wish this naming – between those who deny others the right to speak their word and those whose right to speak has been denied them. Those who have been denied their primordial right to speak their word must first reclaim this right and prevent the continuation of this dehumanizing aggression.

---

44 Action/Reflection – word=work=praxis, Sacrifice of action = verbalism, Sacrifice of reflection = activism

45 Some of these reflections emerged as a result of conversations with Professor Ernani Maria Fiori.

46 I obviously do not refer to the silence of profound meditation, in which men only apparently leave the world, withdrawing from it in order to consider it in its totality, and thus remaining with it. But this type of retreat is only authentic when the meditator is 'bathed' in reality; not when the retreat signifies contempt for the world and flight from it, in a type of 'historical schizophrenia.'

> If it is in speaking their word that people, by naming the world, transform it dialogue imposes itself as the way by which they achieve significance as human beings. Dialogue is thus an existential necessity. And since dialogue is the encounter in which the united reflection and action of the dialoguers are addressed to the world which is to be transformed and humanized, this dialogue cannot be reduced to the act of one person's 'depositing' ideas in another; nor can it become a simple exchange of ideas to be 'consumed' by the discussants. Nor yet is it a hostile, polemical argument between those who are committed neither to the naming of the world, nor to the search for truth, but rather to the imposition of their own truth. Because dialogue is an encounter among women and men who name the world, it must not be a situation where some name on behalf of others. It is an act of creation; it must not serve as a crafty instrument for the domination of one person by another. The domination implicit in dialogue is that of the world by the dialoguers; it is conquest of the world for the liberation of humankind.' (Freire, P. 2000).[47]

Paulo Freire's conception of dialogue goes beyond the didactic model of communication where two or more actors exchange their views. Dialogue is a triadic enterprise for him where actors correlate with each other while they refer to the external word as well. The act of naming, i.e. categorising the phenomena of the external world, is at the beginning of any action. From a Christian point of view, the spoken or used word is important. Marxists often argue about concepts and repeatedly seek new concepts for a more precise description of social processes. The words as well as the concepts shape our analysis of society and refer to individual and socially accepted values at the same time.

How we analyze society, how we set goals and formulate strategies, depends on our mental frameworks. Commercial and political marketing is shaping public opinion in our times; we are manipulated by 'fake news' and 'alternative truths'. Groups in dialogue are islands of sobriety and rationality nowadays, islands seeking new connecting, clear and understandable language. New global phenomena need new categories in any case, and a common fallacy is to articulate them in old, misleading terms. Examples of this could be migrations (How are the persons termed – refugees, migrants, immigrants, illegal migrants?), the authoritarian regimes of Eastern Europe

47 Read the whole 3. Chapter on Dialogue here: https://selforganizedseminar.files.wordpress.com/2011/08/freire_pedagogy_oppresed1.pdf

(Are they dictators, illiberal regimes, centralized democracies?) or the term, national sovereignty.

The Need for a New Marxist-Christian Dialogue

The world is out of control. The global crises of 2008/2009 led to gigantic redistribution and a further concentration of wealth worldwide at the expense of the weakest in society. Economic and social differences have now become hardly negotiable, demonstrating the gap between rich and poor; the eight richest billionaires have as much as the poorer half of the world's population.[48]

None of the global problems have been brought closer to a solution in the last ten years – not economic inequalities, nor social polarization between and within the countries of the North and the South, nor the ecological issues, nor climate change, nor the creation of conditions for stable peace.

In view of these developments, the prevailing neo-liberal consensus on globalized freedom, democracy and social protection loses its binding force. With the loss of this consensus – as Gramsci already observed in the 1920s – the ruling class is no longer a leader, but increasingly a ruler, the owner of pure coercive force, as seen in the growth of authoritarian systems worldwide. There is fragmentation instead of cooperation, unpredictability in politics instead of predictable negotiations to secure peaceful solutions to conflicts.

The post-war order has definitely ended with Trump. Civilization's break with German fascism – the Holocaust – was and still is a reminder. Authoritarian regimes are increasingly in power worldwide nevertheless, including Europe. The political right is also growing in Europe and determines the political agenda even where it is not in power. It is changing the political and social atmosphere.

National/nationalist authoritarian regimes are regaining their support wherever there is a lack of perspective in Europe, where the social and personal decline of entire regions is threatened or has set in long ago, where control of one's own life and its predictability is lost. In this way, a Right which despises humanism is acquiring political weight, acting as a creeping

48 Oxfam. https://www.oxfam.de/ueber-uns/aktuelles/2017-01-16-8-maenner-besitzen-so-viel-aermere-haelfte-weltbevoelkerung. 17.1.2017

poison in bourgeois societies where discourse is changing, where it is being directed against the weakest in society, against refugees, against lived diversity and against minorities, against the unemployed and socially excluded.

Both internally and externally, a policy of balancing and bargaining over things loses influence. National isolation, the unpredictability of politics and the rejection of reliable international cooperation characterize the present which is undergoing radical change. It is not disarmament and the search for alternatives fostering peace that shape international affairs, but the power politics of escalating old and new conflicts, as in the Middle East, the enormous ignorance of misery and suffering, of continuing environmental destruction, the denial of climate change and its dramatic consequences. Tendencies of increasingly open barbarization come to light with the unbearable treatment of those who have fled to Europe. It is a time in which new elements of barbarization are emerging, but also possibilities and ways of new solidary practices.

It is a time for radical social and political upheavals where 'the old dies and the new cannot yet be born' (Gramsci, A. 1999) – a period of interregnum, with the decay and reform of society, the weakness of institutions as well as the development of opportunity structures and the repositioning of actors along new lines of conflict.

It is also a time when the social discussion of ideological questions is growing, when societal values and the relationships among democracy, freedom, equality and solidarity are being renegotiated.

The supposedly consolidated social consensus of multicultural, open, post-conflict Western European societies is debatable. Increasing isolation from other cultures and religions seems to be the new cornerstone of authoritarian social systems instead of openness.

A new anti-Muslim racism is thus closely linked to a leading 'new' national culture in which what is national is combined with very selectively interpreted values of the 'Judeo-Christian West', deliberately delimiting and distinguishing other religions. The conflicts between national-conservative and libertarian values increase on the question of an open, pluralized immigration society for example, and this includes the fundamental right to asylum of course. This means establishing social alliances.

Establishing a position is not enough; resistant alliances are required to defend an open, pluralistic society.

Actors in the Dialogue for Fundamental Social Change

In times of social upheaval, the transition or interregnum is when the old dies but the new cannot yet be born. As the Marxist, Gramsci, says, 'the great masses break away from the traditional ideologies' and no longer believe 'what they believed in before'. It is the time for opportunity structures to emerge, for new alliances and new forms of socio-political organization, and of political entrepreneurship which can build on people's dissatisfaction with the prevailing conditions. The belief in the neoliberal promise of freedom – freedom and deregulation of the markets combined with flexibilisation of work as a necessary precondition for social advancement or social security is not fulfilled for large parts of society.

This is reflected in the discontent and anger characterizing the middle or lower social strata of society. There is awareness that the next generation will not get better, that fundamental problems of global development such as global warming are not being resolved, that wars and terrorism are possible at any time – endangering one's own life in general, that social standards and public services will be further reduced along with fear and insecurity, that social conditions are unsatisfactory. This dissatisfaction characterizes the protests on streets and squares, like in Spain on International Women's Day, in France against the new labour market laws, in Hamburg against the policies of the G20 countries, in Poland against the dismantling of the democratic constitution of the country. It is reflected in countless initiatives to support refugees, in protests by tenants, in the fight to defend open pluralistic societies. Anger is increasingly openly turning against the weakest in one segment of society however.

This means that on the level of the nation in the socio-political field, socially, politically and culturally divided societies demand the restoration of control over their lives and that of their children at the expense of the weakest in society. And there are those who are looking in solidarity for social alternatives to these developments, in view of the many life-threatening developments all over the world.

Christian-Marxist dialogue is meant to strengthen those committed to defending an open, pluralistic society, a society of solidarity. It must entail the search for societal alternatives and for this the promotion of the ideas of freedom, equality and solidarity. It is about explicitly discussing Marxist and Christian ideas to explore the possibility of shared commitment to peace, nonviolence, social justice, democracy and ecological transformation. Dialogue is useful as a teaching method and as a philosophical analytical tool.

What are the Difficulties and Dangers for Dialogue?

One of the foundations for transversal dialogue is the ability to cooperate with the knowledge of differences between cooperation partners. Difference here means those formative differences between the groups of actors that go beyond the diversity within their own 'actor group'; they are constitutive.

In philosophical language, this can mean that not every thought of the other is fully understood. The non-believer will not be able to comprehend the creed or reflections from experienced spirituality as much as the believer. This applies analogously of course to the diversity of cultural and philosophical paths for theory development, to the development of independent ways to organize, and to social practices.

The resulting differences are not only bearable, but they are to be used as a means to enrich diversity. For there are different ways and methods to appropriate the world and so there are also ideologically-philosophically different reasons for peace, freedom, democracy, justice and the preservation of people's livelihoods.

For example, Rosa Luxemburg had already pointed out that freedom (of thought and commerce) always includes the other's freedom – that is, respect for those who think differently.

Dialogue does not mean renunciation of criticism or critical reflections, but it links them to a respectful approach, to the fundamental respect and recognition of the other's philosophical or religious foundations – especially in those questions where one does not agree.

The Catholic Church's fight against atheism, Communism and secularization was the dominant narrative not too many years ago. The institutional Church's battle against liberal theologians was the sub-narrative. The Second Vatican Council introduced a remarkable change in this respect. Among other important innovations, a more participatory mode of church life took hold for 15 years or so after the council. It was expressed in terms of dialogue, collegiality and a synodal working style. What was less recognized about Vatican II, though it is as significant as the halting steps on governance, is that it took account of the world outside the church. For the first time, the church validated the principle of religious freedom and rejected all forms of civil discrimination based on religious grounds.

Sixty years after the Council we find a diversified landscape of dialogue, collaboration and polarization in the Catholic Church. The overriding narrative seems to concern the Catholic Church's conflict within itself. In an increasingly divided world, the Church appears to represent something very different from a community of unity and reconciled diversities. In the Western world this phenomenon takes different shapes and has different histories. Intra-Catholic polarization in the United States, Australia, the United Kingdom, and continental Europe, is not exactly the same in each place. But there is a consensus that it started as political polarization among Catholics, especially around hot-button 'life issues such as gender, contraception and abortion most of all. Pope Francis's reforms have provoked misunderstandings and resistance in many believers.

On one hand there is increasing communion among ecclesial movements and new communities which is something new in the Church's history. On the Vigil of Pentecost, May 30, 1998, John Paul II invited the movements and new ecclesial communities to give a united witness in Saint Peter's Square. Upon Pope Francis's initiative, the world meeting of social movements was held for the third time in 2017. At the 2016 meeting they formulated the most important tasks: the need for change, a change of structures, for the sake of a decent life. We also spoke of how you, the popular movements, are sowing the seeds of change, promoting a process involving millions of actions, great and small, creatively intertwined like words in a poem. That is why I wanted to call you 'social poets'. We also listed three tasks which are essential to progressing toward a humane alternative to the globalization of indifference: (1) putting the economy at the service of people; (2) working for peace and justice; and (3) defending Mother Earth. Pope Francis recalls the basic demands: dignified employment for those excluded from the labour market; land for campesinos and the native peoples; housing for homeless families; urban integration in poorer neighbourhoods; the elimination of discrimination, violence against women and other new forms of enslavement; an end to all wars, organized crime and repression; freedom of expression and democratic communication; putting science and technology at the service of peoples (Pope Francis, 2016).

On What Can this Dialogue Be Based? Ways, Experiences and Tools

A Framework

For us, what are the underlying conditions and principles for such a dialogue?

- A face-to-face dialogue with respect;
- The ability to empathize and to think the other, to try to understand the 'language' of the other which may be unfamiliar;
- The ability to reflect critically on the heritage of Christian-Marxist dialogue;
- Curiosity and openness, the fun and the joy of a common search for social alternatives and the development of alternative practices and projects;
- The search for forms of cooperation where something can be achieved that the groups cannot achieve on their own, through the interaction among differences.

Upon examining the writings of the Old Testament and the New Testament as well as the writings of the classics of Marxism, and upon examining the legacy pointing to common humanistic reason, one finds astounding things:

'Overturning all relationships. ... And knocking the powerful from the throne' (Ramminger, M.; Segbers F. 2018), is the title of a book by Michael Ramminger and Franz Segbers, which refers to the common heritage of Christians and Marxists. Karl Marx wrote in the introduction to the Critique of Hegel's Philosophy of Right: The criticism of religion ends with the teaching that man is the highest essence for man – hence, with the categorical imperative to overthrow all relations in which man is a debased, enslaved, abandoned, despicable essence, relations which cannot be better described than by the cry of a Frenchman when it was planned to introduce a tax on dogs: Poor dogs! They want to treat you as human beings! Not the gods in heaven, but the false gods on earth are the subject of his critique of society.

This Marxist quotation and the quotation from Luke: 1:46-55 (the Magnificat) spring from the same humanistic idea: the equality of men and rebellion against oppression. The idea of God's image also offers access to Marx's thesis that man is to be established as the highest being for man, and not false gods like the market, money and profits.

Pope Francis's use of terminology from the Marxist criticism of capitalism is remarkable: 'This economy kills'. So it is logical that he picks up the option for the poor and establishes it as the standard for social action in the tradition of the Second Vatican Council, proclaiming not only service to the weakest in society, but change of these societies. He calls for new alliances, including a dialogue between Christians and Marxists. The societal analysis based on Marx and Engels, the development of social alternatives and the thorough study of the contradictory process of the history of liberation especially in the Old Testament can also be helpful in this way. The view of society's structures as well as the view of the individual human being, who is sometimes lost by the left in the context of class or milieu affiliation, belong together.

Both are needed to work on a corporate design based on an economy of life, a social-ecological transformation. This can very well be based on different philosophical foundations, just as justice, peace and the preservation of the environment can reasonably be justified in different ways.

So, Where to Start?

The dialogue among different world views must take the side of the weakest in society, with those who have little or no voice. It must intervene effectively where the rule of capital puts into question or even annihilates the very existence of human coexistence and human life. The leftist dialogue must challenge the neoliberal rule therefore, the 'religion of capitalism', that is, the fetishism of goods, money and capital, and the structures aimed at maintaining power.

It is about common practices as they exist, in peace building for example or initiatives to welcome, support and integrate refugees. It's about projects that promote a socio-ecological transformation.

The shared emancipatory heritage is great, as are the common challenges. Common practices are important, building trust and even opening space for difficult issues where there are no facile resolutions.

The participants in this summer university are diverse. The organizers have provided a place which is equally pluralistic – in terms of positions, origins and organizations.

Dialogue is work: Thinking with others, to develop our own thinking.

Dialogue is learning: when you find your own thoughts with others in a new way.

Dialogue is fun: when dreams and ideas become real projects

Dialogue is a way of looking ahead, with healthy constructive breaks on the beaches of Syros.

II. An Example of Christian-Marxist Dialogue

Different Interpretations of the Magnificat among Christians and Marxists

The Magnificat is a passage in the Bible, in Luke's Gospel (Lk 1: 26-56). A few days after the angel, Gabriel's proclamation, the young lady, Mary, visits her cousin Elizabeth according to the text. Elizabeth is pregnant with John the Baptist at the time. This event is called the Virgin Mary's Visitation. Upon Elisabeth's welcome, Mary greets her with a song of praise where she describes God as the one who turns to her and other people of low standing – the powerless and hungry – to raise their status and push the powerful, the rich and the proud from their thrones.

The text of The Magnificat (Lk 1: 46b-55):

> My soul proclaims the greatness of the Lord,/my spirit rejoices in God my Savior,/ for he has looked with favor on his humble servant./From this day all generations will call me blessed, /the Almighty has done great things for me, /and holy is his Name. / He has mercy on those who fear Him/ in every generation. /He has shown the strength of his arm, / he has scattered the proud in their conceit. / He has cast down the mighty from their thrones, /and has lifted up the humble. /He has filled the hungry with good things, /and the rich he has sent away empty. / He has come to the help of his servant Israel/ for he has remembered his promise of mercy, / the promise he made to our fathers, / to Abraham and his children forever. / Glory to the Father, and to the Son, and to the Holy Spirit, / as it was in the beginning, is now, and will be forever. / Amen. Alleluia[49]

[49] For other translations see https://en.wikipedia.org/wiki/Magnificat

Why Should Marxists Know this Text?
Why Should Christians Discuss this Text with Marxists?

From a Marxist perspective the Magnificat is one of those texts in the New Testament with the 'clearest political and liberating content'. It is praise of the Lord and a 'protest song' at the same time, resistance against the prevailing conditions and the need to change them fundamentally. It praises the God of the Bible, who performs the deed: He scatters those who are full of arrogance in the heart and He brings down the powerful from their thrones and raises the lower ones.

Such a radical idea! To overthrow the powerful from their throne is similar to the categorical imperative of Karl Marx, which demands that all conditions should be reversed in which man is a degraded, enslaved, abandoned being.

It is interesting that in the Magnificat and in Marx as well, the view of the weakest in society leads to demand for a fundamental change.

The praise of Mary – the Mother of Jesus Christ – and thus the most important woman in biblical history – is addressed to a God who strengthens the gaze on those who are exploited, in need, in poverty, and hardship, whose access to the riches of this World is denied, whose voices are too weak to be heard, to draw attention to their distress and misery – their intolerable conditions.

The historical context in which the Magnificat is pronounced is 1st century Palestine. It is a small country on the edge of the Roman Empire – the Roman slave-holding society. People suffer from poverty and hunger in political powerlessness under the Roman occupation.

Mary proclaims herself in two ways as a handmaid of God and as a young woman without possessions, of lower rank. She, who otherwise experiences contempt and disdain, is exalted. And while she is raised up, the hitherto exalted shall fall from their thrones. Mary's praise thus becomes an almost revolutionary place in the New Testament from a Marxist point of view.

The perspective on the exploited and humiliated is combined with the need for change through the fundamental transformation of domination, the abolition of conditions in which man is degraded, enslaved, abandoned, and contemptible.

This is the perspective of another world which should be possible. Changes must be imagined from the bottom or the margins of society. From a Marxist point of view, there are many texts which represent the perspective of the weakest in society. There is a repeated reference to the 'damned of this earth'. Marx's friend and colleague, Friedrich Engels, impressively describes the situation of hardship and misery in his book on The Situation of Working Class in England. Marx and Engels focus primarily on those who are down, but at the same time have the potential to redeem themselves from misery. The decisive force is the proletariat for them, the only one which can liberate itself, but only if it liberates all other classes as well.

This path of liberation – according to Marx and Engels in the Communist Manifesto – leads to the formation of the proletariat as a class. In the process of industrial production, this class is directly opposed as the producing class. It is simultaneously exploited and oppressed by the bourgeoisie – the class of capital.

The working class must fundamentally change the process of production and reproduction therefore if it wants to free itself.

Marx's focus on the proletariat, which today is much more differentiated, more feminine, more migratory, makes it easier to understand the opposition of the class with other interests. This focus is in danger of overlooking those outside of production, people excluded in various ways or disdained individuals. That is why the proposition by Marx and Engels is so important, 'in which the free development of each is the condition for the free development of all.'[50]

They do not focus their attention on the proletariat alone of course. They do not overlook those who are passive or who are looking for other ways to resist, like the Russian village communities. But the central focus remains on the proletariat.

The Marxist-Christian dialogue offers the opportunity to interpret Mary as a representative of the oppressed exploited class and at the same time it gives the abstract concept of class a concrete face, an individual story. Mary is subjected to hurt, the mother and the strong woman who draws her strength from belief in the transformation of earthly conditions.

---

50 Sources of the communist manifesto: 'in place of the old bourgois society, with its classes and classes antagonisms, we shall have an association, in which the free development of each is the condition for the free development of all.'

Pope Francis also focuses his attention on the weakest and most vulnerable members of society, who are no longer just exploited today, but are viewed as 'leftovers', as the result of an economy of exclusion and a disposable culture:

Human beings are themselves considered consumer goods to be used and then discarded. We have created a 'throw away' culture which is now spreading. It is no longer simply about exploitation and oppression, but something new. Exclusion ultimately has to do with what it means to be a part of the society in which we live; those excluded are no longer society's underside or its fringes or its disenfranchised – they are no longer even a part of it. The excluded are not the 'exploited' but the outcast, the 'leftovers'. (EG 53).

Their opinion is not sought; they have no voice, no real right to life, while global wealth is increasingly concentrated. The eight richest billionaires in the world today have accumulated more capital than is available to the poorer 50 percent of the world's population. But it is not just the question of concentration of wealth; it is also the issue of access to the basic goods to live. Sixty-five million people are fleeing from hardship, misery, and war today. Almost 750 million people have no access to clean drinking water. Eight hundred fifteen million people are starving; 2 billion are suffering from malnutrition. These unbearable conditions demand change.

Just as Mary urges her exaltation to draw the powerful from their thrones in her song of praise, so in the later time of prevailing industrial capitalism, the analysis of the current capitalist society leads to the need to overturn all conditions. It is no longer just a question of improving the given conditions because if 'it goes on like this' it will lead to catastrophe.

The new and old wars should be named to underpin this development, the unresolved and escalating conflicts like those in the Middle East, the never-ending stream of refugees fleeing war, misery, and persecution, the weakening power of solidarity as a socializing and integrating force.

Only the transformation of the entire bourgeois society, including its property relations as well as its entire mode of production, creates the premises for a just society, formulated by Marx and Engels in the Communist Manifesto. For them, the yardstick for a correlation between the free and the equal, which is to emerge from this revolution, is that 'the free development of everyone is the condition for the free development of all' (Marx K.; Engels F. 1959, p. 482).

Questions

But how does one overthrow the rulers from their thrones today and how can one design a society in which society's wealth is equally distributed? ... in other words, a society where the hungry man is bestowed with fundamental goods to live, and only what is necessary remains for the rich man for a life of freedom? How do we preserve the richness of nature and fundamental natural resources for human life?

How can we establish a just society today? What projects are needed to get started for such a comprehensive transformation?

An important part of this task will have to be to produce the basic goods of society that enable and guarantee a life of dignity in such a way that they reach everyone and do not damage the natural foundations of life.

But where should we start now?

Pál: A Culture of Sharing and the Economy of Communion

In the Christian spiritual and theological heritage you can find different interpretations of Mary's Song stemming from different schools of thought and life. In a Christian vision however, the Magnificat's principal actor is God. He is the one who 'has cast down the mighty from their thrones and has lifted up the humble.' The question arises: What is the human contribution to this radical change of social relationships? In what sense are women and men agents of their own destiny?

I would like to offer the understanding of the Magnificat in the experience of the Focolare Movement for reflection. This evokes an original interpretation of this important Biblical text. Chiara Lubich, the founder of the Focolare, affirms:

> The Magna Carta of Christian social doctrine begins where Mary sings: 'He has overthrown the powerful from their thrones, has raised the humble, has filled the hungry with good things, has sent the rich away empty' (Lk 1: 52-53).

> In the Gospel there is the highest and overwhelming revolution. And perhaps it is in God's plans that, even in this age, immersed in the solution of social problems, may Our Lady give us all Christians a hand to build, consolidate, erect and show the world a new society in which Magnificat echoes mightily.

At the beginnings of the movement during the second world war, you can find an awareness in its proponents that living the Gospel in the light of the collective spirituality proposed by Chiara can provide answers to the concrete social challenges of every time and place. This 'discovery' subsequently encouraged men and women to face the problems of modern society with foresight and competence, to heal wounds and to highlight the potential of individual communities. The spiritual dimension has never been disconnected from the social dimension in the life of the Movement. Ever since 1943 Chiara herself dreamed of 'resolving Trent's social problem' and with her first companions they went around the city to heal both the spiritual and material wounds of those who had survived the bombings, to comfort the ones who had been left all alone, to distribute food and clothing to those who needed them.

One of the first spiritual intuitions Chiara Lubich had was the understanding of God as Love. She recalls the experience writing in 1949:

> To me God was manifested as Love. Since then I have seemed to conceive of religion in a completely different way from how I first conceived it. Religion is to look first to the Father. The discovery of the Father has been a conversion for us.
>
> Jesus, our model, taught us two things alone, and which are one: to be children of only one Father and to be brothers and sisters to each other... (Lubich, C. 2008).

And in 1979 she wrote:

> You can only respond to Love with love, love for God, as a response to His Love for us and you do this by immediately doing something out of love for your neighbour. Whoever we met in our life was given our full attention, our care, our kindness.[51]

The first target for these young girls to help were the poorest. They were sure that behind the sad and troubled faces of these people was Jesus' hidden face. As the community around them grew, they were able to give more help to whoever needed it. They did this for several months. It was natural in this small and yet great revolution of social care to help not just the poor but all of humanity: 'There were those who needed feeding, dressing, something to drink and also those who needed teaching, advising,

[51] https://www.focolare.org/en/all-opera/impegno-sociale/page/7/

support and those who needed prayers'. And so they became aware of the power that the charism of unity contained, seeing its effect in the world.

For Chiara Mary was the role model for all Christians in her living out the teachings of her son perfectly. Chiara was convinced that living the Gospel consistently would lead to a real social revolution. Here is an excerpt from a talk in 1975:

> 'I was thinking to myself that the Gospel is not truly understood, it's not understood. Because if the Gospel were truly understood, we wouldn't need anything else. Even to bring about a social revolution, we wouldn't need anything else.
>
> There's a phrase in the Gospel that says: 'Set your hearts on his kingdom first, and on his righteousness, and all these other things will be given to you as well' (Mt 6:33), or again: 'Anyone who has left house, brothers, sisters, father, children or land for my sake (and all of us have to leave them, not concretely, but spiritually, so that we can have God in the first place) and for the sake of the Gospel will be repaid a hundred times over… in this present time and, in the world to come, eternal life' (Mk 10: 29-30). Or take yet another: 'Whatever you ask for in my name, I will do' (Jn 14:13). And then another: 'If you have faith, everything you ask for in prayer you will receive' (Mt 21:22). These four phrases would be enough to resolve all the social problems.
>
> You might ask: 'But Chiara, what's that got to do with this?' It is relevant, because when Jesus said: 'Set your hearts on his kingdom first, and on his righteousness, and all these other things will be given to you as well,' the 'other things' he was talking about were bread, a house to live in, food to eat, clothes to wear, a good family: all of this was to be given to those who seek his kingdom. And when he speaks about the hundredfold he intends a hundredfold of fathers, a hundredfold of houses, brothers, sisters, mothers, etc. Then he goes on and says: 'Ask, and it will be given to you' (Mt 7:7). He is a God who can give you everything.
>
> The fact is this: we look at the Gospel in its spiritual dimension. But the Gospel has, in I don't know how many phrases, in almost all of them a human dimension, because Jesus is the Man-God. (…) Now, I understand that it's possible to deduce a Christian social doctrine, that we can study economic systems, and so on, but who has had the courage to start a revolution based on the words of God? Nobody, in my opinion.
>
> But, you see, we are alone, we are small… . Yet we have a treasure that one of these days will explode, I'm convinced. It was Our Lady who gave me this conviction with her Magnificat, which says: 'He has pulled down princes from their thrones and exalted the lowly. The hungry he has filled with good things,

> the rich sent empty away' (Lk 1: 52-53). This then is the social revolution: fill the hungry with many goods and send the rich away empty-handed, without armed revolution, without shooting them; it's enough to send them away empty-handed.[52]

The movement has brought about a sort of a culture of sharing based on the realization of different words of the Gospel among its followers over the years – a communion of material goods according to the lifestyle of the first Christian communities:

> 'Now the full number of those who believed were of one heart and soul, and no one said that any of the things that belonged to him was his own, but they had everything in common.' (Acts 4, 32)

Spiritual and material goods were also involved in this sharing during regular meetings to exchange experiences of living out the word. This praxis of sharing material and mental goods is dialogue in the deepest sense of the word.

During the years numerous wealthy persons joined the Movement and gave to the poor from their wealth in order to get closer to the condition of the community of Jerusalem: 'There was not a needy person among them' (Acts 4,33).

During her visit to San Paolo in 1991, Chiara founded the Economy of Communion (EoC), a concrete initiative to address acute social problems by creating businesses that are integral parts of their communities. The EoC draws entrepreneurs, workers, directors, consumers, investors, citizens, scholars, economists – all involved at various levels – to promote a practice and an economic culture characterized by communion, gratuity and reciprocity. Through their own example, they offer an alternative lifestyle in contrast with the dominant one in our capitalistic system.

In concrete terms, the EoC invites us to:

- Live and spread a new civil and economic culture, from the youngest to the oldest among us;
- Prepare new entrepreneurs and renew present ones who are willing to share their profit to sustain the goals of the EoC – reduction of exclu-

52 *The social revolution*. Rocca di Papa, January 25, 1975. Downloadable on http://centro chiaralubich.org/en/

sion and its subsequent poverty, diffusion of the culture of giving and of communion, development of businesses and creation of new jobs; these are business people who conceive and live their activity as a vocation and service for the common good, oriented to those who are excluded in every part of the world and every social context;
- Fight various forms of indigence, exclusion and poverty with a twofold inclusion – productive and communitarian.

To make this project possible, the Economy of Communion is working on a vast project to educate people for the culture of giving – through schools, meetings, formative events geared to young people, workers, business people and citizens.[53]

For a broader knowledge of this idea see the social movement, Prophetic Economy, in order to spread the culture of giving and inclusive economic behaviour on a larger scale.[54]

From 26 to 28 March 2020 the city of Assisi will host The Economy of Francis, an international event oriented to young economists, entrepreneurs and change-makers engaged in thinking and practising a different type of economics. The invitation to participate has come directly from Pope Francis, who issued a letter today inviting young economists from all over the world to the City of St Francis, which is a symbol of humanism and fraternity. There is no distinction among these economists in terms of creed or nationality. This event will initiate a process of global change with them so that today's and tomorrow's economy is more just, inclusive and sustainable, without leaving anyone behind.

The movement also promotes other similar initiatives based on the logic of collaboration and dialogue, for example, the Movement for Unity in Politics and Policy http://www.mppu.org/en

Questions

Can a grassroot non-violent initiative like the EoC become a real game-changer in society?

---

53 Read more on the Economy of Communion on http://www.edc-online.org); or https: //en.wikipedia.org/wiki/Economy_of_Communion

54 https://www.propheticeconomy.org/

Believers and non-believers may have diverse motivations; will it be possible for them to collaborate in the quest for a global change in economic trends?

Europe
Collaboration
Participation
Democracy
Justice
Peace
Solidarity
Belarus
Denmark
Ireland
Slovenia
Latvia
Hungary
Italy
Malta
Albania
NorthernMacedonia
Slovakia
Sweden
Croatia
Luxembourg
Greece
Great
Serbia
Spain
Austria
Norway
Ukraine
Bosnia
Portugal
Bulgaria
Poland
Belgium
Iceland
Lithuania
CzechRepublic
Kosovo
Estonia
Germany
France
Switzerland
Britain
Montenegro
Romania
Netherlands
Cyprus

TOWARDS A PARTICIPATIVE EUROPE

(Re)Thinking Europe

A Contribution to the Future of the European Project

Léonce Bekemans[55]

Introduction

Throughout its history, Europe has developed as a dynamic and evolving entity, showing many faces, multiple identities and various forms of co-operation. It presents a diversified societal model in crisis today, looking for its role and future in the world amidst growing internal and external tensions. In this complex global order political courage, inspiration and citizen-centred practices are needed to (re)shape Europe's future.

The European Union is a community of values founded after World War II by six countries (Belgium, the Netherlands, Luxemburg, Germany, France and Italy) with the long-term goal of a political federation. This project ensured peace to its member countries for over 70 years. It has been expanded to today's Union of 28 member states and more than 500 million citizens. Its Founding Fathers laid the foundations for a civilizational project based on values and on a human-centered political perspective.

Europe is now going through a hectic period of challenge and change, and the EU project is facing an existential crisis. The sense of community

[55] The author is a Jean Monnet professor ad personam, holding the JM Chair 'Globalisation, Europeanisation, Human Development' at the University of Padua (It) (2007-2019). He teaches at various European universities and collaborates with European organisations. Currently, he is President of Europahuis 'Ryckevelde' in Bruges (B) and a member of various international scientific and advisory boards. He has written many articles and edited books on issues related to Europe.

has also been weakened over time in spite of its motto, 'united in diversity'; diversity is often perceived as a threat today. In fact, growing diversity within and among EU Member States regarding specific policies makes it increasingly difficult to agree on common policies. On one hand, economic and financial crises, threats to internal security, geo-political shifts along with the ongoing uncertainty of Brexit and the questioning of Western values within the European Union are all exerting pressure on mainstream politics. Nationalism, populism and xenophobia are on the rise on the other hand.

A vision is needed for a more cohesive, democratic, fair and sustainable future. Only by working together at various institutional levels can the EU deliver valid policies. Moreover, credible policy arguments are required to counterbalance the criticism of populist-led Euroscepticism against the process of globalisation, the environmental crisis and increasing inequality. What is at stake is a European model that combines social security and economic solidarity with shared values of freedom, democracy and the rule of law.

This contribution is structured in three parts. The first part puts the European future in a historical perspective. It refers to the development of the integration process from a mainly economic project to a sui generis international organization. The second part presents a forward-looking analysis of Europe's role, prospects and challenges in a rapidly changing world. In the third and final part some building blocks for a value-driven European future are presented, identifying Europe as a community and viewing education as a lifelong multi-level process with a European dimension.

I. The Process of European Integration

A Historically Embedded Context

Now in the midst of a radically changing economic, social and political landscape, the process for European integration still needs to be understood in its conceptual, theoretical and historical context. The actual role of Europe can be assessed from a global perspective only in this way. Departure points for such a broad understanding refer to: – Europe as a visual expression of diversity in unity in a variety of areas and dimensions; – Europe as a civilization and model of society; – Europe as a (changing) historical and geographical (loose) entity; and – Europe as a community of values and principles: its raison d'être is linked to the principles of peace, safety and security, unity and equality, fundamental freedoms, economic and social solidarity, respect for cultural diversity/identities as well as for the European cultural heritage, etc.

In the first place Europe is a two thousand-year old civilization. Paul Valéry, the French poet and philosopher, describes the common characteristics of Europe in his essay 'The Crisis of the Mind'. He calls it a Europe of the spirit, shaped by the legacies of Rome, Athens and Jerusalem. It has made humanism its foundation and is rooted in Christianity. This means that Europe presents a world of religious, mythical and artistic references exhibiting different expressions and experiencing various historical and political stages throughout the centuries.

It first developed into a geo-political entity under Alexander the Great. It was inspired by the Aristotelian paradigm of linking the individual and the community through the 'ethos'. Europe shifted its power centre to the West with the Roman Empire, and slowly developed into the Christian era in the Middle Ages where the sense of community became the binding and exclusive element of European peoples. With the Renaissance and the rebirth of Greek classics through Arab influence, commercial routes and artistic exchanges made city states flourish into flexible linkages and cooperation such as the Hanseatic League. With the Treaties of Westphalia (1648) and Vienna (1815) the role of nation states in international relations was legally defined and the boundaries of states were fixed. Napoleon tried in vain to integrate Europe with military means in the 19th century. The dramatic consequences of the two World Wars finally led to an American financed voluntary economic integration of former European enemies. The economic community of the founding member states has evolved during the last 60 years of phased development into a European Union of 28 member countries and more than 500 million citizens.

Europe never was united for a long period after the fall of the Roman Empire, although many military, economic, political and cultural attempts were made to integrate European territory. Through these various (dis)integration and cooperation attempts Europe has developed over the years into a vague geographical and historical framework with specific characteristics. Given its current unique process of integration, we are convinced that Europe should remain a responsible actor In today's world, promoting principles of freedom, democracy, equality and diversity within and outside Europe.

The European Integration Process: Origin and Development

The originality of the European Union is derived from the special way its different constituent parts have evolved since the first European treaties after World War II. The European Communities consisting of the European Coal and Steel Community/ECSC (1951), the European Economic Community/EEC (1957) and European Atomic Energy Community/ Euratom (1957) were born from the desire for a united Europe, an idea which gradually took shape as a direct response to the events that had shattered the continent. They were established to integrate strategic industries, in particular the steel and coal industry. Threatened by the East-West confrontation, the future of Europe lay in Franco-German reconciliation.

As specialized organizations, each of the three communities only held those powers attributed to them by member states. The principle of attribution required that each community 'shall act within the limits of the powers conferred upon it [. . .] and of the objectives assigned to it' by the treaties which established them (i.e. Treaty of Paris establishing the ECSC and the Rome Treaties establishing the EEC and EURATOM). Similarly, each community institution, i.e. Parliament, Council, Commission, Court of Justice, Court of Auditors, assisted by an Economic and Social Committee and a Committee of the Regions, had to 'act within the limits of the powers conferred upon it' by the Treaties.

The EU came into being with the adoption of the Maastricht Treaty in 1992. It brought together the three original organizations established in the 1950s with the goal of further integrating policies in specific sectors and cooperating in the areas of common foreign and security policy and justice and home affairs. The resulting structure has been described as one built on three pillars. The first, comprised of the three communities, is supranational; each has its own legal personality. The other two pillars pertain to intergovernmental cooperation.

The EU has been the first 'general-purpose' international organization to be derived from the pooling of some of those policies under the umbrella of the European Communities, not from a coordination of its members' national policies. The result of this pooling of policies was an innovative type of body, i.e. a supranational authority, formed by the voluntary transfer of certain sovereign powers by its member states. The member states did not surrender their powers, but decided to exercise them jointly at a higher level where there were common institutions.

With the aim of creating an ever-closer union among the peoples of Europe, integration has proceeded step by step, first by merging policy on certain sectors of member states' national economies, then by the creation of a common market, followed in turn by the gradual introduction of an economic and monetary union. Notwithstanding its economic foundations, the objective of the European Union was a priori political. The neo-functional approach taken by the 'Founding Fathers' of the communities, Jean Monnet and Robert Schuman, meant that it was necessary to move from the economic to the political sphere. The interconnectedness and interdependence between economic and political sectors raised spillover issues which required political choices.

Thus, the completion of a common market in which there was the free movement of goods raised the question of the movement of people, services and capital, requiring the introduction of a number of accompanying policies in the areas of competition, industry, agriculture, transportation, research, etc. Ultimately, complementary policies addressing the problems of highly sensitive national prerogatives were gradually adopted. This was the case with social and fiscal policy. In addition to the EEC's internal policies, its subjection to international law impacted its dealings with non-member states and other international organizations such as the World Trade Organization, the World Bank, the International Monetary Fund, etc. It forged external relations in the areas of world trade, development aid, immigration, defense, etc. as a result.

While the European community has been constantly evolving since its creation, the degree of integration achieved at each stage has been the result of an ongoing compromise among various modes and interpretations of integration and cooperation. With their own particular economic and social background and national susceptibilities, each of the member states has often been struggling between the benefits of integration and the drawbacks of having their political and budgetary autonomy curtailed, something often perceived as a surrender of national sovereignty.

Meanwhile the EU managed the two inseparable processes of expanding and growing in depth at the same time: expanding through the various enlargement phases and growing in depth by extending its powers and institutional procedures. The major issue in these developments was the confrontation between the expectations of applicant countries and the operational efficiency of the common institutions. The collective agreements put in place by the founding Treaties have evolved pragmatically over time as a consequence. This reflects the diversified structure of the organization, the priorities of the various players in the process of building Europe, and the changes in the geopolitical environment.

Major reforms to the founding treaties were made with the adoption of the Single European Act in 1986 and the signing of the Maastricht (1992), Amsterdam (1997) and Nice (2001) Treaties. The Maastricht Treaty indicated major momentum in the European integration process with a radical structural change of the EEC. It renamed the 'European Economic Community' the 'European Community' to reflect its expanded responsibilities beyond economic matters; it established the European Union with its three pillar-based structure and placed the European Community (EC) at the heart of European construction. After a long and difficult process of institutional discussions and negotiations the European Council adopted the Treaty of Lisbon on 13 December 2007, amending the Treaty on the European Union and the Treaty establishing the European Community (renamed 'Treaty on the Functioning of the European Union'; the term 'Community' was replaced by 'Union').

The Lisbon Treaty began as a constitutional project at the end of 2001 (European Council Declaration on the Future of the European Union, or the Laeken Declaration). It was followed up in 2002 and 2003 by the European Convention, comprised of representatives of the heads of state or governments, the national parliaments, the European Parliament and the European Commission. The former French President Giscard d'Estaing presided over it. It introduced a new method to reform the Union, offering greater transparency and more participation for the players involved. It drafted the treaty establishing a Constitution for Europe which was signed in Rome in 2004.

However, the process finally leading to the Lisbon Treaty was the result of the negative outcomes of the French and Dutch referenda on the new Treaty in 2004 and the negative result of the Irish referendum on the

'Reform Treaty' in 2007. The European Council responded with a two-year 'period of reflection'. The global finance crisis aggravated the economic and political situation but simultaneously opened up new possibilities for stronger political and economic European integration within the global landscape. On the basis of the Berlin declaration of March 2007 finally, the European Council of 21-23 June 2007 adopted a detailed mandate for a subsequent Intergovernmental Conference (IGC) under the Portuguese presidency. The IGC concluded its work in October 2007. After the signature in Lisbon and its ratification by all member states the Treaty of Lisbon entered into force on 1 December 2009, providing the legal basis for its further development.

In short, the European integration process shows a dynamic and evolving reality with many faces, multiple identities and diversified forms of mixed intergovernmental and supranational cooperation. Today this process is at a crossroads, navigating between pessimism, optimism and realism, shaped by a confrontation between developments of globalisation and Europeanisation in the midst of a rapidly changing international landscape. (Bekemans, L. 2013).Its destiny is at stake. The prospects and challenges facing the project of European integration are both internal and external and therefore require timely critical analysis.

II. Europe in Today's Changing World: Contextual and Forward-looking Analysis

Prospects

What is Europe's relevance today? What are its cultural heritage, its values and norms, its societal model? The answer to these fundamental questions will shape the future of Europe and the building of our European societies. Is Europe still an inspiring idea(l) of a values-driven society worth pursuing? Themes such as the European borders, European citizenship, cultural diversity, and the role and purpose of Europe in a global framework all require a vision of what Europe is and should be.

Europe is at a crucial intersection in its history and at a decisive moment in the process of European integration. Its diversified socio-economic model is in crisis today. 'Europe' has never been so needed and yet Europe has never been in such danger. In this rapidly changing world, political courage, inspiration and a citizen-centred perspective are needed to shape a new European Renaissance. In a February 2016 EurActiv interview the French sociologist and philosopher, Edgar Morin, speaks of a 'global crisis' and the need 'to change civilization' to address the complexity of today's world.

This reality certainly implies a rethinking and actualising of the pluralistic European narrative in a new and radically changing context. Europe is at a turning point between its past, present and future. We are now confronted by a number of (internal and external) challenges to the European model of socio-economic cohesion and cultural and regional diversity. We believe that the various crises Europe faces are indeed symptoms of a broader systemic crisis confronting society.

Europe still has a mission and responsibility nevertheless in the world undergoing globalisation. It has an appointment with its destiny. Its model of society, based on fundamental human rights, on culture as a vehicle for emancipation, on sustainable development and socio-economic cohesion, and on a multilateral vision of the world order, is under strain and pressure. In other words, we experience a confrontation between the actual confusing (political, economic, cultural and institutional) European reality and the global responsibility Europe has in the context of ever increasing globalisation.

Europe's capacity to respond will depend on its ability to adopt an open-ended vision and a forward-looking narrative. To consolidate and develop the EU's role of building peace on a global scale and at the same time strengthen its democratic dimension, the European elections in late May 2019 offered European citizens a historic opportunity to regain full sovereignty, defend their interests and contribute to building a fairer and more just international society. The new European Commission led by Ursula Von der Leyen seems to have understood this changing reality in its structure and determination of priorities.

Challenges

What are the main (internal and external) challenges facing Europe today? They include rising global exposure, threats to economic and social cohesion, growing cultural diversity, increasing complexity, an expanding political agenda, the climate crisis, and last but not least – imperiled legitimacy and trust.

The prolonged 'Brexit' negotiations have created more uncertainty, and the outcome is still unknown. Our democracy is in crisis and EU citizens are losing faith in it because political leaders cannot deliver their promises on a national level. The state is no longer the exclusive actor and power has been globalised and society individualised and fragmented in the meantime, defying attempts to return to national solutions and exclusive citizenship building, as the populist drive throughout Europe illustrates, particularly in the case of the 'migration crisis'.

There are many challenges within and outside the EU. To respond to these challenges requires a new mobilising myth for Europe, i.e. a project for further European integration that guarantees institutional governing structures and financing mechanisms with internal and external European solidarity. Only such a vision can inspire the commitment of citizens and undoubtedly young people as well, and thereby strengthen Europe's role in the world undergoing globalisation. Recent political signals are not very hopeful however. Today's policy approaches and answers to the migration issue demonstrate a lot of tension and misunderstanding among member states, falling short of the human rights principles and European values.

How Do We Define the Current European Situation in the Changing World?

Europe moves prudently as a global actor in the midst of complex and interconnected transformations at all levels. The international system is more complex, more interdependent and more fragmented, involving diverse actors. We are searching hard for a proper European setting, role and responsibility in the global world to respond to the 'global commons'.

The EU plays a global role, mainly in trade, development, environmental and social issues, and more recently in security strategy as well. It made an important step towards strengthening its global aspirations with the Lisbon Treaty. Chaos, fear and uncertainty reign nevertheless, although the EU is still the world's leading exporter of goods, the largest trader of services and the biggest provider of development and humanitarian aid, the second largest foreign investor and a main destination for migrants. We may speak of a European malaise, a decline in its economic, political and moral power and the EU's weakened position as a global actor.

This weakening is related to external factors, such as increasing competition at the global level and the management of complexity, along with internal factors such as demographic developments, migration issues, climate crisis, secularisation, democratic deficits and populist movements. Nevertheless, the EU seems to gradually take up measures for better and more efficient governance amid many doubts and differences.

Two essential and distinctive dimensions of the EU's contribution to global issues can be distinguished: its influence as a model of national and supranational democracy and its impact on international democratisation. Since its creation in the 1950s, the European Community (now the EU) has played a key role in a gradual strengthening of democratic processes throughout its several expansions from the Mediterranean to central and eastern Europe. It is also gradually applying democratic practices at a regional level through its own institutions and policies.

However, we should not forget that the global implications of the European contribution towards peacebuilding have been addressed over the centuries by political thinkers, from Immanuel Kant to Jürgen Habermas, Ulrich Beck and Zygmunt Bauman. European studies have become a specialisation in international studies and the EU is perceived as a unique, sui generis model of integration–a work in progress used as a reference point for other regional organisations in the world.

III. A Values-driven 'Rethinking' of Europe

What is needed to understand Europe in a changing world and to act accordingly and responsively?

In a rapidly changing world, political courage, leadership, inspiration and human-centred practices are needed to shape and strengthen the values which are connected with 'Europe' as a never-ending story. As Václav Havel put it,

> 'Without commonly entrenched moral values and obligations, neither the law, nor democratic government, nor even the market economy will function properly.' (Havel, V. 1992, p. 146).

Europe has a mission and a responsibility to find a new equilibrium between diversity and unity in a world undergoing globalisation. It is confronted with the moral responsibility to maintain its model of integration and diversity within a radically changing world system. We should ask whether Europe can guarantee both internal solidarity within a unifying European economic space – while allowing states, regions, communities and persons to live their diversity, as well as external solidarity as expressed in its international relations and activities.

This twofold task contains internal and external aspects. We witness that various economic, political, social and cultural challenges in the era of globalisation have a drastic and diversified impact on societies, states, peoples, communities and persons across Europe every day. Acknowledging this growing complexity and interconnection among and within societies in the global world should be an important departure point in all the European dialogical frameworks

1. What Are the Expected Trajectories?

If Europe wants to respond adequately to the global challenges and to the newly emerging world order, it needs a stronger open-ended vision and a new forward-looking storyline. One can think of two (interrelated) tracks that could further strengthen Europe's position in the multipolar world of tomorrow: (1) differentiated and deepening integration and (2) acting as an agent of change within the multilateral system. Both approaches require commitment of course, along with courage and determination to take advantage of Europe's role in the world.

– Differentiated and Deepening Integration

As size matters for both economic and political power, being divided into a multiplicity of small actors does not help much to respond to global challenges. Increased European integration in certain specific policy areas (such as trade, competition, cooperation for development, economic, monetary and financial issues, and 'human' security) seems to be the only way forward. The national interest of member states will become part of the overall European interest only then – unity in diversity within a well-defined international and legal order. In other words, we need a multi-level and multiple actor approach in order to manage various challenges and issues while respecting diversity.

It seems natural for the European construction to use patterns of differentiated integration[56] therefore, so as to be able to act in an effective manner while taking this diversity into account. Examples of differentiated integration processes launched during recent decades are numerous, such as illustrated by the cases of the Schengen area and the Eurozone or defense policy.

Differentiated integration should not only focus on effectiveness however, but also on issues of legitimacy (Bertoncini, Y. 2017, p. 16) which are key for the EU to function and succeed at a time when it is confronted by global challenges, but also fragmented along several divides among states and peoples. Philosophical, political and institutional conditions should be provided to allow a legitimate sharpening of differentiation within the EU. (Pirozzi, N. et al. 2017, p. 24). A differentiation based on sound political foundations should be able to serve the interests of the European peoples then, regarding collective security issues for example, or the Economic and Monetary Union or the Stability Pact.

– Acting as an Agent of Change in the International System

In the emerging new international world order, states, international and regional organisations, transnational policy networks and non-governmental actors are the building blocks for the multilateral system. In other words, states are mere players among others. Furthermore, the interaction among all these actors is not organized in a hierarchical way, but as a network which often addresses specific issues with variable coalitions. This implies that there is no single centre of power thereby blurring the centre-periphery framework.

Instead, there is a fluid web of relationships, alliances and partnerships among different types of actors at different levels of governance – from the neighbourhood, city, region and state to the European and international level. The new Global Strategy for the EU's Foreign and Security Policy (2016) (Mogherini, F. 2016), proposed by Federica Mogherini, the former High Representative of the European Union for Foreign Affairs and Security Policy and Vice-President of the European Commission, has certainly

56 On the concept of 'differentiation' in the EU, see in particular Gaëtan Ricard-Nihoul, *Pour une Fédération européenne d'États-nations. La vision de Jacques Delors revisitée*, Bruxelles: Larcier, 2012.

been a step forward in delineating the EU as a prudent agent of change in international relations.

2. What Should Be the Vision Guaranteeing these Forward-looking Trajectories?

As mentioned earlier, Europe's model of society and its future role in the changing world is under much stress; it is being challenged by internal and external forces. The radical transformation of European societies is subject to globalising, Europeanising, regionalising and localising dynamics. Questions about identity, citizenship, governance, borders, democracy and dialogue require proper answers therefore.

The EU is in danger of falling apart due to political short-sightedness, the inadequacy of its institutions, a lack of democracy, of citizen participation and of respectful dialogue. Walls are built on the basis of national and regional selfishness. They undermine Europe's common future and make internal and external solidarity more difficult. The common European House, as expressed in the Ventotene Manifesto (Castellina, L. 2016) and favoured by the human-centred political project of the Founding Fathers, is subject to a lot of criticism in this context. The logic of fear seems to take the lead at the expense of the logic of hope.

There is a hope to change course and to strengthen cross-border cooperation and diversified integration within the European project nevertheless. This can be done by involving the citizen more in the Europe of tomorrow, at local, regional, national and European levels. This requires that policy reflect inspiration, conviction and courage. (Bekemans, L. 2018, pp. 47-70)

On March 1st, 2017, the European Commission presented a White Paper on the Future of Europe (European Commission, 2017), as a contribution to the 60th anniversary of the Treaty of Rome. It set out five possible future paths, corresponding to different degrees of integration: Carrying On (i.e. the EU27 focuses on delivering its positive reform agenda); Nothing but the Single Market (i.e. the EU27 is gradually re-centred on the single market); Those Who Want More To Do (i.e. the EU27 allows willing member states to do more together in specific areas); Doing Less More Efficiently (i.e. the EU27 focuses on delivering more, faster in selected policy areas, while doing less elsewhere); Doing Much More Together (i.e. member states decide to do much more together across policy areas).

Although the EU cannot be comprehended in one rule, it is a special political structure with intergovernmental and supranational characteristics. The debate about the nature of European cooperation still appears to be strongly determined by a confrontation between federalists and intergovernmentalists. It remains a project in the making however. A new inspiring and mobilizing story is needed today where the quality of immaterial well-being is not subordinated to the mere quantity of material welfare. This is very well illustrated by the whole climate debate, very much guided by the younger generations. The EU should definitely take the lead in the environment; it has become a priority political issue and global challenge of the greatest importance.

What is important is that a forward-looking vision should encapsulate a sense of belonging and offer true added value to EU citizens, even in times of transformation and confusion. Such a vision should be based on a values-driven community, respecting Europe as a multi-faceted and multi-dimensional space exhibiting diverse characteristics. We should be aware that these aspects have to be understood, contextualised and translated to a diversified citizenry within a context that often produces radically changing and paradoxical realities. These realities have an impact on current European identity, citizenship and the effort to build solidarity. They also shape the framework for internal and external dialogue among and within countries, regions, communities and citizens.

In the fast-changing global landscape, Europe is confronted with the preoccupation, but also with the moral responsibility, to maintain its model of integration and diversity within a world system undergoing radical transformation. This requires a new operational equilibrium between diversity and unity in a world undergoing globalisation, taking into account the economic, historic, social and political changes on an international level, but remaining faithful to its principles of internal and external solidarity as made explicit in international and European law.

In short, we need to convey a true message with a positive and dynamic vision. This implies a view that is embedded in a community of shared values, supports the strength of a diversified European integration process, and recognises the positive heritage as well as the complexity of a multifaceted Europe as an additional value in the European project.

The European elections of May 2019 were undoubtedly a struggle, not only among the traditional parties of the Right, Left and centre, but especially among those who believed in the benefits of continued cooperation and integration at the level of the EU and those who wanted to repeal the integration efforts of the past 70 years. The doubts do not concern the project so much, but rather the trajectory, the course along which Europe must develop further. Although the populists did not achieve the result they desired, the European political landscape was severely shaken. The new European Commission seems to have understood the challenges we are facing nevertheless, with the establishment of its structural priorities – the green and digital deals.

Reform, Transform or Rethink Europe implies recognition of far more complexity within our societies, further development of a diverse citizenship within multiple identities, and the development of multi-level and multi-actor practices. This suggests all the stakeholders' participation and involvement in building the society. Member states, regional and local authorities as well as civil society organisations have an important task in this.

Europe is still essentially a civilisation project in spite of all the dramatic events and radical changes. It is characterised by a rich intellectual (material and immaterial) cultural heritage and a community of common values that need to be further developed. It means that the relationship between the institutional fabric of the EU and its citizens should be a priority focus; essentially, it is a union of states and citizens evolving toward European democracy. (Hoeksma, J.A. 2018).

3. Value Premises as a Departure Point: Europe as Community

The complex internal and external reality certainly involves full recognition and constant updating of the European narrative within a radically changing context. This must be elaborated on the basis of generally shared and widespread moral values and obligations. A vision for Europe's future relies very much on the concept of community, therefore.

We are convinced that the original vision of the Founding Fathers can inspire a renewed impulse for integration. They worked for a European project embedded in a long-term vision after all, but it was driven by a pragmatic approach. This vision can be summarized in Robert Schuman's definition of 'community'. (Bekemans, L. et al. 2018. 38-55). Europe must not only be seen as a socio-economic community therefore, but also as a community with a vision, mission and responsibility.

Our main departure point to recognise Europe as a values-based Community is legally embedded in Art. 2 of the Lisbon Treaty (TEU):

> The Union is founded on the values of respect for human dignity, freedom, democracy, equality, the rule of law and respect for human rights, including the rights of persons belonging to minorities. These values are common to the Member States in a society in which pluralism, non-discrimination, tolerance, justice, solidarity and equality between women and men prevail.

What are the characteristics of such a values-based European community?

- As a community with a destiny, Europe is a unique project for peace. It has the strength, experience and resources to play an active, substantial and constructive role in world affairs, including the issues of the environment, climate and information technology. The process of European integration has led to increasing interdependence and complexity in the interactions and relations that shape our common destiny in a world undergoing globalisation. The maintenance of peace, the conservation of the environment, and the means for people to live their lives with dignity all demand common policies and respect for diversity. All Europeans are called upon to work together responsibly to build a peaceful European order in dialogue.

And yet, the concrete realities of everyday life manifest growing tension, division and frustration about Europe's role in the world in the middle of today's 'migration crisis' and politically motivated violence.

- As a community of values, Europe should safeguard, strengthen and care for the values it shares as a community. These values are rooted in common legal principles and norms which acknowledge both the freedom of individuals and their social responsibility. Fundamental European values refer to human dignity, the rule of law, tolerance, humanity, dialogue, fraternity and hospitality. These principles have opened the way to a free and peaceful future in international relations.

In today's Europe however, these values seem to be put into question by national(ist) and populist reactions which are often driven by the 'blind' feelings of sovereignty.

- As a community of life, the EU should be made up of citizens, with citizens and for citizens. By becoming a citizens' Europe, it should develop into a tangible and living community. To that end, citizens should be given the opportunity to participate more fully in the European process through various kinds of dialogues and encounters. More democratic structures are needed in order to build up a real Habermasian European public space. The 2017 European Commission's Report, Reaching out to EU Citizens: A New Opportunity (Van den Brande, L. 2017, p. 35), tried to respond to this need. Its concrete policy proposals very much focused on vertical and horizontal dialogue about policy, youth, intergenerational solidarity and education.

• As an economic and social community, the first steps were taken when six countries founded the European Coal and Steel Community where industries were placed under a common Authority. This neo-functional approach resulted in the European Economic Community, and eventually developed into the European Union, bringing peace among Member States and producing higher living standards.

European integration has been very much economically driven from its beginning in 1957, however. The current crisis has made it clear that economic integration is not a sufficient basis for further development. Only a socio-economic community that is also culturally inspired can produce sustainable and cohesive European societies.

• As a community of purpose and responsibility, Europe should bear particular responsibility in today's world which is subject to globalisation and accentuated individualism. The EU has close economic, political and cultural ties with many regions of the world, often formalised in cooperation agreements. Europe can only effectively respond to global and European challenges through cooperation and internal and external solidarity.

Conflicts and crises threaten all European states and citizens alike, whether within or beyond Europe. Responsibility should be expressed through a common foreign and security policy, neighborhood development policy, and particularly in the politically sensitive area of migration. The absence of true European refugee and asylum policies creates frustration and leads to a lot of political discord and chaos in the way the migrant issue is managed.

• As a community and meeting place for diverse identities, Europe should foster freedom, peace, human dignity, equality and social justice as its greatest common goods. Europe needs a morally acceptable political structure and citizen-driven policies to protect and further develop these goals. This should strengthen the sense of common purpose and belonging, while establishing the credibility of the EU and making its citizens proud to be Europeans. Recognition of the wealth stemming from diverse identities should be further developed through exchange programmes and places to meet together (Bekemans, L. 2013b, pp. 305-317).

However, most Europeans are still very much bound to the territorial dimension and the environment in which they have lived and built their identity. As a consequence, they are afraid of the 'other'. This makes Europe less hospitable and more closed. In this context, cities and multicultural learning spaces are very important to be able to live together in harmony.

- As a community for multicultural learning, Europe should further reinforce the common background and future of citizens' dialogue and participation in order to demonstrate the value of the additional dimension of the European identity. This suggests taking into account the specific multilayered and diversified institutional and cultural European environment in education and learning.

We clearly affirm Europe's value premises therefore, while simultaneously acknowledging negative reactions and criticism of the failure to apply and implement the existing legal framework. Europe is a multi-purpose community requiring the ongoing rethinking of its many tasks.

4. Role for Education in Rethinking Europe

(Bekemans, L. 2018b, pp. 22-51).

General Context

As explained above, the conceptual framework still needs to be translated into a workable and forward-looking reality amidst a radically changing world. Education's role is fundamental as a permanent vehicle to learn to live together in Europe and the world. We should recognise moreover that the learning environment has drastically changed; it is more competitive, complex and fragmented, with a wide variety of learning sources.

We define education as a dynamic learning process that creates added value, fosters a person's integral development and/or arouses curiosity. It plays a significant role in the development of both human beings and modern societies as it enhances social, cultural and economic development, favours active citizenship and possibly highlights ethical values. The right to education was universally proclaimed and clearly emphasized in Article

26 of the Universal Declaration of Human Rights (1948) as a means for the full development of the human personality.

We strongly believe that new, innovative and person-oriented (human-centred) approaches are needed to respond to the challenges of fragmented and disturbed societies. There is a substantial urgent need therefore to re-examine the role and increased responsibility of education in culturally diverse and complex societies. This new culture for education embodies a respect for integral human development, including various (formal, informal and non-formal) learning places and environments.

This implies learning to cope with changes, uncertainties and risks. Focus on learning competences, life skills, practices, pedagogies, case histories, testimonies and exercises are needed to stimulate creativity and imagination. Such learning should be oriented to bridging existing educational gaps and changing rigid mind-sets. It should be a vehicle to prepare people to live together by acting together to tackle complex issues and to deal with diversity. This requires a variety of life competences – values, attitudes, skills and behaviours. New forms and places should be considered for dialogue, learning and study for a variety of new and old actors.

European Context

Education was formally recognised for the first time in the European context in the 1992 Maastricht Treaty. The current legal context for education in the EU is reflected in Art 165 of the Lisbon Treaty which also explicates its objectives.[57] We firmly believe that education and education programmes can concretely contribute to the reconsideration and reform of Europe. On the occasion of the 25th anniversary of the Maastricht Treaty (9/12/2016) European Commission President Juncker said:

> 'We cannot explain the European Union, the European project, simply by going back to the history... we want to convince younger people that the EU is a must today ... we have to explain the European history in a perspective: What is Europe today and what will it be tomorrow and the day after tomorrow?'

[57] Art 165, paragraph 1 says that: '*The Union shall contribute to the development of quality education by encouraging cooperation between Member States and, if necessary, by supporting and supplementing their action, while fully respecting the responsibility of the Member States for the content of teaching and the organisation of education systems and their cultural and linguistic diversity.*'

The importance and relevance of education in building and strengthening Europe's future in a global context are very well illustrated by the EU 2020 Strategy which is focused on 'smart, sustainable, inclusive growth,'[58] the EU's specific Strategy on European Cooperation in Education and Training (ET 2020)[59] and the Erasmus+ programme (2014-2020).

Finally, building a strong European Education and Lifelong Learning Area is vital for Europe's future. We favour a broadly-defined European studies curriculum which encompasses all levels, sectors and forms of learning – formal, non-formal and informal – in order to truly benefit all EU citizens and foster active and responsible EU citizenship. This should strengthen the European dimension of national education systems and programmes as well as the EU's own lifelong learning agenda. Not all young people are students after all, and not all students are young people. However, support for inclusive European-oriented education about responsible citizenship, multiple identities and dialogue among citizens should deal with differentiated discourses, general and specific curriculum content and the social and cultural relevance of education projects. We need education policies at a national level and European education programmes that match the 21st century reality to be able to live as Europeans in a world undergoing globalisation.

Conclusion

Four fundamental tasks

In conclusion, I am convinced that the 'Europe' project is still a valid working place to define the European common good and to develop a unique institutional and operational framework in this changing world, in spite of its failures and imperfections. This leads me to distinguish four fundamental tasks.

- Firstly, Europe has the moral responsibility to build a best practice of cooperation internally and externally. Individual and collective well-being depends more and more on an understanding of man's capacity to read the signs of time and act accordingly in the pursuit of economic and social welfare within a world of global competition. We need a radical

[58] European Union: EU 2020 Strategy, Sept. 2015.

[59] European Union: ET 2020. Feb. 2016.

change in vision and method to survive as European civilisation. Real progress must be valued and made visible to the citizen therefore. This requires a stronger, more direct and positive communication of the European project. (Van den Brande, L. 2017, p. 36).

- Secondly, Europeans have the moral responsibility to show that people can live together in the world, despite differences in language, culture, religion, origin, etc. EU citizens still need to show practically that they can form an international public space where cultural diaspora can exist in mutual respect, tolerance and dialogue. This implies education for citizens' participation in a variety of learning spaces.
- Thirdly, European countries and regions have to constantly strive to make their social and economic systems more efficient so that the weaknesses of one can be compensated with the strength of the others. This implies the importance of encouraging individual initiative, of seeking a broad and just distribution of the benefits of economic welfare and giving weight to the sense of responsibility in a values-driven education with a European dimension.
- Finally, Europeans should play a more courageous and dynamic role in the international political scene by defending its model for peace and transnational cooperation and by strengthening its method of collaboration with other macro regions. Europe should work for a transition of the traditional management of geopolitical and global economic conflicts to a new transversal policy in the global political and economic landscape. This also implies being a global leader on the environment – much in line with the Paris climate agreement.

Expectations of Hope and Fear

The EU needs a renewed political project embedded in a long-term vision in the current era of globalisation. The increasing influence of national interests in European policy-making can only be blocked in this way, in favour of the 'European commons'. Otherwise, faced with citizens' growing frustration, criticism and even indifference, the danger is that the EU will become a mere union of economic interests or disintegrate into national and sub-regional entities.

Undermining the foundation of the European integration model would mean undermining Europe's economic, social and environmental achievements and ultimately lead to its marginalisation in the global system. The crisis of European solidarity – illustrated very well by the absence of a European refugee policy – can only be overcome if initiatives and measures are taken which restore citizens' confidence in the European institutions within a framework of 'shared sovereignty'.

A mobilising vision that can generate a new impetus and a strengthened connection with the citizen is crucial. The EU's Founding Fathers' pragmatic vision is certainly relevant; they worked for a European project with a long-term vision but driven at the same time by a pragmatic approach. Economic arguments supported the political objective. However, European integration should remain the common destination to respond to the various challenges of a world undergoing globalisation.

That is why Europe needs bridge-builders who can complete the rhetoric of the European narrative, underline the European ideals of peace, unity in diversity, freedom and solidarity and mobilise young people for the European model of society. Yet the rhetoric must be translated into a workable and future-oriented reality where citizens feel at home. Broad and committed participation in European elections and beyond are an important driver for political change.

The role of education and learning is fundamental in this (Bekemans, L. 2012, pp. 263-287). Only through integral human development in education and learning processes can a genuine dialogue among citizens be developed and European citizenship be linked to democracy. However, the creation of transnational decision levels requires identification and loyalty if European democracy is to work. Education for inclusive European citizenship is part of the integral social development that Europe must promote therefore. New forms and places of learning, dialogue, active citizenship and cooperation also have a place in this.

Where Europe Comes from

The European Policy of Unity and Alexander's Policy of Omonia

Spyros Syropoulos[60]

It is undoubtedly easy to conclude that Alexander was superior and greater than Philip II; Alexander conquered the largest empire of the known world and expanded it even further, whereas Philip had managed to create Macedonia and only initiate the expedition against Persia. Nowadays however, we are more inclined to recognize Philip's superior military and political intellect and a number of works have managed to do justice to Philip's achievements.[61] It is one thing to accept Philip's superior intellect however, and another to acknowledge a most instructive fact: it was Philip alone who provided Alexander with the first model of an integrated society as a basis for the unity of the empire.[62] Moreover, Alexander was definitely in-

60 Professor of Ancient Greek Literature, Department of Mediterranean Studies, University of the Aegean; Director of the the MA Course 'Ancient Greek Theatre: Educational and Philological Approaches', Former Vice Rector of the University of the Aegean (2014-2018), General Secretary of the Greek Rectors Conference at the European University Association (2013-2019)

61 For such works one could turn easily to Nicholas Hammond, *The Miracle that was Macedonia*, Singwick and Jackson, London, and Nicholas Hammond, *Philip of Macedon,* Gerald Duckworth & Co. Ltd, 1995.

62 Indeed, Philip had proven the efficiency of many policies that Alexander adopted later. First of all, political marriages: Then, use of local upper classes of subdued areas, who cooperated with him, ensuring stable local administration and provision of their armies to the army of Philip. Cf. A. Bosworth, *Conquest and Empire, the Reign of Alexander the* Great, Cambrigde University Press, 1988 [here utilized the translation in Greek by. K. Μακρής, Κατακτήσεις και Αυτοκρατορία του Μεγάλου Αλεξάνδρου, εκδ.

fluenced by the integration policies of Darius the Great (Dārayava(h)uš, 550–486 BC), who had laid the foundations for the rule of vast, socially heterogeneous kingdoms such as his own empire. Setting aside common methodological problems, such as the subjectivity and originality of ancient sources, I will refer to these sources as a reliable and constructive corpus of valid information and compare Alexander's famous policy of Omonoia or universalism to that of contemporary policies concerning Europe. The methodological merits of this approach were stressed by Wight, who also proposed that we should view organizations such as Alexander's Empire or even the modern European Union, as being comprised of nations, i.e. independent political bodies (united or federal), which recognize no one else as superior to them and only acknowledge the same rights to independence in other states that belong to the same system.[63]

The vision of an empire where the conquerors would not feel like conquerors and the conquered would not feel like the conquered was the challenge Alexander strove to resolve throughout his short life. The problem was graphically captured in Plutarch's description of Alexander's alleged meeting with a Brahman wise-man, Kalanos; using a dried goatskin, he called Alexander to step on each of its corners, showing him that every time he put his foot on one side, the other side would rise in the air.[64] Alexander had to come up with innovative ways to establish political cohesion if his empire was to stand a chance of longevity. He had three basic problems to solve in order to achieve this: a) the establishment of a strong central government for his new empire, b) the establishment of functional and stable local administrations and c) the unity of his empire.

Οδυσσέας, 1998, p. 33].

63 M. Wight (with introduction by M. Bull), *Systems of States,* Leicester, Leicester University Press, 1977, for essays on the Graec-Persian and the European system of administration. Quoted by. Adam Watson, *The Evolution of International Society. A comparative historical analysis,* Taylor and Francis Book L.t.d., 2006 [Here utilized the translation in Greek: *Η εξέλιξη της διεθνούς κοινωνίας. Μια συγκριτική ιστορική ανάλυση*, μτφ. Λ. Στροίκου, επιμ. Χ. Παπασωτηρίου – Π. ' Ηφαιστος, εκδ. Ποιότητα, Αθήνα 2006], p. 21.

64 Plutarch, *Parallel Lives, Alexander-Caesar,* 66. I have argued aspects of this realization in the information of Alexander's policies in Σ. Συρόπουλος, Το Δέρμα του Τράγου, Ηρόδοτος, Θεσσαλονίκη 2003.

The Establishment of Secure Central Government

In the 6th paragraph of the so-called stone or stēlē of Behistun[65], Darius claims the legacy of his sovereignty as being derived straight from Ahura-Mazda.[66] Divine origin and protection had characterized all Egyptian and Persian rulers.

Most of our ancient sources agree that what Alexander really wanted from his visit to Ammun was confirmation of his divine patronage and his right to rule the world.[67] It is the story recorded by Curtius Rufus, who describes the famous slip of the tongue by the priest of Ammun when he greeted Alexander as son of Zeus, simply by changing the final 'n' of the vocative case into an 's', thus turning it into a genitive, translated as 'Hail, son of Zeus!' instead of 'Hail, young man!" Curtius Rufus concludes his anecdote by informing us that Alexander not only allowed everyone to address him as Son of Zeus, but he also gave orders that this should be carried out.[68] Plutarch states that, 'nothing happened to Alexander, nor was he drunk; he was merely using the fame of his divinity only to subdue others.'[69] Curtius also agrees that by doing this, Alexander simply wanted to boast the glory of his achievements.[70] What was his motivation?

If Alexander wanted to legalize his ascendancy to the throne of Persia as a legal heir of the Achaemenid line of Kings, he had to demonstrate his divine origin to his local subjects, just like their previous rulers. This led to great conflicts with his Macedonian associates of course. According to Curtius, they 'turned their back to their king, who was persistently talking about his immortality, making them feel awkward.'[71] It is true that the

---

65 The text of the stēlē was first published by L. W. King & R. C. Thompson, *The Sculptures and Inscriptions of Darius the Great on the Rock of Behistoun in Persia*, 1907.

66 A. T. Olmstead, *History of the Persian Empire,* University of Chicago 1948 [here utilized the translation in Greek by E. Πέππα, Ιστορία της Περσικής Αυτοκρατορίας, εκδ. Οδυσσέας, Αθήνα 2002] 216.

67 Plutarch, *Life of Alexander* 27; Diodorus, XVII, 51,3; Curtius IV, 7, 28; Justin XI, 11, 10. Only Arrian does not refer to any details with regards to the visit of Alexander to the temple and claims that the only thing Alexander wanted to know was about the future (Arrian, III, 3.2).

68 Curtius, XI, 11, 10.

69 Plutarch, *Life of Alexander* 28.

70 Curtius, IV, 7. 30.

71 Curtius, IV, 7. 31.

only unresolved problem for Alexander was to make his associates accept his visionary concept of the progressive joint administration of their new empire.

The Satrapy as a Basis for Effective Local Administration

The system of integration was not as totalitarian as it seemed. Despite the fact that Alexander treated the peoples and nations who comprised his newly founded empire as equal members, and not as subjects, there never was the pretense of everyone's equal participation in the upper echelons of the administration and defense system; Alexander obviously believed in the cultural superiority of two nations: the Macedonians and the Persians. Offices of grave importance for the administration of the empire were only reserved for Greeks and Persians. (Cartledge, P. 2004, p. 187) The need for a common army comprised of Greeks and Persians was realistic however, since Alexander realized that he would not have been able to master the control of his vast empire with only the limited number of troops he had brought from Macedonia.[72] By the end of 328 he had taken advantage of the superb Iranian cavalry and he had formed units of Bactrian and Sogdian riders. In 327 he had also recruited 30,000 young Iranians, arranging their instruction in Greek and the superior Macedonian military tactics. Paul Cartlege sees in these the realization of a policy of integration. It was a policy that died out with Alexander however, just like the forced mass weddings at Susa (Cartledge, P. 2004, pp. 254f).

The question is raised here about the equal participation of every member of this empire or commonwealth in the administration of this organization. It is safe to deduce that Alexander never meant equal participation in the central government for every culture of his new empire. It was principally Macedonian rule with Persian aid, especially from the upper classes, that would ensure the longevity of the new empire. 'The Greek and Macedonian fans of hegemony, just like the Persians, demanded three things from the communities whose external relations they regulated. The three requirements were: a contribution to the imperial treasury, a military or naval force

[72] For the need to incorporate local troops in the Macedonian units, not only for practical reasons but also for political, see. J. F. Fuller, *The Generalship of Alexander the Great*, Wordsworth Editions [here utilized the translation in Greek by Κ. Κολιόπουλος, Η ιδιοφυής στρατηγική του Μεγάλου Αλεξάνδρου, εκδ. Ποιότητα, 2004, p. 509-510].

that they would be available when required, and the presence of an imperial commissioner or satrap and a military commander.'[73]

Another issue that Alexander tackled was the issue of people's trust in central government. A number of satraps who did not perform their duties as expected were simply executed; during the winter of 325/4, Astaspes of Carmania, Orxines of Persis, Avoulites and Oxathres at Susiana and Paraceten were charged with incompetence and bad management (Bosworth, A.B. 1998, pp. 16-43). Higgins had suggested that punishments like these probably served other purposes and helped Alexander get rid of potentially subversive administrative elements. (Higgins, W. E. 1980, pp. 129-152). Even so, they reinforced his subjects' faith in the administration's fair system and subsequently reinforced their faith in Alexander – especially in the case of punishment of the Macedonians mentioned above, rather than Iranian satraps. It was in Medēa where Cleander, Sitalkes (and possibly Agathon) were brought to trial; they were charged by their subjects with sacrilege and oppression and they were condemned to death immediately.[74] The system of a trustworthy administration where no one is above the law was stressed by Ronald Heifetz in a recent interview with a Greek journal: 'Restoring confidence is important because without it, the leadership cannot mobilize the collective intelligence and create prosperity. To restore the course requires a number of changes mainly in the justice system and especially to stop the impunity of politicians. Two or three token gestures are not enough to restore the credibility and trust within society' (Heifetz, R. 2012, 44-49, p. 47)[75]

---

73 For a meticulous study of the evolution of common alliances to a hegemony of multiple dependencies with a central governing state, see Adam Watson (2006) esp. 95-146 for the transition from a Persian to a Macedonian and Hellenistic system of administrating the empire.

74 Arrian VI.27.4; Curtius X.I.1-9. Both of these sources agree that there was mismanagement although those rulers they were not the only ones responsible for this. It is more likely that they had proved disobedient to central administration (Curtius, X.1.7). They had been involved in the execution of Parmenio and the army, faithful to Parmenio, welcomed their punishment. It is worth noting that the Iranian co-satrap of Medea maintained his post, as he had proved his devotion to Alexander by turning against his compatriots.

75 Ronald Heifetz is King Hussein bin Talal Senior Lecturer in Public Leadership at JFK School of Government, Harvard.

Three Factors for Unity

Alexander had to acknowledge that his great predecessor on Persia's throne, not Darius the III but Dārayava(h)uš the Great, had indeed acted on extremely progressive policies – religious tolerance, respect for local traditions, freedom of languages and fair taxation. (Συρόπουλος, Σ. Δ. 2004, 38-59 and Olmstead, T. 1948, pp. 205-226). While preserving a functional peace by respecting the cultural differences of his subjects however, he failed to create a homogenous social foundation for his empire. The feeling of hostility toward Persian government, no matter how enlightened or tolerant it was, was evident the many times Alexander did not need to fight but was welcomed as a liberator from the Persians (as in Egypt). Alexander would have to solve this problem if he was to avoid past mistakes. If he were to try to achieve homogeneity, he would have to act as no one had done before. There was no point in trying to violently uproot cultural distinctiveness. History had already proven – and would certainly do so in the future – that in cases like this, people tend to defend whatever constitutes their cultural difference with more zeal. Without depriving his subjects of their individual cultures therefore, Alexander would have to offer them common points of reference.

Common Currency

From what we know about the Persian Empire it depended on a system of drawing heavy taxes in kind from its subjects. We know that there had not been uniformity in the economic growth of the subject areas, since production was somewhat primitive; trade consisted mainly of luxury items and wealth was accumulated in the hands of few. Iranian areas and the remote east satrapies in particular were considered especially poor in comparison to the big administrative centers. (Gafurof, B. et al. 1982, p. 194) One way to develop the economy was the extensive use of coinage.

Coercion also fostered monetary uniformity, and there is no denying that Alexander imposed a common currency – widely used even during the first years of the Roman expansion – because it also served as a means for propaganda.[76] Bosworth has no doubt that Alexander's primary goals were

---

[76] 'Coins were by far the best propaganda weapon available for advertising Greek, Roman or any other civilization in the days before mechanical printing was invented.' (Davies,

political, seeking to mint a currency that would advertize his sovereignty throughout his empire. (Bosworth, A.B. 1998, p. 407). Even Aristotle observed in his Oeconomicus that the circulation of new coins is the first expression of a royal economy, which is totally distinguished from satrap administration.[77] The extensive use of coinage would replace the traditional trade economy of course; it would make the circulation of wealth and monetary control easier and it would boost his subjects' trade and prosperity. But it also served as a most effective tool to spread Alexander's image to the outermost peripheries of his empire.

Benedict Anderson offered an interesting definition of a nation in his influential book, Imagined Communities: 'it is an imagined political community – and imagined as both inherently limited and sovereign. It is imagined because the members of even the smallest nation will never know most of their fellow-members, meet them, or even hear of them, yet in the minds of each lives the image of their communion' (Anderson, B. 2006). The appreciation of the propagandistic power of his coinage becomes obvious if this notion is applied to Alexander's empire; comprised of a mosaic of nations and cultures, Alexander's newly founded empire would always lack homogeneity. Just as in the days of the Persian predominance to put it simply, Persians would be Persians, while Phrygians would by Phrygians; Babylonians would be Babylonians and Egyptians would be Egyptians, and so forth. The only thing that those people had in common was their king, a king that most of them would probably never see personally. However, every time that the subject from the most remote corner of this empire would pay his taxes, or buy food, or drink, any time he would use a coin, he would be reminded that the person minted on this coin is not only his master, but also the one common element he shared with the rest of the peoples who comprised this empire.

Contemporary numismatic policies in Europe were definitely based on the same principles. When the EU was founded as the European Economic Community in 1958, it had one goal – the creation of a common agricultural market. It evolved into a broader, united economic market which was almost complete by 1993. The numismatic unity of Europe was about united numismatic policies and a common currency, the Euro. The establishment

G. 2002, 85-86)

[77] Aristotle, *Oeconomicus* 1345b20 ff.

of a common currency at Maastricht, Holland, in December 1991 and numismatic integration in the EU resulted in growth, internal productivity and economic resilience benefitting every nation independently, subsequently leading to even more growth and the creation of more jobs in the EU.

This common currency could not have survived or practically functioned if Alexander had not secured a stable political system with unity. Ian Traynor, the Editor of Europe, observed in a recent post that David Cameron and George Osborne had realized together that the 'remorseless logic' of sharing a currency is based on the notion of political unity in Europe. He suggested in his article that 'the leaders may even run out of time, exhausting the reserves of brinkmanship and last-minute calls that have characterized the 'crisis management' of the past 30 months. But they hope that by unveiling a medium-term strategy for a fiscal and political union in the eurozone they will convince the financial markets of their resolve to save the euro, that the currency is irreversible, and that the heat will be off. The impact of 'the project' will be immense, if it takes off' (Traynor, I. 2012).

Common Language

In Imaginary Communities Anderson had also argued that all national identities form around a common tongue. Given the diversity of languages in Europe and the absence of a common language, is there a chance of creating a common identity that would lead to a united Europe? The question was answered by Leonard Orban, the former European Commissioner of Multilingualism,[78] who commented, 'I think yes, it is possible. I don't think that the variety of languages in Europe creates division. The divisions are sometimes created by different stakeholders trying to promote their own agenda; an agenda which is not similar to the agenda of the European Union. I do think it's important to consolidate a kind of European citizenship, but let's be very clear (and this was also my main message when I was a Commissioner): only by respecting the diversity of languages in Europe can we ensure a feeling of common identity. It looks a little strange that, on the

[78] Leonard Orban is the Romanian Minister of European Affairs and former European Commissioner for Multilingualism. His response on the question of common European identity is found at http://www.debatingeurope.eu/2011/12/19/is-a-european-identity-possible/.

one hand we are supporting diversity but on the other we want to create such a feeling of European citizenship, but by defending the language of different people living in the European Union, we may offer this feeling of being really a European'. Orban rejected the idea of establishing a version of 'Esperanto' in the same response, or any other artificial language while admitting that, 'English is an excellent language, and it helps one have a direct dialogue with people from different member-states'.[79]

It seems that Alexander had already acknowledged the issue of language as a culturally unifying factor in a multicultural organization. It had to be a language which was easy to use, functional and perhaps spoken by many people already. It is interesting to observe that Alexander did not impose the use of the Macedonian dialect in contrast with all notions of modern imperialism. He opted for the Attic dialect instead, perhaps because it was already widely used for trade throughout the Mediterranean world. (Horrocks, G. 2001, 457-467, p. 457). In fact, the Hellenistic Common was the language of the middle and upper classes and certainly the language for administration especially towards the end of the Hellenistic era. This is verified by the numerous dialectic epigraphs for a purely local purpose, which were increasingly invaded by the Hellenistic Common. (Ib., p. 458)

Common Traditions

Tradition is a strong cultural bond and Alexander could not have failed to observe its unifying potential. Religion was a strong means to establish new traditions. Alexander's visit to the temple of Ammun after the battle of Granicus, not only legalized his royal status among the indigenous popula-

[79] Leonard Orban, Op.cit. English is spoken by more than 50% of Europeans today either as first or second language. Interestingly enough, the report *Europeans and their Languages,* published in *Special Eurobarometer* 386 in June 2012, states that: a) at a national level English is the most widely spoken foreign language in 19 of the 25 Member States where it is not an official language (i.e. excluding the UK and Ireland). (p. 12), and b) German is the most widely spoken, with 16% of Europeans saying it is their first language, followed by Italian and English (13% each), French (12%), then Spanish and Polish (8% each) (p... 12), c) Two thirds of Europeans (67%) think that English is one of the two most useful languages. It is much more likely to be considered useful for personal development than any other language. Less than one in five Europeans mention German (17%), French (16%) and Spanish (14%), p. 71. The whole text can be obtained from http://ec.europa.eu/public_opinion/archives/ebs/ebs_386_en.pdf.

tions, but it may have marked the first case of official religious syncretism characterizing the Hellenistic era.[80] Ammun was identified by the Greeks as a form of Zeus during Alexander's occupation, and he continued to be the principal local deity of Thebes.[81]

The case of Sarapis (or Serapis)[82] is far more interesting. Most scholars agree that Sarapis was part of the official Ptolemaic policy with regard to an integrated society. Ptolemy Lagos may have been the first ruler who made the cult of Sarapis official. (Brady, T. A. 1935).[83] C. Welles went further than this, suggesting that it was indeed Alexander who established this cult, commonly revered by western and eastern cultures. (Welles, C. B. 1962, pp. 271ff). If this was the case, then we can safely speak about a most visionary policy that would eradicate religious differences, so often a source of social and political trouble in the East.

We should certainly not exaggerate the role of religious syncretism as an element for cultural fusion. As Gehrke pointed out, there has never been a mystery-cult in Egypt which was common for both the Egyptians and the Greeks; Greeks could be initiated into the mystery cults of the East but they could never be enrolled among the clergy, which continued to be exclusively Egyptian.[84] The failure of such a policy does not rule out the intention on the part of either the Ptolemies or Alexander however. Religion is a strong cultural factor and Alexander and his successors could not ignore

---

80 Gehrke (2000) 270-275.

81 Pausanias, *Description of Greece* iii.18 §2

82 The Greeks fused this Egyptian deity with a number of Hellenistic deities, including Zeus, Helios, Dionysus, Hades and Asklepius to form Serapis or Sarapis. Eventually, these Hellenistic deities would predominate the god's final form. He then emerged as a supreme god of divine majesty and the sun (Zeus and Helios), fertility (Dionysos) the underworld and afterlife, as well as healing (Hades and Asklepius). For his association with the Sun cf. Macrobius *Saturnalia* 1.20.13. In the same passage Macrobius states that 'In the city on the borders of Egypt which boasts Alexander of Macedon as its founder, Sarapis and Isis are worshiped with a reverence that is almost fanatical'. For Sarapis, see Wilkinson, R. H. (2003).

83 For opposing views cf. P. Fraser, 'Two Studies on the Cult of Sarapis in the Hellenistic World', *OAth* 3 (1960) 23ff.

84 Gehrke (2000) 268.

it.[85] The Roman and the Byzantine Empire would later rely on the unifying factor of religion with varying degrees of success.[86]

The creation of common points of reference in culture and traditions was probably one of the things that Alexander had in his mind when he initiated the mass weddings at Susa. 10.000 of his men were married to Persian women. The converse never occurred. If Alexander wanted to create a new elite of people having the best of both cultural backgrounds, but with the culture of the father being dominant, then he would have to mix Greek men with local women, and not vice-versa.

Conclusions

From what is indicated above it becomes obvious that Alexander's most progressive idea was to achieve social and national integration of the numerous cultures he ruled. 'Alexander's idea of cooperation among peoples became the basis of the Euthydemian kingdom in Bactria and India and, on the philosophical side, was picked up by Zeno and St. Paul to constitute a standing challenge to all posterity'. (Robinson Jr., C. A. 1957, 326-344, p. 344). We can safely say that the successors to this quest included the great empires of Rome, the United States of America and Europe – in this specific order. All three of them applied extensive policies to create common cultural points of reference for the culturally heterogeneous nations they ruled, and all of them used a common language, a common currency and common traditions in order to unite their peoples, without uprooting the distinguishing characteristics of each. The varying results of such policies today stem from the most unforeseen factor of all, the one that even Alexander had failed to harness: human nature.[87]

---

[85] For the respect of Ptolemies and their policy of blending local cults with aspects of Greek religion, see Koenen, L. (1982), Bulloch, A. et al. (Eds.) (1993), 25-115.

[86] Betz, amongst others, argued for the Hellenistic foundations of Christian religion, or at least the interpretation of certain Hellenistic religion aspects under the light of Christianity. (Betz, H. D. (1994), 1-25).

[87] Also worth quoting Mason Hammond who said that 'the problem which ancient imperialism poses to the modern world is not that of creating a world state; the Persians and Alexander showed that this could be done, while Augustus founded one whose endurance still challenges the imagination of mankind. Rather, the problem is to combine the surrender of sovereignty to a world state with the preservation of responsibility

From what we have seen, the main points of this argument can be summarized as follows:

a) The model for Alexander's administration of his vast empire was based on Philip's political experiments in northern Greece; in its turn this was inspired by the Persian system of administration, known quite well by both Philip and Alexander.
b) The principles for the administration of Alexander's empire focused on the development of strong poles for cultural integration with the sole purpose of gradually eliminating awareness of cultural difference, namely a common language, a common currency and common traditions.
c) Previous systems to administer culturally heterogeneous cultures had failed (the Delian League, the Persian Empire) and the problems of such delicate unions can even be grasped in recent European history (the breakdown of Yugoslavia).
d) The conscious effort to achieve the unity of contemporary Europe draws many of its principles from the system modeled by Alexander the Great.

Hans Morgenthau had observed that during the times when large trans-national and trans-state empires predominated, less powerful collective entities never ceased striving for collective freedom and political supremacy. Most of these empires shared another characteristic; they barely outlived their founder. (Morgenthau, H. J. 1948, p. 63). Alexander's policies indicated the recognition of such difficulties and constituted the first systematic attempt to resolve them. It is not the failure or success of such policies that constitute someone as great at the end of the day, but the adoption of such policies by all the major subsequent collective political bodies, whether they succeeded or not. Alexander's political thought was the link between the past and – not the present, but – the future. In the words of Mary Butt, the great lost English Modernist, there are people who epitomize an era and there are people who start another. Alexander did both.[88]

---

to the will not merely of the people, but of many peoples, each eager to protect its own economic, social, political, and cultural integrity' (Hammond, M. (1948), 105-161, 124-125).

88 Mary Butts, *The Macedonian,* 1931. Reprinted with a foreword by Thomas McEvilley, as *The Classical Novels*. Butts, M. (1994).

Where should Europe Go?

Democracy in Europe

Michael Löwy

Let us begin with a quote from an essay on bourgeois democracy in Russia, written in 1906 after the defeat of the first Russian revolution:

> 'It is highly ridiculous to believe that there is an elective affinity between grand capitalism today, as it is presently imported into Russia, and well established in the United States [...] and 'democracy' or 'liberty' (in all the possible meanings of the word); the real question should be: how are these things even 'possible', in the long term, under capitalist domination?' (Weber, M., 1906, p. 353).

Who is the author of this insightful comment? Lenin, Trotsky, or perhaps Plekhanov? In fact, it is Max Weber, the well-known liberal sociologist. Although Weber never developed this insight, he is suggesting here that there is an intrinsic contradiction between capitalism and democracy.

The history of the twentieth century seems to confirm Weber's opinion: very often, when the power of the ruling classes seemed threatened by the people, democracy was pushed aside as an unaffordable luxury and replaced by fascism – as in Europe in the 1920s and 1930s or military dictatorships in Latin America in the 1960s and 1970s.

Fortunately, this is not the case in Europe today; rather, we now have, particularly during the last decades with the triumph of neoliberalism, a *low-intensity democracy,* a democracy without social content which has become an empty shell. To be sure, we still have elections, but there seems to be only one party, the U.M.P. or United Market Party, with two variants differing in having only limited ways: the right-wing neoliberal version, and the centre-left social liberal one.

The decline of democracy is particularly visible in the oligarchic functioning of the European Union, where the European Parliament has very little influence while power is firmly in the hands of non-elected bodies, such as the European Commission or the Central European Bank. According to Giandomenico Majone, Professor at the Europen Institute of Florence and one of the semi-official theoreticians of the Union, Europe needs 'non-majoritarian institutions', i.e., 'public institutions that are, on purpose, not responsible either towards electors or elected officials': this is the only way to protect us against 'the tyranny of the majority'. In such institutions 'qualities such as expertise, professional discretion and coherence [. . .] are much more important than the direct democratic responsibility".[89] One could hardly imagine a more blatant apology of the oligarchic and antidemocratic nature of the Union.

With the present economic crisis, democracy has been reduced to its lowest level. In a recent editorial, the French newspaper *Le Figaro* wrote that the present situation is exceptional, that this explains why democratic procedures cannot be always respected; and that when normal times return, we can re-establish democratic legitimacy. We have therefore a sort of economic/political 'state of exception' in Carl Schmitt's sense. But who is the sovereign that now has the right to proclaim a Schmittian state of exception?

In Europe the absolute and total sovereign today is, as we all know, the global financial market. Financial markets dictate to each country wages pensions, cuts in social expenses, privatisations, and the rate of unemployment. More recently, they directly nominate the heads of government (Greece and Italy), picking so-called 'experts' who are faithful servants of the financial markets.

Let us have a closer look at some of these all-powerful 'experts'. Where do they come from? Mario Draghi, until recently president of the Central European Bank, is a former manager of Goldman Sachs; Mario Monti, former European Commissioner, is also a former adviser to Goldman Sachs. Monti and Lucas Papademos are members of the Trilateral Commission, a very select club of politicians and bankers that discuss future policy. The

---

89 Quoted in Anderson, P. (2011), pp. 154, 158.

Honorary Chairman of the European Trilateral was Peter Sutherland, former European Commissioner, and former manager at Goldman Sachs; the vice-president of the Trilateral, Vladimír Dlouhý, former Czech Minister of Economy, is now adviser to Goldman Sachs for Eastern Europe. In other words, the 'experts' in charge of saving Europe from the crisis have worked at one time or another for one of the banks directly responsible for the subprime crisis in the United States. This does not mean that there is a conspiracy to deliver Europe to Goldman Sachs; it only illustrates the oligarchic nature of the 'expert' elite governing the Union.

The governments of Europe are indifferent to public protest, strikes, and mass demonstrations, and the populations' opinions or feelings; they only care about, and are extremely sensitive to, the opinion and the feelings of the financial markets and their employees, the credit rating agencies. In Europe's pseudo-democracy, to consult the people via referendums is a dangerous heresy, even worse, a crime against the Holy Market. Any political leader that entertains – for whatever opportunistic reasons – such an explosive idea is unanimously considered by the European oligarchy to be a public danger who must be immediately removed from office and replaced by some reliable expert, preferably a bank manager.

While the crisis worsens and public outrage grows, there is for many governments an increasing temptation to shift public attention towards a scapegoat: the immigrants. Thus, undocumented foreigners, non-communitarian immigrants, Muslims, Roms and Sintis are being presented as the main threat to the country. This of course presents great opportunities to racist, xenophobic, semi-fascist, or outright fascist parties, which are growing and in several countries are already part of the government – a very serious threat to democracy in Europe.

The only hope is the growing aspiration for another Europe, beyond savage competition, brutal austerity policies, and eternal debt peonage. Another Europe is possible, a democratic, ecological and social Europe! Yet, it cannot be achieved without a common struggle of the European populations, beyond ethnic borders and the narrow limits of the nation-state. In other words, our hope for the future is popular *indignation,* which has been on the rise particularly among youth and women in several countries. For the 'indignado' protesters, it is becoming increasingly obvious that the struggle for democracy is a struggle against neoliberalism, and, in the last analysis, against capitalism itself, an inherently antidemocratic system, as Max Weber already pointed out a hundred years ago.

A Different Europe?

Constructive Critique of a Passionate European

Luciana Castellina

If we are to build a better European Union than the one that was born 60 years ago, the most important thing we can do is to free it from the unbearable rhetoric that has accompanied it, which has blocked any constructive criticism, as it is immediately branded as 'anti-European sentiment' and a nostalgic attachment to a world of little nations responsible for all wars.

The first real confusion that occurred to the detriment of the European project was the belief that the project launched in 1957 was spawned by the Ventotene Manifesto, the declaration drafted by a respected group of Italian anti-fascists on the island where they were imprisoned by Mussolini. The Manifesto did have a significant influence on the drafting of Italy's 1948 Constitution, but no influence at all on the many European Treaties. Indeed, at the Community's official baptism ceremony, which took place at the Teatro Adriano in Rome on 23 March 1957, Altiero Spinelli's federalists threw leaflets down from the gallery onto the stalls where the authorities were sitting, with the message that they did not recognise the 'monster' that was emerging. Indeed, it was the Italian Constitution – which is fairly unique in the West in imposing strict restrictions on the right to own property and declaring war illegal if it is not to defend against invaders – which posed an obstacle to Italy's entry into the then embryonic Europe. One of the witnesses to the negotiations at the time, Professor Paolo Elia, a respected Christian Democrat leader, said that it was particularly Germany's minister of finance Ludwig Erhard who would have liked to exclude our country, precisely because of our republic's founding document. He did not get his way; if he had, it would have been impossible to perpetuate the myth that the 'monster' was inspired by the Ventotene Manifesto.

A movement that aims to transform Europe can benefit from a consideration of the EU's early development. We can begin with the dissemination of the Ventotene Manifesto. To begin with, re-reading the Ventotene Manifesto, looking at how it was disseminated, and registering how different the current European Union is from its vision can help counteract the toxic effects of pro-European rhetoric.

Nobody remembers that the first legislative act – proposed by John Foster Dulles, the powerful head of US diplomacy (and brother of CIA director Allen) favouring European union came not from our continent but from the US Congress (approved 11 March 1947 by the Senate and 23 March by the Congress). It is true that this vote was accompanied by the simultaneous launch of the Marshall Plan, an option which turned out in reality to be forward-looking and managed to defeat those who, in America, opposed it and for fear of European economic competition wanted to see a weakened Europe. Instead, Washington opted for a Europe that was strong enough to make a good trading partner and, despite the political obligations the plan imposed on the countries involved (one of the reasons why it could not be accepted by countries in the east); it was a plan that was good for the US and Europe. Yet it is also, or rather above all, true that this US endorsement was also one of the first acts in the Cold War, as the project helped build a western fortress, which, rather than uniting Europe, was to break it into two opposed parts. It also meant that the public, still smarting from the war, would have to swallow German rearmament. This was one of the main reasons that caused the left – not only Italian communists and socialists but also a large part of social democracy – to oppose the project for a long time.

In short, Altiero Spinelli was not the father of the EU but was always committed to a different model. We need only read his critical remarks on the preparation of the first federalist movement congress in The Hague in 1948. He refused to participate in it if the only high level figure present was Churchill, the inventor of the Cold War, a move that would brand the initiative with the same stamp. Spinelli's supporters reiterated the non-bloc alternative, a 'third way' for Europe.

There has been no reflection on what was being built in Europe and how it was being done, even in recent years. Not even in 2005, when the citizens of two founding Member States, France and the Netherlands, were asked to decide on the new Lisbon Treaty in a referendum and did not approve it. In this case also, the peoples of the two countries concerned were accused of resurgent nationalism. The accusation was not completely inaccurate, but it is not at all true to say that the rejection was based only or fundamentally on nationalist sentiment.

As a result, a committee was established to organise a process of reflection. Unfortunately, it did nothing of the kind. Instead, two years later in the capital of Portugal a Treaty was launched that was almost a carbon copy of the awful document born 15 years earlier in Maastricht.

It is due to this 'illegitimate birth' – which was never endorsed by the authors of the Ventotene Manifesto – that Europe has never become popular. Indeed, in 1955 when the first blueprint was conceived, almost nobody noticed: the location chosen to launch it was, significantly, Messina – not to project a sacrosanct desire to open up to the Mediterranean but for a more trivial reason. There were local elections looming, which were of great interest to our Gaetano Martino, Minister of Foreign Affairs in the dreadful Scelba government. (The astonishment in the north at the peculiar location was expressed with particular irony by a Belgian correspondent: 'Why not move the Council of ministers to Alaska or Tierra del Fuego then?' As for the interest generated by the event, just consider the remark from Paul Spaak – who was tasked with preparing Europe's real 'baptism' – two years later in Rome: 'public opinion towards us was not hostile, it was indifferent').

The rest of the story is well known. From one treaty to another, right up to Lisbon, the DNA of the embryo hasn't changed, nor has the indifference: the Maastricht Treaty, which is by far the most significant – because it unleashed the legal horror of constitutionalising a specific policy choice, liberal policy, thus exempting it from parliamentary decision – was ratified in Italy after a parliamentary debate lasting half a day. The only opposing votes came from the members of the Communist Refoundation Party (which in subsequent years did did little to oppose the treaty). This was despite the fact that they were faced with adopting competitiveness as the Union's overriding principle, thus making any sort of market regulation illegal, and introducing a substantial limit on the welfare state.

The EU project thus proceeded step-by-step to deliberately destroy any obstacle to full liberalisation. What is worse is that it produced a silent but complete acquiescence within a large part of the left, both those in government in their respective Member States and a good number of the opposition. Instead they noisily denounced any criticism or counter-proposal as a disgraceful offence against the 'holy European fathers'.

Indifference was so widespread that there was no effort – in almost all of the Member States nor in virtually any of the political groups – for a way to drive forward proposals that, if accepted, could have made the EU less ugly. Just think of those brought to the table by Delors himself, for example, including long-term and youth unemployment in the convergence criteria of the Stability Pact as one of the indicators that 'best revealed the difficulties that a country may be experiencing'; or Vredeling's proposal for a directive, in which he called for the establishment of works councils in companies with more than 1,000 employees located in two or more countries, to allow workers facing closures or relocations to benefit from information provided by management boards who were often far away and no longer direct counterparties to company claims (which would have been particularly helpful to the Fiat workers). There was also the proposal by the French economist Fitoussi: calculate the public deficit minus public investments in development.

Let us not forget how the foolish enlargement of the EU to include some 28 countries was also swallowed, a process in which any suggestion of full political union – which was obviously impossible given such a huge diversity of structures – was buried. Rather than seeking new forms of co-operation with the eastern states, they were incorporated pure and simple. This project was dictated above all by the attractiveness of these markets and by their readiness to align unconditionally with the rules of liberalism. By also, immediately, arranging their entry to the Union to coincide with the parallel enlargement of NATO (as today it would like to do with Ukraine), the Union became the cornerstone of western identity, translated into a string of missile bases.

Even here the left preferred to believe and promote the belief that only selfishness could stop all peoples on earth from having their slice of the splendid European cake. Thus, they aroused hopeless appetites in countries and regions ready to abandon their original identities to be able to join the 'exclusive club'. (The breakup of Yugoslavia began in this way, without any negotiation as provided for by the Treaty on European Security and only by expanding the people's right to self-determination – exactly what is considered illegal today with regard to Crimea).

Is it still possible to salvage the spirit of Ventotene, and is the slogan 'another Europe is possible" that we all continue to proclaim still meaningful? I believe so; in fact, I think it's essential that we try. But rather than also engaging in discussion over the institutional architecture in order to determine what changes should be brought to treaties and regulations – many are already doing this – I would prefer to talk here about us and our left, which although never (yet) in government, is not exempt from blame.

First of all, for not being seriously committed to building a European social and political entity, able to change – at EU level – the current balance of power, form alliances, establish hegemony and deepen its mooring in civil society, or to become a key player in political battles, at least as far as possible at the national level where democracy exists.

This 'entity' – and I call it 'entity' and not 'people' or demos in order to avoid the risk of cultural (or worse 'Schmidian') misunderstandings – doesn't exist: the story of Europe is the story of its nations, our monuments were erected to celebrate victories which, across borders, remind us of disasters. The idea that a shared historical culture exists is also hot air: Christianity generated endless religious wars and the Enlightenment led to further splits. With regard to the famous legacy of Greco-Judeo- Christian civilisation (the separation of religion and politics, respect for the individual, etc.), this is now the heritage of the whole Western world; it is not a specific characteristic of our continent. In addition, we speak 26 different languages and each people is rightly protective of its own.

In particular, 'intermediary bodies' are missing at European level – trade unions, parties, media, and associations – which in the individual nations ensure greater levels of democracy, by acting as channels of communication between civil society and the institutions. These bodies allow the public to make their voices heard and thereby influence executive power. It was this sacrosanct tradition that drove the German Constitutional Court to declare the admission of Federal Germany to the European Union born with the Maastricht Treaty inadmissible: this was because – as we read in Judge Grimm's judgement – the basic law of the country prevents it from joining a non-democratic supranational organisation. A manoeuvre was found to overcome this substantial objection, but the Court of Karlsruhe renewed its judgement again in relation to the Lisbon Treaty.

These are important observations: we all know that European-level trade unions exist almost only on paper, operating from a beautiful building in Brussels, where they promote interesting studies but do not organise any real joint trade union action. (Just consider basic income – also known as inclusion income, minimum income, among other names –, which is a rallying cry in all European countries; however, I am not aware of anything that has been done to formulate a joint proposal or to fight for it at the EU level). With regard to the political parties, I remember when Willy Brandt said that the meeting of European socialists was the best place to go to read the newspaper. Since then not much has changed: there is hardly even any information on what European member organisations are doing in their respective countries. Not to mention the media: there is no real European TV and only a few Member States are involved in the tiny Euronews channel. Each country has its own broadcaster abroad and there is no standard supplement to be included in like-minded newspapers. As a consequence, European public opinion does not exist. There is only public opinion in individual Member States and it is easy to play them off against one another, meaning that EU legislators and policy makers do not really have to meet anyone's needs.

Under these conditions it is difficult for Europeans to feel that they are part of a common good, which forms the basis for democratic participation. Nor does it make any sense to call for solidarity between Member States and ask that the treaties be changed to abolish the horrible 'no bailout' clause, which lays down the rule that each country must tend to its own affairs and cannot be called upon to help another country struggling with economic problems. We will never manage to change the terrible competition rules (the opposite of solidarity) that underpin the treaties unless we first build a community (even if Schäuble does retire).

We must also correct (and this has also been done very little) the concept of democracy that Brussels has tried to endorse over the years – with some scholarly support – namely, the notion that there is no people in the European Union, just citizens. Although, in the Nice Charter, the Union lays down many individual rights (even more in many cases than are provided at the national level) it does not include the key right in any democracy: a collective right. This means the power to take part in the deliberations on general decisions.

The complexity to create a European political subject, in light of the deep differences characterising the nations that are part of the EU, is aggravated today by the intense immigration coming from other continents, which leads to further and much deeper ethnic, cultural, and religious heterogeneities. The origin of the racist wave, as the backdrop of this phenomenon, is undoubtedly rooted in the sense of insecurity caused by the economic crisis and by the inequalities produced by the neoliberal policies that have been adopted after the crisis. It is not surprising that the most widespread rejection of immigrants is coming from the Eastern European Countries – countries that are still experiencing the trauma of a radical system change that has exposed their populations to the harshest form of capitalism.

Much has been said about the immediate measures that must be adopted in order to tackle the migratory flow and many proposals have been made by those opposing the horrific policy adopted by the EU in this field. But little consideration has been given to the necessary changes to be effected when it is be definitively established that this level of immigration represents, for the most part, an irreversible process (there can be no freedom of movement for capital and goods without freedom of movement for people). After all, an unexpected degree of mobility also characterises the European populations nowadays: increasingly – generally highly qualified – young people are leaving their countries of birth to find jobs in other countries. (In the south of Italy this emigration surpasses the number of immigrants.)

In light of the above, it is necessary to rethink the concept of citizenship by conceiving a notion of 'multiple citizenship' that preserves the persons' own roots while introducing a European dimension, which is tied to the European territory where the person is rightfully living, but decoupled from a single nation.

Much more needs to be done for enabling people to consider themselves as citizens, hence holders of this common good called Europe – perceived as a community of goals, based on its own specific model, and not as a mere geographic/bureaucratic space. To this regard, it is necessary, first of all, to start calling the immigrants 'new Europeans' and no longer 'third-country nationals', and to strengthen the idea that Europe is a community.

The term 'common' is also important, because in this era of globalisation when everyone trades with everyone else the idea of a common market – which might have seemed like a good idea in the 1950s – is almost ridiculous. Thus, either we answer the reasonable question – why Europe? – or nobody will take action. Quite the opposite, the illusion of the 'little homelands' will continue to resurface.

I also believe that one of the reasons why interest in the EU has further declined is the fact that Europe has lost its uniqueness and we have become just one piece of the global market. I am referring to our post-war national constitutions and welfare, based on the non-sanctity of private property and not demonising the public. I also have in mind the characteristic that Karl Marx ascribed to Europe in the *Grundrisse*: the discreet distance maintained by society from the commodification of all aspects of life, a critical distance guaranteed by the persistence of pre-capitalist vestiges – such as the rural world, the Church and the aristocracy – and of their values, which remained active during the development of the capitalism. These historical entities continued to not completely accept the new society that was evolving and still produced reactionary effects but at the same time impeded the reduction of everything to a mere marketplace.

To demonstrate the accuracy of this Marxian observation, it is enough to think of gastronomy. It is not without reason that we, as the Committee for Culture and Education of the European Parliament, decided to use it as a reference point in defining a common European identity. During the first big demonstration against globalisation at the WTO Summit in Seattle in 1999 the notorious symbol of the protest was Roquefort cheese, which was seized on by José Bové as a banner of resistance. It symbolised the idea that Europe was proud of its thousands of varieties of cheese even if market forces were pushing for a homogenisation: an assembly line for a single anonymous kind of dairy.

If this model and its values are dismantled, Europe also loses its meaning.

That is why the action we must take to save Europe is entirely political and cultural, rather than economic. Of course, motivating our own activists to fight for a different Europe is not easy, nor is it easy to construct the entity that this battle may aim at creating. The events of recent years in particular suggest that we should give up the project, with everyone looking for a way to save themselves. But we should realise that alone every one of our little countries would drown in the ocean unless it convinced its inhabitants to return to a pastoral economy. Although there is still hope of recovering some form of democracy in our era, this certainly will not be done at global level, – global democratic institutions are difficult to imagine – but rather only by focusing on macro-regions. Despite all, Europe is perhaps the easiest one of these regions to build on, even with all its faults, given that, as Etienne Balibar notes, it is the richest in social and individual rights, with its embedded history of struggles and revolutions.

Gramsci critically noted that there was a defect common to both the social-democratic tradition and the communist workers' movement: statism. That is, an obsessive focus on the control of central power, whether through parliamentary elections or the storming of the Winter Palace, while at the same time under-valuing society itself as a site of politics. The same can be said today, particulary in terms of Europe, where the left has been more concerned about Brussels and has taken very little interest in European society. In my view, it is essential that we take care of European society and commit to building agents of change at this level.

The
Secular State as a Religious Necessity

An Islamic Perspective

Adnane Mokrani

Challenges to religion

Religions face the challenges of modernity in different ways today, particularly in relation to politics and democracy. These challenges are part of a larger issue, i.e., the relationship between revelation and history, between the eternal and the temporal. The problem is how to distinguish between principles and values and their historical forms and modes of application. The world has changed radically and classical religious thought is rooted in a historical phase that no longer exists. Therefore, a radical reform and a profound renewal are needed to enable religion to be more open, particularly to dialogue with the world's new realities. It entails a radical innovative effort, *ijtihād*, and not merely a simple superficial reform. The history of political thought has known great changes and developments. We have experienced the following epochs:

First, the classical state, where the criterion for belonging to the state was to be a member of the governing religious community or tribal coalition and where the followers of the other groups and communities were considered second class subjects (and not citizens). To a certain extent, this is the case of the current hered-itary monarchies, which persist today in many ways, even de-spite the abolition of the caliphate in 1924. Second, the postcolonial national state that represents an intermediate phase situated between the classical and modern phases – a dictatorial state, often with a democratic or ideological façade. Like the classical state, the national one carries an exclusivist character, in the sense that those belonging to other ethnic groups, linguistic and cultural minorities are considered second-class citizens, though this is often not officially declared (incomplete citizenship). Atatürk in Turkey, Reza Shah in Iran, Bourguiba in Tunisia are clear examples; also included are the liberation movements, often secular leftists, such as the FLN in Algeria. Third, after the failure of the national state and its secular leadership to achieve the promised development – full independence and liberation – militant Islamism invaded the political scene as a radical opposition force in the 1970s and 1980s. The Iranian revolution of 1979 was the culmination of this phase.

Following the terrorist massacres in Algeria in the 1990s and the crisis of the Islamic Republic of Iran, especially after the 2009 elections and the Iranian green movement (the green wave), the Islamist discourse began to lose ground. In my opinion, the appearance of Al-Qaeda on the international political scene is the exception that proves the rule. It is an apocalyptical ideology which does not have any project for the future.

While the initial image of Arab revolutions, the so-called 'Arab spring', reinforced the idea of 'post-Islamism', it seems that we are heading toward a 'neo-Islamism.' But even this wave of Is-lamist post-revolutionary governments seems rather to be a quasi-obligatory passage to reach a real and mature democracy.

The fourth step is represented by the democratic state, based on full citizenship without any discrimination, even though it is a work in process characterized by strong hesitation and resistance. The main sign of change is the growing collective consciousness of a need for democracy, freedom and human rights, especially among young people.

Obstacles on the way towards civil and political maturity

In order to arrive at this level of civil and political maturity, where the human being is at the center of attention and interest, democracy must meet certain challenges:

- Resistance imposed by religious and nationalist systems, especially in a globalized world where fear of losing one's identity is widespread; this fear is nothing other than the persisting desire to maintain the same thought and lifestyle in a world that is rapidly changing. This kind of resistance is the main topic of this paper.

– The dominance of money or 'money-cracy' (and not democracy) or even 'money-latry' (idolatry of money), is another great temptation that takes on powerful forms. This is a serious risk for the development of democracy which becomes reduced to a mere procedural form in the hands of those who have the financial means and who control the mass media.

The fusion of these two types of resistance is obviously possible and is evidently manifested in certain cases, a fact that makes humanity's journey towards a more equal and just society more difficult.

Regarding religious resistance, the question, from a religious perspective, is whether it is necessary and legitimate to attain this democracy based on full and complete citizenship. Are we dealing with a new heresy or a fundamental ethical principle? And if this principle is accepted, how can religions contribute positively to the development of democracy, especially to the development of a democratic culture?

Religious obstacles

In the following I shall discuss some problems which could pose obstacles for the total acceptance of democracy in the area of Islamic culture, given the presence of religion as a determining factor:

First, a certain image of God, as an absolute king sitting on the throne, ('Doer of whatever He wills', Qur'an 11:107 and 85:16), could directly or indirectly influence despotic thought. The same problem arises with the metaphorical image of hell (or paradise) in the Qur'an, full of terrible torture; if this is understood literally, it is incompatible with modern human rights.

We have a dominant theology that confirms God's freedom at the expense of human freedom. This is for instance illustrated by the debate between the Mu'tazili school of theology and the Ash'ari one about the creation of human acts and the rational capacity of human beings to distinguish between good and evil.

The same concerns are true with regard to a certain understanding of God's sovereignty, *ḥākimiyya*, based on Qur'anic verses, such as: 'Judgment (the command, power, all authority to govern) belongs only to God,' Qur'an 6:57 and 12:40, 67, see also Qur'an 5:44, 45, 47. The slogan entered the political sphere for the first time with the Kharijites, as a slogan against the acceptance of arbitration by 'Ali b. Abī Ṭālib during the battle of Ṣiffīn in the year 657. In this context, Imam 'Ali famously commented, 'This slogan is right but they are taking its meaning wrong.' The same slogan returned with the Islamist movements of the twentieth century.[90]

In the juridical approach to religion, a political theory based on this concept inevitably assigns a key role to jurists, *fuqahā'*, as the only élite capable of transforming fundamental texts, the Qur'an and the Sunnah, to a series of commandments and norms that organize the entire life of the believer from morning to night, from birth to death, covering every detail in his daily life. The extreme effect of the religious legalism is the education of a passive citizen, unable to take initiatives and decisions, always preferring that others, in this case jurists, decide for them. This is what can be called '*fatwa* politics.'

The problem that can arise from this perspective is the choice between God's sovereignty of and people's sovereignty. The traditional image of the common people, the masses, is rather negative; power is very elitist according to the traditional definition. Governance was the task of *ahl al-ḥall wa al-'aqd*, literally, men who 'dissolve and tie the knots,' i.e., 'those who have binding authority,' the decision-making élite *de jure* or *de facto.*[91] Leadership in classical political theory is considered the task of the élite and not of the crowd or common people, considering that number is not the criterion of Truth. The expression *akthar al-nās*, 'most of the people', which could be heard as 'the majority of the people', appears in twenty verses of the Qur'an (2:243; 7:187; 11:17; 12:21, 38, 40, 68, 103; 13:1, 16, 38; 17:89; 25:50; 30:6, 30; 34:36; 40:57, 59, 61; 45:26), and is always accompanied by negative qualities, such as 'most people have no knowledge'.

This religious approach to politics became more complicated because of the challenge of modernity and the cultural and political clash with the

---

[90] Sayyid Qutb (1906–1966) is considered one of the most important theorists of this trend. See Khatab, S. (2009).

[91] Classical Islamic political theory deviated from sagacious and religious legitimacy, preferably with the consent of the people, towards the factual legitimacy based on power to avoid civil war and social disorder giving priority to unity based on the governor's legitimacy. This theory became the theory of the Sunnis for many centuries, as represented in the school of thought of al-Māwardī (972–1058) in his book, Wafaa Wahba (trans.), *The Ordinances of Government: al-ahkām al-sultāniyya w'al-wilāyāt al-dīniyya* (Reading: Garnet Publishing, 2000).

West. Democratization is seen by some conservative Muslims as Westernization therefore, introducing foreign laws and models of government.

In cases where parliament is legitimated, it remains controlled and conditioned by sharia law through a constitutional council of jurists or 'the Guardianship of the Jurist', *wilāyat al faqīh*, the political religious theory of Khomeini (1902-1989) which has been operative in Iran since 1979.

Many constitutions in the Islamic world include clauses such as 'the religion of the state is Islam' and/or 'sharia is a/the primary source of legislation'. This is a way of confirming that the sovereignty of the parliament is actually under the sovereignty of God, even when the application of sharia is limited to the 'island' of family law.

The expression 'Islamic state' did not appear until the twentieth century, and then in a polemical context. A state is an institution that should govern the public affairs of society and not a person who may or may not believe. (See: An-Na'im, A.A. 2009, pp. 157-169).

Conceptual ambiguity of 'secular state'

The ambiguity of the concept of the 'secular state' was a problem of definition when the modern concept was first introduced in the Muslim world. In the European context, secularity originally meant 'the separation between state and church', which is meaningless in the Islamic context, because there is no formal hierarchy in Islam. The second definition that secularity is 'the separation between state and religion' is also unacceptable for people who believe that ethics are essentially religious; it is like saying 'a state without religion' or 'a state without ethics', practically saying 'a corrupt state', which the Islamist movements try to Islamize and moralize. From this perspective, 'the Islamic state' means an honest, just and uncorrupted state.

Secularity has not only been inadequately presented as a political theory but also implemented in a very questionable way by certain regimes declaring themselves as secular but having nothing to do with democracy. So-called secular and sometimes anti-religious despots have led to a strong prejudice against secularity seen as secularism, as an ideology, a sort of 'masked atheism'. Another important point to consider concerning secularity and modern democracy is their diverse meanings and forms that are rooted in European and Western history. To some Muslims, this justifies the use of cultural and religious particularisms or a certain independence and cultural autonomy in rejecting a system considered foreign. The problem also exists in a wider context, posing the questions: When is cultural particularism a true condition to guarantee pluralism in a world threatened by global homogeneity? When is this same particularism used as a pretext to justify dictatorship and conservative politics?

Possible solutions

It is not my task to answer all these difficult questions and resolve all these complex problems. Neither I nor any Muslims on their own could achieve this, since part of the problem is common to all religions–with diverse nuances and shades. I therefore consider it my task to propose the right questions and present issues for reflection, which I believe are of a particular importance. There are some fundamental concepts that might prove helpful.

Principles not systems

First of all, we do not find well-defined political and economic theories or systems in the fundamental textual sources of Islam; on the contrary, what we find are general ethical principles and guidelines. Such flexibility should allow creativity and adaptation of new ideas and systems. There is an interpretative space for juridical discernment; this space is not because of an accidental slip or an oversight but, rather, due to mercy and freedom. The key verse for this aspect is: '[They conduct] their affairs by mutual consultation' Qur'an 42:38. This verse does not indicate the manner of the consultation, neither who conducts it, nor its subject. Historically, each of the four Caliphs (successors) of Prophet Muhammad was chosen in a different way. The Umayyads in Damascus adopted the Byzantine hereditary system while the Abbasids in Baghdad were nearer to the Persian Sassanid version of government.

It is important to explore and to put into practice all the theological and political implications and potential of some Qur'anic verses (which were historically neglected or limited), like the verse of the consultation mentioned above, or the verses about religious freedom:

> There is no compulsion in religion (Qur'an 2:256).

> Therefore do remind, for you are only a reminder. You have no control over them (You are not a dictator over them) (Qur'an 88:21-22).

Other verses confirm religious pluralism as a legitimate fact desired by God:

> To every one of you We have assigned a right way and an open road. If God had so willed, He would have made you one community, but He wanted to test you through that which He has given you, so race to do good deeds: you will all return to God and He will make clear to you the matters you differed about (Quran 5:48, see also: Qur'an 2:148 and 42:8).

From this perspective, the only political system that guarantees coexistence and harmonious collaboration between different religions, in our time, is the secular state. This does not refer to a secular ideology however, like a 'pseudo-religion', replacing religion.

Rethinking the mission of religion

It is not the role of religion to offer a political system but rather to educate and prepare the human being for being a good citizen: a person free from egoism, ready to serve, full of love and altruism, constructive and not violent, with a critical mind. This is not the task of politics, nor of the parliament. It is a religious task *par excellence*; it is the religious mission of religion, its real mission. The object of religion is truth, it is a question of free conscience and pure hearts; the object of politics is the administration of public interests. The first is not dependent on numbers or votes, while the second requires votes and consensus.

Many historical reasons favor the dominance of a juridical vision of religion (both in the past and in the present with ideological and populist tendencies) marginalizing other conceptions. There is a need to restore the balance between the various approaches towards religion, to reconsider the moral and spiritual ones and to radically review the juridical system as it has been understood historically.[92]

---

92 In this context a moratorium on corporal punishment, for instance, is needed as the first stage of reform even if it will not suffice as a solution. In 2005, Tariq Ramadan launched 'an International call for a Moratorium on corporal punishment, stoning and the death penalty in the Islamic World,' which was opposed by some institutions and religious leaders in the Arab world in a very polemical and aggressive way to the point of accusing him of apostasy. See http://tariqramadan.com/blog/2005/04/05/an-international-call-for-moratorium-on

It is important to give priority to the spiritual and theological approach of religion. Islamic theology includes a fundamental pillar, coming right after the doctrine of the Oneness of God. This is justice.[93] The duty and mission of the believer is to realize the model closest to justice, and, consequently, any form or practice that experience proves to be unjust or disrespectful to this sacred principle must be eliminated or modified. This is what is meant by theology taking priority over law; the latter should be inspired by fundamental Islamic principles and should not become a creed in itself. Other important concepts in Islamic legal theory such as *maṣlaḥa*, public interest, and *'urf*, custom, could be developed in order to embrace new concepts and systems, like democracy as part of the 'heritage of humanity', as a 'common good'. There is no notion, including religion, which does not have an environment from which it originates; however, when it shows its concrete validity in everyday experience, it can go beyond its own limits: human history is full of these fruitful exchanges. This is the case with democracy.

It follows that we have to look for positive definitions of secularity and democracy that find resonance in Islamic thought. This obviously only applies to someone who does not see an insurmountable contradiction between secularity and Islam, if we perceive the secular state as a guarantor of justice and equality, two fundamental principles in Islamic ethics. This allows for going beyond the pragmatic and utilitarian approach towards secularity (religious minorities are generally pro-secular in order to escape from the dominion of the majority), adopting a more comprehensive and insightful concept. The laws and rules of a country can be accepted as *status quo,* with an attitude of honesty and civil discipline. This is what we consider the minimum level of integration, which does not come in conflict with the basic values of democracy. A profound integration demands a cultural intelligence that goes beyond form, orienting itself towards the spirit and the foundation of the norms themselves. One cannot reach this step without a formation which is profoundly Islamic and, at the same time, profoundly European.

-corporal-punishment-stoning-and-the-death-penalty-in-the-islamic-world/

93 The first school of systematic Islamic theology, the Mu'tazilites, was called 'the people of justice and unity [of God],' *ahl al-'adl wa al-tawhīd*. This was within the context of protests against the injustice of the Umayyads.

To demonstrate the substantial link between secularity and democracy is crucial, especially after the failure of the nationalist and Islamist ideologies and models of government, and after the growing awareness of the importance of democracy among young people. Historical experience has confirmed the validity and utility of democracy, even though it still needs continuing improvement. Slogans and empty rhetoric no longer suffice for new generations, as long as the political system does not offer the possibility of peacefully influencing politics through free and transparent elections that make the alternation of power possible. True democracy does not exist without true citizenship based on equality before the law, and only the secular state can serve as a guarantee against any type of discrimination. This is what authoritarian or Mafia regimes, nationalist or religious, even with their democratic façade, cannot offer. (An-Na'im, A.A. 2008).

The secular state is not a non-religious or anti-religious state but rather a neutral one which treats all citizens equally. The need to recognize the neutrality of the state is a religious and Islamic imperative; it is a neutrality that allows the full expression and actualization of religious values with conviction and freedom, considering that forced faith is nothing but hypocrisy, *nifāq,* a phenomenon condemned repeatedly and severely in the Qur'an (see for instance: 2:8–20).

Especially during the era of its founders, the Islamic juridical system was established independently of the state, if not to say in opposition to the state. Almost all the founders of the juridical schools were persecuted by the governors of their time.[94] For this reason, Islamic jurisprudence developed as a moral ideal with no executive power, an alternative to the corrupted state which was no longer following the prophetic example. This happened in spite of successive compromises between state and jurists.

Every state system adopted by Muslims throughout history has been a system developed by human beings. All interpretations of the sharia are human efforts in fact, which can be subject to critique and reform. The problem of fundamentalist governments on one hand, lies in the fact that they have adopted the worst of the state models mentioned above, the modern totalitarian regime. No empire or state in Islamic history has ever reached this level of control. On the other hand, fundamentalist governments have

---

94 It is the case of Abū Hanīfa (699-765), al-Awzā'ī (707-774), Mālik b. Anas (713-795), Ahmad b. Hanbal (780-855) and others, all are founders of juridical schools.

adopted the Western idea of one juridical code as their own, a novelty in Islamic law which has always recognized immense juridical diversity and pluralism.

Democracy, Christianity and Pluralism

In the Face of Global Interdependence

Alberto Lo Presti[95]

Historical Premises

1. The relationship between Catholicism and democracy has often been viewed as contradictory. In fact, some historical interpretations observe the hostility of the Catholic Church to the affirmation of the political principles of the modern world. Although it may be admitted that there have been currents of Catholicism that contributed to the development of democracy, their role is considered rather insignificant in comparison to that of liberal and socialist perspectives, for example. Indeed, this assessment applies only at an abstract level, serving merely ideological propaganda. Democratic thought is as varied and multifaceted as the historical paths that led to the development of numerous forms of democracy in the modern world. It is impossible to attribute credit without considering the various paths involved in the evolution of different political doctrines and numerous historical and cultural contexts. The contributions of some Catholic scholars in the weaving of the historical paths that led to the development of democracy are recognizable. Among the best-known names (including some mistakenly considered as conservative) are Alexis de Tocqueville, Antonio Rosmini, Jaimes Balmes, Wilhelm Emmanuel von Ketteler, Karl Vogelsang, Juan Donoso Cortés, Daniel O'Connell, Charles de Montalembert and Jean-Baptiste Henry Lacordaire. Furthermore, these representatives of 19th century political Catholicism refer to some of their predecessors who in pre-

95 Prof. Dr., born 1966 in Rome, teaches History of Political Thought at the Lumsa – University of Rome, and Political Contemporary Theory at the Sophia University Institute (Incisa, Figline Val d'Arno).

vious centuries laid the foundation for the fundamental rights of the person and the principles of freedom, equality and solidarity. The list includes Girolamo Savonarola, Francisco De Vitoria, Bartolomé de Las Casas, Francisco Suárez, Johannes Althusius, Giambattista Vico, Montesquieu and Edmund Burke, to name a few.

2. The core theory these precursors believed in is highly critical towards any form of political power that goes beyond the limits of the law ordained by God. This tends to happen when power is sought as a pure manifestation of human will, being transformed into a force that oppresses man and tramples on his dignity. Their ideas stemmed from the consideration that sovereignty over creation belongs to God alone, who recognizes men's freedom. Political authority must adopt the model of God's sovereignty as the principle of its action and therefore must recognise the freedom of individuals and social actors. Since Divine order must be gradually discovered and developed by human thought, they believed that history represents a slow but progressive affirmation of Christian principles. This is why political Catholicism of the eighteenth and nineteenth centuries rejected the modern idea of constructing a social order, ex novo, by a reason critically aware of itself. One cannot govern with the illusion of making a tabula rasa (clean slate), i.e. not taking into account the history, tradition and culture of the community.

3. Hence, at the beginning of its formation, Catholic political thought, originator of democratic ideas, refuted the unlimited power of the monarch, who is not subject to the law. At the same time, it carefully avoided letting the people's sovereignty become an absolute power. The moral order precedes the political order. It decrees the inalienable dignity of the human person bestowing innate and inviolable rights that could not be renounced by individuals even if they wanted to. Any public power, even if representing unanimous popular consensus, must accept an insurmountable limit. Setting limitations to sovereignty and reaffirming the moral framework for the dignity of the human person affirms that from a political government's point of view, the common good can never be subordinated to the reason of State, or worse, to the reason of party. During the nineteenth century, the distance between Catholic thought and the main ideologies was reflected in the emergence of the democratic order. The socialist (Ferdinand Lassalle) or even the social democratic (Eduard Bernstein) perspective, con-

ceived democracy as a means to hand over the political and parliamentary majority to the working masses. That meant that once in government, the working class could have been able to implement policies that reflected the interests of the labour force and not those of the capitalist world by the re-distribution of property and the socialization of material resources. Catholic ethics repeatedly denounced this risky political program revolving around social conflict and generating violence. Furthermore, the idea that in democracy – the will of the majority – the natural right of property could be arbitrarily discarded, was a mistake from the theological point of view. The conflict between capital and labour revealed the risky nature of democratic governance where working classes could prevail in the electoral confrontation. For this reason, pursuant to the reflections of Tocqueville and John Stuart Mill on inevitable democratic development, the liberal democracies of the nineteenth and early twentieth century did not favour the extension of electoral suffrage and continued to select the parliamentary class based on wealth.

The Catholic Conception of Democracy

4. The common good, the raison d'etre of the political community, offers a set of social conditions so that each player in society (person, family, group) can be fulfilled and perfected. Democracy, like any other form of government, is therefore conceived by Catholic ethics as a means and not an end (EV 70). The inherent aims of the common good are just and lasting peace, authentic freedom, solidarity, and an end to poverty. For this reason, the social thought of the Church has no particular doctrinal emphasis nor is it ideologically triumphalistic when it considers democracy. Instead, it is assessed on the basis of its appropriateness in achieving the goal of good public life. It does not constitute a self-sufficient ideal principle. For example, the encyclical letter Centesimus annus clearly states:

> The Church values the democratic system inasmuch as it ensures the participation of citizens in making political choices, guarantees to the governed the possibility both of electing and holding accountable those who govern them, and of replacing them through peaceful means when appropriate. Thus she cannot encourage the formation of narrow ruling groups which usurp the power of the State for individual interests or for ideological ends. Authentic democracy is possible only in a State ruled by law and on the basis of a correct conception of

> the human person. It requires that the necessary conditions be present for the advancement both of the individual through education and formation in true ideals, and of the 'subjectivity' of society through the creation of structures of participation and shared responsibility. (CA 46)

Therefore, the system of democracy is 'appreciated', but not in every circumstance. The decisive elements include political participation, the responsibility of rulers, negative consideration concerning the role of power elites, and peaceful relations. While explaining democracy as a political system Centesimus annus establishes the criteria of the rule of law, the dignity of the human person and the principle of subsidiarity. These values and principles precisely distinguish the concept of democracy of Catholic thought from other theoretical currents.

Political Participation and Elites

5. Not all political conceptions consider political participation a decisive element of democracy, for example, the schools of thought that can be traced back to Friedrich von Hajek and John Gray. In general, these theoretical currents conceive democracy as the best system to guarantee individual rights, which can be made possible by setting limits that the state must not transgress. Affirming involvement in public life or participation in the affairs of the state, as an indicator of a good citizen, is considered a disturbance to individual free existence and a threat to the freedoms of the person for them. On the contrary, Catholic ethics speaks of participation as a right and a duty to promote the common good (PT 50; GS 75). Participation is one of the characteristics of the human person who – representing both the foundation and the goal of political coexistence – is fulfilled in relationship with others. Therefore, 'social life is not something external to man'. (GS 25). It means that democratic participation is not a threat to individual rights or a burden to be removed, but an essential dimension of the dignity of the human person.

6. Catholic ethics is critical of the role of power elites in government. If the goal is the common good and the principle is the participation of citizens, then each group acting politically to make its exclusive interest prevail represents a pathology for the political order. The situation worsens when these groups influence the mechanism of a democratic election

through ideological deception for example. Hence, being fully accountable for one's work implies a clear and non-manipulable relationship between political representatives and voters. In other words, it is necessary to allow voters to choose their representatives after evaluating their work rationally and conscientiously.

7. Some theoretical currents have reconciled elites and democracy (Gaetano Mosca, Max Weber, Robert Dahl), while others have denounced democratic hypocrisy viewing the latter as the latest outcome of an old story – the struggle for power – disguised in new ideals and updated in accordance with modern civil needs (Vilfredo Pareto, Robert Michels, Joseph Schumpeter); still others have produced a negative vision of democracy precisely because of the advent of the masses on the political scene (Gustave Le Bon, Scipio Sighele). In general, such theoretical perspectives consider democracy as a tool in the hands of the upper classes. Its values of equality and freedom are only instruments, useful to achieve consensus needed for domination. Catholic ethics treats these theories with particular rigour. In fact, their persistence over time and their regeneration call attention to the point of explaining the mechanisms of hereditary, cultural or simply the economic transmission of acquired power. Therefore, they must be seen within the context of 'structures of sin', systems of action in which personal sins become institutionalized social practices, capable of surpassing individual conduct and existences to be propagated over time and space. In particular, an acknowledged characteristic of the structures of sin is 'the hunger for power with the intention of imposing one's own will on others.'(SRS 37)

Rule of Law and Subsidiarity

8. Since the time of Rerum Novarum, the social thought of the Church considers the state a means to serve the common good to ensure the realization of the human person. The human person, being prior to any civil consortium and in particular the state (RN 6), limits the power of the latter as per the natural law of the person (RN 10-11). Therefore, intervention is justified in pursuing a general interest, meaning the ethical idea of the common good that safeguards the dignity of the human person. For this reason, Catholic ethics believes that 'every form of power should preferably be balanced out by other powers and spheres of competence, in order to keep it within its

proper limits. This is the principle of the 'rule of law', in which the law is sovereign and not the arbitrary will of men.' (See: CA 44; CIV 41) This preference presents the criterion for distinguishing an authentic democracy. In fact, democracy has generated multiple experiences, sometimes contradictory. For example, it is necessary to recognize the exploitation carried out by authoritarian and totalitarian regimes – so-called democratic political systems – that actually lacked the prerequisites for a healthy democracy. At times, it becomes necessary to clarify the concept of democracy when it is applied to cultures and traditions exercising different principles of the rule of law, such as democratic traditions in other cultural and civil contexts (Sen, A. 2004). In the case of the Islamic Republic of Iran for instance, the religious form of the state can also be derived from the will of all its citizens, but in the absence of a framework based on the legal guarantees of minorities, the meaning of democracy loses many important theoretical references and the use of the term can be confusing (Khatami M. 1999).

9. Political Catholicism played a decisive role in the elaboration of the principle of subsidiarity. This was the result of the historical need to claim autonomous space where the modern state demanded hegemony on social and civil terrain. The centuries-old story of the struggles within Christendom had disruptive social effects. In order to bring order back, the state presented itself as the supreme body, regulating ethical and religious differences. In some countries, the state tried to condition the function of the Catholic Church to meet national interests and any form of resistance led to criticism concerning Catholic 'ultramontanism'. Also because of this – and not only by reason of the theological conception concerning the limits of sovereign power – Catholic ethics has reiterated that the State cannot expect to assimilate all individual realities, groups or associations, which play a role in civil society.[96] The evolution of the democratic form of government is very important today in the context of its constitution, as it acts as a principle of regulation among different levels of government. It is at the service of reforms around institutional decentralization, welfare systems and, in general, the forms that guarantee social autonomy. The theoretical current of structural functionalism was intended instead to study the relationship between the state and other actors in civil society, not from the

[96] The first who formulated the idea of a "subsidiary right" against the centralism of the Prussian state, was Wilhelm Emmanuel von Ketteler (1811-1877), the Bishop of Mainz.

point of view of these entities but from the prevailing social processes and civil dynamics. Through the work of individuals such as Talcott Parsons, David Easton and Niklas Luhmann, the pattern of the relationship between the state and civil society was reversed, reducing the state to a sub-system of society, in charge of political decisions. It is another excessive interpretation, which instead of emphasizing the role of the state dissolves it in the mechanisms of the production of public decisions. As a result, it loses its ethical meaning by reason of the common good conceived in relation to the organic nature of social coexistence.

The Idea of Democracy in the Face of Ethical-religious Pluralism

10. The main challenge of any democracy is to harmonize different interests present in civil society. A prerequisite for democracy is that it consider the interests of all its citizens equally. The State does not discriminate the interests of its citizens (provided they are legitimate), nor decide how they should pursue their happiness. (Dahl, R.A. 1989). This affirms that the state cannot be 'paternalistic'; every citizen, irrespective of their social background, level of education, professional status, etc., must be seen as the best spokesperson for his or her own interests. Catholic ethics, as such, does not deny the validity of such theoretical positions, as long as democracy also assumes the onus of supporting the formation of its citizen in the positive values of the human social dimension – the common good, solidarity, subsidiarity and the universal destination of goods. In the affirmation of these democratic principles, the social thought of the Church recognizes the temptation of ethical-political relativism, according to which there are no objective criteria to determine a hierarchy of political goals. It warns of the risk that 'if there is no ultimate truth that guides and directs political action, then ideas and beliefs can easily be exploited for power. A democracy without values – history shows – simply becomes open or devious totalitarianism.' (CA 46)

11. Today democracies are beset by unprecedented challenges. In fact, they not only present conflicting interests – i.e. different ways of conceiving the common good and the aims of the political community – but also hold within themselves a variety of moral conceptions, philosophical doctrines and religious beliefs that may become antagonist, if not in mutual oppo-

sition. So what does the future hold for democracy in the era of ethical-religious pluralism? Political theorists have focused on this particular question in recent years. The answers of John Rawls and Jürgen Habermas are the best known and the most debated. Rawls's solution marks a significant distance from Catholic ethics as it is based on the idea that liberalism, in order to encourage the coexistence of different ethics, must simply let go any ethical reference so as to seek purely political motivation. From this stems 'the democratic idea of tolerance' (Rawls, J. 1993, p. 58), based on the observation that if an ethical doctrine is reasonable, then it will have the same need to exist as the others and, therefore, to recognize the existence of others. Thus an appropriate democracy is structured in the era of ethical-religious pluralism. However, the alternative idea of Habermas gives rise to discursive democracy. For him democracy is based on the assumption that the rules that govern the civil consortium, in order to be democratic, must arise from precisely and rigorously institutionalized discursive processes that are capable of generating a legitimate right, insofar it is discursively founded. If popular sovereignty is understood as a great discursive process (institutionalized in procedures and norms) then it also presupposes that the individuals who participate in it have their freedom and rights protected; therefore, the rights of individuals, in one sense, are a condition for the democratic process – an indispensable prerequisite for its development – while in another sense they are also the result since democratic citizens attribute their rights to themselves. The fundamental rights that define the structure of a democratic state must, therefore, be considered as mutually recognized rights by the citizens, when they decide to legitimately regulate their coexistence with legal instruments; therefore, while rights do not pre-exist in a political community, it cannot disregard them either.

12. From the point of view of Catholic ethics, understanding democracy as a discursive process is not to be disapproved. Strengthening the dialogue among the social partners and different faith communities has been one of the longstanding goals of the Catholic Church (Consider ES). However, it sees danger in the forms of 'discursive democracy'. For example, in Habermas, it is made possible through a structure of fundamental rights that – in the absence of a reference to natural law – must be the fruit of dialogue and interaction among different cultures. The danger is that in the midst of this hermeneutical circularity, the ethical sense of democracy is lost; it is likely

to become an exercise of continuous negotiation and indefinite discourse (CIV 73). In other words, it is a democracy that has stopped seeking its own foundation, considering any attempt of the sort futile (Richard Rorty, Gianni Vattimo).

For a Democracy Based on Global Solidarity

13. Catholic ethics sees the advent of ethical-religious pluralism as an opportunity and not a threat. Many scholars and researchers of human-social disciplines have almost simultaneously highlighted the emergence of a 'global web of mutual dependency.' (Bauman, Z. 2008, p. 72). This can be paralleled to the principle of interdependence – according to which nothing of what happens elsewhere can be considered a priori irrelevant here and now – and the principle of the common destiny of all the peoples of the Earth (GS 25). Catholic ethics can apply these two principles to democratic theory. The one of interdependence teaches us that all potentially affect all, so it would be perilous to leave anyone out of the political process of representation and deliberation at the different levels of the articulation of interests. This means that the principle of interdependence goes beyond any problem regarding suffrage, participation and configuration of the demos. Democracy becomes a dynamic process aimed at individual, social and cultural inclusion. Its goal is to spread until it fills every tiny space because an effect, capable of influencing history, can arise from it. It is an idea of democracy that is never satisfied with any results achieved because it is conceived as a vital form of community organization based not on political participation – if anything, that is a goal – but on the person.

In other words, the task of democracy is to encourage every single person – irrespective of the political and electoral law, age and citizenship – to represent their legitimate interests in the political community. It must activate processes to intercept, above all, various voices within the community, i.e. the latent needs that are pushed to the background by a series of cultural influences that, today, determine priorities to solve problems. Some of these are the needs of minorities that are sometimes pushed to the opaque zones of active citizenship, stakeholders who are excluded from the loop of political representation (for example foreign nationals living in a community) or minors who do not have access to the electoral law, etc. By extension however, in its information and performance process, democracy should involve the requests of the foreign communities that are present in the territory and whose future affect it. Furthermore, democracy should be able to introduce in its political sphere the concept of world civilization, which does not really mean including a greater number of foreign policy issues in its government programs, but identifying specific forms that could place the global community at the centre of the deliberative process.

14. In the era of interdependence, the principle of the common destiny theoretically states that any idea of the common good must respect the good of others.[97] (Any attempt to omit this can be dangerous – even fatal. Regardless of any ethical exhortations it contains and the linguistic context in which it is proposed, cyclical financial crises from which no reality can be considered immune – even though, in the end, it is always the weaker section of society that's hit the worst – clearly demonstrate the need for the principal today. Considering the wellbeing of others as one's own is decisive for our own destiny; no one can save himself; it is impossible to believe that our happy little island can remain so despite the widespread suffering all around us (I. Giordani, I. 1945). Both of these principles are a basis for a concept of any democratic theory. If democracy is imagined as a form of government in which the order and organization of associated life are regulated by the associates themselves, then it is necessary to understand who and how many associates are at play. It is the problem of demos, of the people. So far, classical theories have always been confronted with the fear of encountering the margins of its composition. Now the concern needs to be reversed – to prevent the formation of these margins, to circumvent the self-referentiality between political power and the people subject to its obligations. Pope Francis expresses this need with great emphasis: 'When a society – whether local, national or global – is willing to leave a part of itself on the fringes, no political programs or resources spent on law enforcement or surveillance systems can indefinitely guarantee tranquility. This is not the case simply because inequality provokes a violent reaction from those excluded from the system, but because the socioeconomic system is unjust at its root. Just as goodness tends to spread, the toleration of evil, which is injustice, tends to expand its baneful influence and quietly to undermine any political and social system, no matter how solid it may appear.' (EG 59)

---

97 Another formulation is that we should seek the good of others as if it were our own.

15. Already in the mid-twentieth century after the tragedy of the world wars, Jacques Maritain had sensed the urgency of giving a soul to democracy. It is a task that Christian culture must make its own, as democracy is the natural evolution of civil relations that fit within the fold of Christianity (Maritain, J. 1943). It's an important responsibility for the Catholic Church, which also has the means to perform it: 'the light of love proper to faith can illumine the questions of our own time about truth. Truth nowadays is often reduced to the subjective authenticity of the individual, valid only for the life of the individual. A common truth intimidates us, for we identify it with the intransigent demands of totalitarian systems. But if truth is a truth of love, if it is a truth disclosed in personal encounter with the Other and with others, then it can be set free from its enclosure in individuals and become part of the common good' (LF 34).

κοινές τιμές közös értékek luachanna coiteanna

общие значения shared values

algemeene warden valores comuns gemeinsame werte

skupne vedrosti kopigas vertibas valores comunes

wspólne wartosci общи ценности

A FUTURE
OF
SHARED VALUES

Conceiving a New World in the Twilight of Neoliberalism

A Marxist View

Walter Baier

Theological and philosophical reflections on the situation of humanity and the world can seem tiresome and abstract unless they are grounded in a fresh analysis of our present situation, which is in many ways unprecedented in the history of humanity. There is a widespread sense that the Covid-19 crisis and the ensuing virtually global standstill of social and economic life are game changers in modern world history. To the extent that we believe there can be no return to what had been seen as capitalist business as usual we share this perception.

As this text is being written, the capitalist world finds itself in an incipient global recession whose duration and depth nobody can predict. In theory, we could of course imagine a rebound of the economies after the end of the lockdown with a quick return to normality. In reality, however, this is unlikely, even without the distinct possibility of a second wave of the pandemic. In fact, the global economy, already before Covid-19, burdened by growing geopolitical tensions, had entered crisis mode. Moreover, capitalist societies are facing a Gordian knot of critical developments ranging from the environmental crisis to the digital revolution, and all this in a geopolitical order in upheaval.

Thus, the world is clearly undergoing a transition, but where it will all end is an object of an increasingly intensive conflict between colliding tendencies in the economy, in politics, culture, religion, and philosophy, which are in danger of leading to violent confrontation.

The term 'world disorder' has been circulating among the think tanks associated with the power elites.[98] The helplessness into which the Cold War released its victors cannot provide Schadenfreude even to the vanquished – not only due to the instability of a world overloaded with weapons of mass destruction but above all because it brings out all the more starkly the lack of an interpretation of the world situation which could be the basis of a consensus sufficient to lay the basis for common effective action against the dangers that are threatening civilisation as a whole.

The logjam of the international system, which the failure of the UN Climate Conference has laid bare last year in Madrid, contrasts with the existential intensification of global crises, the most dramatic being the climate crisis because it leaves its mark on all the other crises through the scarcity of vitally important resources, global social inequality, and immigration flows.

The danger stemming from the destruction of the environment has been sufficiently documented scientifically, as has the time timeframe available for the by now well-known, necessary countermeasures. The responsibility of people today is clear from the fact they can know that their actions or neglect will have irreversible consequences that will affect future generations.

This historic constellation, which the Dutch chemist and Nobel Prize winner Paul Crutzen has called 'anthropocene' (see Altvater, E. 2013), requires a universalist and cosmopolitan ethic that the worldwide movement of the youth is calling for. But if the new ethic is to be more than an appeal to the powerful in the world it must become political in order to overcome the objective and subjective obstacles it encounters.

Capitalism

The worldwide recession towards which capitalist societies are now heading is reflected in the data published by the International Labour Organization (ILO). At the end of June it observed a 14 per cent drop in global working hours during the second quarter of 2020, equivalent to the loss of 400 million full-time jobs; and, even in the best scenario, a recovery in the second half of the year will not trigger enough economic dynamic to allow employment to return to pre-pandemic levels. Instead, there is a danger of continuing large-scale job losses (ILO Monitor, 2020). The experts and the

98 See for example Masala, C. (2018).

politicians no less than world opinion formed by the mass media are poorly prepared for a crisis of this dimension.

On the political left, overoptimistic as it tends to be, many thought that the Great Recession of 2008 finished off Francis Fukuyama's assertion of the End of history (Fukuyama, F. 1992). 'But ten years of economic growth have [...] overshadowed the memory of the 'nastiness of the Great Recession' (McCloskey, D.N. 2016, p. 53). Economists began again to idealise the age of capitalism as the era of 'the Great Enrichment'(ib. p. 8), which, as the figures show, certainly is true for the upper one per cent of the world population.

With stunning candor Deirdre N. McCloskey, a renowned US academic author, lays bare neoliberalism's ethical background as she explains: 'it does not matter ethically whether the poor have the same number of diamond bracelets or Porsche automobiles as do owners of hedge funds. It does, however, matter ethically whether they have the same opportunities to vote or to learn to read or to have a roof over their heads' (Ib., p. 46). Therefore drop the ugly 'word "capitalism", which is misleading' and substitute it with the 'non-snappy but accurate "trade-tested betterment" – or if you want a single word, "innovism".(Ib. p. 93)

Joseph Stiglitz's résumé of capitalism's most recent period is more critical than that of his US colleague McCloskey: 'The elites claimed that their promise was based on scientific economic models and "evidence-based research". After forty years we now have the figures: Growth has slowed, and the fruits of this growth went overwhelmingly to the few at the very top. In view of stagnating wages and flourishing stock markets, income and assets flowed upward instead of trickling down.' (Stieglitz, J.E. 2019)

But if the reality is so unambiguously what Stiglitz judges it to be, how can we explain that the neoliberal elites came through the crisis politically reinforced and, with the nationalist right-wing forces, were even able to create a strategic reserve, which penetrates to the middle of society?

Where is the defect in the Left's analysis? Marx would probably have said that the chief defect of economists, the critical ones included, is that they view the capitalist economy only as an object and not as sensuous activity, not as the praxis of the people who live in it, consume, and labour.[99]

---

[99] Marx, K. 1976 (1845). The English translation published in the *Collected Works* of the first sentence of the first thesis reads: 'The chief defect of all previous materialism (that

An aspect of contemporary life in developed, and in this respect, privileged capitalist societies that increasingly influences all of our lives has been called by some US economists surveillance capitalism, 'a novel economic mutation [. . .] bred from the clandestine coupling of the vast powers of the digital with the radical indifference and intrinsic narcissism of financial capitalism and its neoliberal vision' (Zuboff, S. 2016, p. 6).

David Harvey originated the term 'accumulation by dispossession', and Shoshana Zuboff applies it to surveillance capitalism: 'accumulation by dispossession that claims it right to ignore every boundary in its thirst for knowledge of and influence over the most detailed nuances of our behaviours' (Ib. p. 6). 'Dispossession by surveillance' has generated a deeply anti-democratic power, as Zuboff writes: 'It challenges principles and practices of self-determination – in psychic life and social relations, politics and governance – for which humanity has suffered long and sacrificed much.'(Ib. p. 17f)

Surveillance capitalism does not erode these decision-making rights – along with their causes and their effects – but rather it redistributes them. Instead of many people having some rights, these rights have been concentrated within the surveillance regime opening an entirely new dimension of social inequality. (Ib. p. 17)

Internet, big data, and social media have above all unleashed a new wave of concentration of capital. Since 2016 Google, Apple, Facebook, and Amazon ('GAFAM') have been the world's top five corporations in terms of market value; in 2017 two of China's GAFAM counterparts, Alibaba and Tencent, joined them to be among the world's top ten. (Staab P. 2016, p. 81)

Beyond this 'a kind of linguistic convergence mirrored the centralised structure of monopoly-finance capital in the age of digital surveillance with "securitization" increasingly standing simultaneously for a world dominated by: (1) financial derivatives trading, (2) a network of public and private surveillance, (3) the militarization of security-control systems, and (4) the removal of judicial processes from effective civilian control'. (Foster J.B. and McChesney, R. W. 2014, p. 22).

---

of Feuerbach included) is that things [Gegenstand], reality, sensuousness are conceived only in the form of the object, or of contemplation, but not as sensuous human activity, practice, not subjectively.' Marx K. and Engels F. (1976), p. 3.

If we take the variations in stock prices in the first half of 2020 as indicators of the way things are developing we can then assume that the GAFAM companies will emerge strengthened from the world economic crisis sparked by the pandemic and will determine the logic of accumulation of the coming period of capitalist growth.

The following can only be intimated here: The analysis of financial-market-driven capitalism needs to be completed by a substantial study of the relations of *cognition*, which not only modify the production and circulation of capital but also make available to the political management of societies hitherto undreamt of spaces and methods. In 2018 the whistle-blower Christopher Wylie exposed how the US/British firm Cambridge Analytica gathered data via Facebook on 90 million of its users in order to create psychological profiles to be deployed in electoral campaigns – information which then contributed, among other things, to Donald Trump's victory and the pro-Brexit vote. The breadth of the operations and their effectiveness gives us an idea of the role big data plays in political left, for example in the worldwide, simultaneous rise of the nationalist radical right.

The working class and global society

The new relations of cognition have prevailed also because the traditional interpretations of social and political contradictions offered by the socialist labour movement are no longer in sync with today's world.

This particularly applies to the notion of labour, which produces a strange paradox. While labour – performed industrially or in the reproduction of people – assumes a central place precisely through the ecological crisis, the concept *working class* has lost its empirical sociological power of distinction in those regions of capitalism in which 90 per cent of the populations depend directly or indirectly on the labour market for their livelihood.

Moreover, the current productive and destructive forces of humanity have lifted the social and political conflicts to a global level. Already in 1955, when the Cold War was in danger of turning into a hot war deploying thermonuclear weapons, on Albert Einstein's and Bertrand Russell's initiative Einstein, Russell and nine of the world's most important natural scientists addressed the international public:

> '[...] the best authorities are unanimous in saying that a war with H-bombs might possibly put an end to the human race. It is feared that if many H-bombs are used there will be universal death, sudden only for a minority, but for the majority a slow torture of disease and disintegration.' (Russell B. et al. 1955).

Although the dangers of 1955 are comparable in scale to what is at stake today, dealing with the environmental crisis requires strategies different from those needed to restrain the danger of nuclear war. The latter danger was able, though not banished, to be kept under control for decades through political management; the solution of the environmental crisis, however, cannot be postponed but demands the speedy intervention of the international community. Moreover, the balance of nuclear powers was based on the maintenance of the political status quo. Yet, a sustainable coping with the environmental crisis can tolerate no status quo; it requires intervention into the mode of operation[100] of societies, a transformation of the relations of property, distribution, and power.

How is a political subject to emerge from all of this, one that has impact on world development?

Is it possible to imagine an eco-socialist transformation, catalysed by a working class defined by its antagonism to capital, though no longer sociologically differentiated from large parts of the working population – as a working class capable of expressing the needs of society as a whole?

The large capitalist enterprise, the place in which the working class was formed in the struggle against capital, was the predominant form of socialised labour throughout the twentieth century. In the age of worldwide, electronically connected value chains the socialisation of labour has taken on a new quality because it has been emancipated from the necessity of concentrating workforces in spatial locations. It has become global socialisation.

Added to this is the fact that this technology makes the production process approach the point adumbrated by Marx in the *Grundrisse*:

> 'the creation of real wealth becomes less dependent upon labour time and the quantity of labour employed than upon the power of the agents set in motion during labour time. And their power – their POWERFUL EFFECTIVE-

[100] Marx and Engels use this term 'Betriebsweise' in the Manifesto of the Communist Party – see *Marx-Engels-Werke*, vol. 4, p. 463 and *Collected Works*, vol. 6, p. 485, where it is translated as 'system'.

> NESS – in turn bears no relation to the immediate labour time which their production costs, but depends, rather, upon the general level of development of science and the progress of technology, or on the application of science to production.' (Marx, K. 1987a, p. 90).

When Marx, extrapolating from the industrial developments of the nineteenth century, anticipated this future production system, what he had in mind was the substitution of handicraft by technology. He had no idea that his prognosis that man will stand 'beside the production process, rather than being its main agent' (Ib. p. 91), would one day involve intellect workers as well, whose cognitive activities would be immeasurably magnified and accelerated through the 'artificial intelligence' programmed in machines.

For several years now, alarming investigations have been making the rounds, according to which 47 per cent of professions in the US will be automatable in the near future. (See: Frey C.B., Osborne, M. 2017, pp. 254-280). Even if there are good reasons to doubt these numbers (Wolter, M.I. et al. 2016) and the road from technical substitutability to the actual substitution of an activity can prove to be long and complicated, we are nevertheless facing a technological rupture whose social and ethical implications have not yet been negotiated, while at the same time the market- and finance-driven deployment of the new technologies have shifted power relations further to the detriment of the dependently employed (or unemployed).

It is not that the large capitalist enterprise ceased being the site of social conflicts. But during the technological revolution the power of shop floor representation and trade unions was in general undermined, although the clout of small, highly skilled work teams has increased in some sectors that are strategic for the maintenance of capital circulation such as the transport.

However, these contradictory tendencies should not obscure the fact that the traditional labour movement, which in the – up to now – privileged part of the capitalist world is consuming itself in necessary defensive struggles to maintain the welfare state, is not giving a socio-political response to the new stage of socialisation. The debates conducted among critical social scientists regarding the commons and basic income have only slowly penetrated to party programmes and leaders who, constrained by daily parliamentary work, are tempted to subordinate what is strategically necessary to what is tactically useful.

The first sentence of the *Communist Manifesto*, according to which all previous history has been the history of class struggles, led to the misunderstanding that social progress occurs via the ruthless enforcement of the interests of an ascendant class. Marx himself contributed to its dissemination through his brutal concept 'dictatorship of the proletariat'.

Surprisingly, to many, it is with Lenin that we find for the first time the notion that the invoked proletariat can only be victorious by creating broad social and political alliances. (Lenin, V. I. 1905). How far he took account of this insight in the revolutionary praxis of 1917 and later is another matter.

Be that as it may, the relativising of the Russian model of a socialist revolution constitutes the essence of Antonio Gramsci's theory of hegemony. To achieve hegemony in a moral and cultural sense, one needs, in contrast to leading through force, to invert the theory of class struggle in the sense indicated by Karl Polanyi: '[. . .] the fate of classes is more frequently determined by the needs of society than the fate of society is determined by the needs of classes' (Polanyi, K. 1944b, p. 159). 'The "challenge" is to society as a whole; the "response" comes through groups, sections, and classes.' (Ib. p. 160).

In other words, if transformative socialist organisations want to be serious about introducing a new societal principle they have to overcome the spontaneous narcissism of caring exclusively about the economic and social interests of the class they claim to represent and become an ideology that relates to the social totality.

Internationalism

The history of the labour movement's internationalism is full of contradictions and metamophoses.

When, in the nineteenth century, the peoples attempted to free themselves through revolutions from the dynasties and the reactionary international order established by the Congress of Vienna, the publication of the *Communist Manifesto* presented them with the prospect of a master plan, which in accordance with the spirit of the times claimed to be scientifically grounded. In fact, with their critique of political economy, Marx and Engels were not only opening the way to a scientific understanding of capitalist society and but also became the founders of a powerful international movement. But the idea of a comprehensive plan for emancipation soon led to paradoxical results. For example, in 1849 Engels attributed a 'non-historical' character to the Central and Southeast European Slavs *tutti quanti*, because their emancipatory strivings ran counter to the course he foresaw the revolution would take.

The International descended from Marx and Engels collapsed in 1914 because it failed to organise international political action to pre-empt the war that had been in gestation for a decade. The more radical elements of the movement then came together in the Communist International, which after a chequered history, was dissolved by Stalin in 1943, ostensibly to appease his allies in the anti-Hitler coalition. This step, however, came all the more naturally to him as many miscarriages had shown that communism had become a force that could not be steered by the central body in Moscow.

The attempt of Communists to give internationalism after 1945 a new and broader form through a system of international front organisations[101] was sacrificed to the logic of the Cold War in which the Soviet Union was involved. In addition, the Communist schisms with Yugoslavia and China and the Eurocommunist dissidence of the 1970s showed that the Soviet-steered diplomacy between the parties which still associated themselves with communism was ineffective in keeping the diverging tendencies together.

How this ended in 1990 and thereafter is well known. Communism as a global political movement with its power centre in Moscow vanished; however the question of a new model based on social equality and commonality is still actual. Thus Communism as a philosophical and cultural current still exists.

Traumatised by the experience of the twentieth century, people appear to be resigning themselves to the condition Jürgen Habermas identified in his famous essay 'The New Obscurity' (Habermas, J. 1986), limiting internationalism to an honourable pacifism and morally motivated solidarisation with the victims of aggression and injustice. However, moralism as a compass in the global transition in whose beginnings we now find ourselves, is too little.

[101] The World Federation of Democratic Youth (founded 1945 in London), the International Union of Students (founded 1946 in Prague), the World Federation of Trade Unions (founded 1945 in Paris), the Women's International Democratic Federation (founded 1945 in Paris), and the World Peace Council (founded 1950 in Warsaw).

The same also applies, however, to the old simplistic formula of traditional 'anti-imperialist campism' which does not hold up in the face of the contemporary world shaken by chaotic convulsions. The authoritarian make-up of most of the protagonists opposing the US, the ruthless actions of the Russian leadership domestically and internationally, its pacts with Europe's right-wing nationalists, North Korea's Byzantinism, or the religious fundamentalism of the regime in Tehran, rule out any idea of political solidarity under the banner of 'anti-imperialism'.

Gramsci called this condition of obscurity an *interregnum* in which a 'great variety of morbid symptoms' appear because the 'old is dying and the new cannot be born' (Gramsci, A. 1971, p. 276). In terms of morbid symptoms we think above all of the worldwide spread of nationalist, fundamentalist, and right-wing radical movements. The dying old describes the declining integrative power of the hegemony of neoliberalism. But with the new that cannot be born the socialist left and all political and cultural forces who do not believe in the 'End of History' come into the picture, with their weak capacity to help bring the new to life through consensus around a radically new civilisational model.

Utopia

Habermas's diagnosis of the age, conceived still before the fall of the Berlin Wall but already taking into account a capitalism that was mutating into neoliberalism, is stunning in its current relevance:

> The future is occupied with the merely negative; on the threshold to the 21st century we find the terrifying panorama of a world-wide threat to the interests of life in general; the spiral of the arms race, uncontrolled proliferations of automatic [nuclear] weapons, structural impoverishment of developing countries, unemployment and growing social imbalance in the developed countries, problems of overburdening the environment, and the nearly catastrophic operations of high technology are the catchphrases that penetrate by way of the mass media into public consciousness. In Europe, the answers of the intellectuals reflect the same helplessness as do those of the politicians. (Habermas, J. 1986, p. 2).

While the prophets of postmodernity announced the end of a rationally based perspective of liberation – Habermas expressly cites Derrida – he himself sees the end only of a 'specific utopian idea, which in the past crystallised itself around the potential of a society based on social labor (Arbeitsgesellschaft)'. (Habermas, J. 1986, pp. 3-4)

The classics of social theory from Marx to Max Weber agreed, he noted, that the structure of bourgeois society is characterised by abstract labour, by the type of paid labour that is managed by the market, 'utilized for purposes of realizing capital, and organized in the form of capitalist enterprise', to which they linked a utopian expectation of the emancipation of labour from external control. (Ib. p. 4)

'The utopian idea of a laboring society of independent producers', in Habermas's view, 'has lost its persuasive power not only because the forces of production have lost their innocence or because the abolition of private ownership of the means of production has clearly not in and of itself resulted in the management of workers by themselves. Above all it is because that utopian idea has lost its point of reference in reality: the power of abstract labor to give structure and form to a society.' The 'power of the factors of labor, production, and profit in determining the state of a society and societal development in general' is declining. (Ib. p. 4)

Conceptions regarding the significance of labour as a component of consciousness still vary widely in today's socialist left. Feminist social science has enriched the discussion through the realisation that masculine-connoted wage labour only describes a minority of the labour necessary for the reproduction of society.[102]

Other authors have pointed out that with his labour-value theory Marx aimed at something other than 'laboring-society' emancipation, when he said the true wealth of a society is 'DISPOSABLE TIME [. . .] time which will not be absorbed in direct productive labour, but will be available for ENJOYMENT, for leisure, thus giving scope for free activity and development. Time is scope for the development of man's FACULTIES.' (Marx, K. 1989, p. 390).

But today the environmental crisis makes the question of the power of determination that belongs to labour in respect to the development of

[102] A comprehensive time-comparison study established that for Germany unpaid labour time for housework, childcare, and elder care surpassed paid work by 1.7 times. German Federal Statistics Office: 'Wo bleibt die Zeit? Die Zeitverwendung der Bevölkerung in Deutschland 2001/2002' [Where Did the Time Go? The German Population's Time Use 2001-2002], 2003, <https://www.bmfsfj.de/>, p. 11. See also the relevant studies by the feminist economist Mascha Madörin, for example: Madörin M. (2010).

societies appear in a new light, as it is nearing the end of the cul-de-sac into which the mode of production driven by capitalist accumulation has channelled it.

The 'utopian idea of a laboring society' dismissed under the banner of post-materialism has been transformed under our eyes into the dystopia of a possibly imminent global environmental catastrophe produced by our own labour. And so today again, the question of what, how, to what end, and how much we want to work, and what price we are willing to pay for it, points to the need 'to work out for ourselves what our own share in social problems is, to establish a balance in ourselves between effect and counter-effect and to freely take on ourselves the task of drawing up an inevitable moral balance sheet of social being' and do so 'consciously [. . .]'.[103] However, the social conditions for the exercise of this sovereignty do not exist. In view of the environment, these conditions require that our *concrete* labour (concrete in the sense of our practical acting upon nature) be released from its subsumption to *abstract* labour (abstract in the sense of its indifference to its specific use-value-creating content and thus to its social and ecological consequences).

A plan

The events of recent months have reminded us once again that the fundamental question of today's politics is the ending of armed conflicts and the prevention of a world war. Although awareness of this is spreading, the risks stemming from progress in weapons technology is to a great extent underestimated. Worldwide military expenditures amount today to almost two trillion USD, spent by the major powers in the development and production of a new generation of sophisticated weapons, some of which will be deployed in the space.

Aside from the threat of a global war, possibly triggered even by mistake or incident, these tremendous expenditures impede the necessary ecological transformation of our civilisation.

– The minimal conditions to cap the environmental crisis are generally known:

[103] Karl Polanyi, 'On Freedom' (transl. Eric Canepa), in: Brie M. and Thomasberger C. (eds) (2018), p. 306.

- by 2030: limiting the rise in temperature relative to the pre-industrial age to a maximum of 1.5 degrees Celsius;
- making economic activity climate-neutral by 2050 (IPCC 2018).

Already in 2019, before the pandemic with its devastating economic impact, the EU Commission stated that 2.8% of the Union's gross domestic product must be devoted to these aims in the next 10 years. This requires an additional investment of 175 to 290 billion euros per year compared to the existing baseline for environmental measures. (European Commission, 2019).

The size of these needed expenditures stands in stark contrast to the generally neoliberal orientation of the EU's financial policy. The Stability and Growth Pact agreed on in 1997 binds the Member States to balanced budgets. And even in the middle-term financial framework of 2020 to 2027, the EU budget is to stay below 1.1% of GDP. The result of these two factors is that the capacity for public investment lies far below what is necessary.

The ECB, responding to the Corona crisis, has in an unorthodox and unprecedented way decided to buy state bonds up to 750 billion Euro, amounting to indirect funding of borrowing carried out by states, which in theory is forbidden by the Treaty of Lisbon. The European Commission, for its part, suspended the Growth and Stability Pact in order to open the way for anti-crisis policies on the part of states. Moreover, it has announced a European recovery programme, which, although providing urgently needed help to the countries in the European South hardest hit by the pandemic, does not provide a financial stimulus strong enough to overcome unemployment and restart the economies.

This is not the only problem.

The UN's Intergovernmental Panel on Climate Control (IPCC) speaks of 'systems transitions', necessary to reach acceptable climate goals, which are 'unprecedented'.(IPCC 2018, p. 15). Nowhere and never in history were such transitions the spontaneous accomplishment of markets left to their own devices. Where they have succeeded they have required robust state intervention.

The US left has called attention to this fact by fighting for the necessary policy changes under the label of the Green New Deal. The allusion is to Franklin Delano Roosevelt's New Deal, which in the 1930s sought a democratic way out of the Great Depression through a social and economic reform programme. The analogy is well chosen, seeing as the environmental crisis demands an equally thoroughgoing reconstruction of the economy, which has to be shaped in a socially acceptable way if it is to succeed.

When Roosevelt was elected as the 32nd president in 1933, the unemployment rate in the US was 24%. There was no social security, and trade unions had no right to negotiate collective contracts. The share of GDP represented by state expenditures, including on the military, was about 20%.

By contrast, today in Europe we see more or less extensive welfare states, with a ratio of government expenditure to GDP of between 40% to 50%. Despite the civilizational progress this represents, we ought not to idealise the European social models. First, because the quality and extent of the social protections vary by nation; second, because thirty years of neoliberalism have substantially weakened the welfare states and led to a general precarisation of living conditions; and, third, because the historic welfare state was, like the US New Deal, oriented to the image of the white, male wage worker, which now makes it vulnerable to justified attack from many sides. Therefore, its defence must go beyond the maintenance of an inadequate status quo. However, precisely this necessity offers an opportunity to think of social progress in a new way and to put the programme of a progressive *ecological welfare state* on the agenda.

Objectively, a green and a red programme converge around these points. But an important difference remains. Most green politicians aim at reconciling neoliberal capitalism with ecological demands – while red politicians understand the Green New Deal as a policy that has to be initiated under the given balance of forces but must then advance to become a programme to fundamentally transform society.

The radical left does not believe in a neoliberalism with a human face. Whatever steps towards social and ecological progress are achieved have to be fought for and defended against neoliberalism, that is, against the very idea that societies have to be subordinated to the despotism of unregulated markets and by consequence to the benefit of the wealthy 1 % of the global population.

A critique of the social conditions that led to the climate crisis more radical than what the greens offer is being discussed today in church milieus. Pope Francis writes in his 2015 encyclical *Laudato Si'*:

Is it realistic to hope that those who are obsessed with maximizing profits will stop to reflect on the environmental damage which they will leave behind for future generations? (LS 190)

Therefore no half-measures will do:

> It is not enough to balance, in the medium term [i.e., by seeking a middle way], the protection of nature with financial gain, or the preservation of the environment with progress. Halfway measures simply delay the inevitable disaster. Put simply, it is a matter of redefining our notion of progress. (LS 194)[104]

According to the Pope, redefining our notion of progress requires assuming the standpoint of the excluded and the poor, who make up the majority of our planet but are viewed as an 'afterthought' in international economic and political discussions, whose misery is seen as 'collateral damage'. This criticism is directed not only against the rulers but also takes in Western intellectuals and scientific elites as a whole:

> This is due partly to the fact that many professionals, opinion makers, communications media and centres of power, being located in affluent urban areas, are far removed from the poor, with little direct contact with their problems. They live and reason from the comfortable position of a high level of development and a quality of life well beyond the reach of the majority of the world's population. (LS 49)

The cynical question Joseph Stalin asked at the Yalta Conference – 'How many divisions does the Pope have?' – demonstrated not an understanding of power but ignorance. It is, however, certainly not an exaggeration to say that the debate the Pope has unleashed among 1.3 billion Catholic Christians represents one of the most important world-political events in modern history. But it is also an example of how the limits that the capitalist system is coming up against are becoming a topic of discussion in ever broader circles.

[104] The Latin 'medias via' and the Spanish 'término medio' are better translated as middle way or middle ground. 'Per mediam viam naturae curam nummariis copiis, vel ambitum servandum progressui conciliare non sufficit. Hoc de argumento mediae viae parum tantum ruinam remorantur. Agitur modo de progressu iterum finiendo.' 'No basta conciliar, en un término medio, el cuidado de la naturaleza con la renta financiera, o la preservación del ambiente con el progreso. En este tema los términos medios son sólo una pequeña demora en el derrumbe. Simplemente se trata de redefinir el progreso.'

And this raises the question of a broad social dialogue on alternatives, in which socialism has something vital to contribute. I think that in view of the gravity of the situation we should conduct this discussion without panic because panic means irrationality and the inability to act.

In the IPCC report we read the following sentences:

> There are a wide range of adaptation options that can reduce the risks of climate change. (IPCC 2018, p. 10)
>
> Mitigation options consistent with 1.5°C pathways are associated with multiple synergies and tradeoffs across the Sustainable Development Goals (SDGs). While the total number of possible synergies exceeds the number of trade-offs, their net effect will depend on the pace and magnitude of changes, the composition of the mitigation portfolio and the management of the transition. (Ib. p. 19)

Thus in the brittle language of natural scientists no inevitable fate is assigned to us but we are called on to act quickly and rationally.

The corona crisis also contains an important lesson: While the pandemic subsides in Europe during the summer months, which is allowing a – possibly temporary – return to an almost normal life in most countries, the infection and mortality rates are continuing to rise worldwide, especially among the disadvantaged members of society. People in Europe are going to learn that no borders or weapons can save them from this disease. Either humanity in its entirety ends this pandemic or the pandemic will vanquish humanity.

In this respect it presents us with the alternative confronting humanity as a practical task.

Commons – Our Common Ground?

Christian and Socialist Perspectives

Petra Steinmair-Pösel and Michael Brie

Are there common grounds between Socialists and Christians? Or are we representing completely oppositional and conflictive worldviews? While in both traditions there are harsh rejections and damnations of the respective other side, Pope Francis has repeatedly pointed out the urgent necessity of a transversal dialogue on topical political, economic and ecological challenges. (Cf. Pope Francis 2014) This article is an intermediate product of such a dialogue between a Catholic social ethicist (Petra Steinmair-Pösel) and a Socialist philosopher (Michael Brie). The question inspiring this dialogue is, whether the maintenance and care for commons could be a common ground shared by Catholics and Socialists alike. In order to explore this question, we start with a shared academic definition of commons: What are commons and how are they addressed in current economic research? (1) In a second step we outline how our respective traditions approached the issue of commons historically. (2 + 3) A third step focuses on present challenges by asking for the structural framework needed to protect and maintain jeopardized commons. (4) The fourth and final step turns to highlighting contemporary approaches to commons from the Socialist and Catholic perspective, thereby addressing anthropological foundations as well as visions and strategies for societies. (5 + 6)

Entering a dialogue presupposes to concede that the other might be right. It is based on the strong will to listen carefully to what the other has to say, how s/he understands her/himself. From both partners it demands emptying oneself and putting aside one's own prejudices and judgements about the other, trying to learn from shared as well as alternative views, from clear-cut positions as well as open questions. Dialogue does not only require strong intentions but also time and enabling structures. Preparing for the summer school but also during the study week we had the structural framework, time, and opportunities to exercise ourselves in this kind of dialogue. However, we are very much aware that this is only a first step – others have to and hopefully will follow.

What are Commons?

Brief introduction to the term and concept

The English term *commons* goes back to the Latin term *communis* – meaning common, ordinary, universal; of or for the community; democratic, representing the common sentiment. It is also related to *munus*, meaning both, 'gift' and 'counter-gift', which is to say, a duty. In our native German, the traditional word for commons is *Allmende* or *Allmein*, a term comprised of *alle* (all) and *Gemeinde* (community) – identifying that which belongs to all in a community. Thus, its etymology points to the very core of the modern discourse on the commons: All those, who belong to one particular community, use resources together and therefore have to agree upon *how* they do this; upon the conjoined rights, duties and responsibilities. (Cf. Helfrich 2011, p. 11)

Historically, the law of the commons can be traced 'back to ancient Egypt and the Roman Empire, and is stitched like a golden thread throughout medieval history in Europe' (Bollier 2014, p. 84). David Bollier, one of the leading commons experts, denotes 'the Magna Carta and its companion Charter of the Forest' as 'landmarks of commons-based law' that are 'deeply embedded in Western law'. (Bollier 2014, p. 84) In medieval England, 'the common was an integral part of the manor and was thus legally part of the estate in land owned by the lord of the manor, but over which certain classes of manorial tenants and others held certain rights. By extension, the term 'commons' has come to be applied to other resources which a community has rights or access to.'[105] Usually it denotes 'shared agricultural fields, grazing lands and forests'[106]. Persons who have a right in or over common land or resources together are called commoners.

Up to the 19th century commons were part of the life reality of many people, but with the agrarian reforms of the 18th and 19th centuries, many former commons were enclosed and done away with. While the UK was quite radical in this[107], some Alpine regions of southwest Germany, Austria and Switzerland, which had the most advanced commons structures, have kept them until today. (Cf. Bertolini 2012) With the widespread structural changes of the 19th century, also the notion 'commons' began to vanish.

Only one hundred years later, in 1968, it gained new prominence due to a famous and controversial article published in the renowned *Science* magazine by biologist Garrett Hardin. The article was titled 'The Tragedy of the Commons' (Cf. Hardin 1968) and argues that in the context of a conjointly used resource, rational man will – for the purpose of personal gain – extract more than s/he is entitled to, which inevitably leads to the depletion of the resource. We will address this thesis of the 'tragedy of the commons' and its validity later. For the moment suffice it to say that Hardin's thesis became formative for the discourse of the following decades. It was politically functionalized by some, and critically contested by others. Anyway, the notion of the 'commons' was back on the agenda and has been gaining attention during the last two decades.[108]

How is the term 'commons' understood and used today? Wikipedia, the free encyclopedia and itself a digital common, offers the following definition:

> 'The commons is the cultural and natural resources accessible to all members of a society, including natural materials such as air, water, and a habitable earth. These resources are held in common, not owned privately. Commons can also be understood as natural resources that groups of people (communities, user groups) manage for individual and collective benefit. Characteris-

[105] https://en.wikipedia.org/wiki/Commons (last accessed 22.08.2019)

[106] https://en.wikipedia.org/wiki/Commons (last accessed 22.08.2019)

[107] However, the UK and the former dominions have till today a large amount of Crown land which often is used for community or conservation purposes. https://en.wikipedia.org/wiki/Commons (last accessed 22.08.2019)

[108] Cf. https://commons.blog/was-sind-commons/ (last accessed 22.08.2019)

> tically, this involves a variety of informal norms and values (social practice) employed for a governance mechanism.'[109]

Silke Helfrich, a German commons-expert who co-authored and edited several volumes on the topic (Cf. Helfrich and Heinrich-Böll-Stiftung 2014; Ostrom and Helfrich 2011) and runs a 'Commons-blog'[110], explains, that the notion of the commons basically refers to two central categories: (1) Finite, material, natural resources like raw materials, energy sources, water, forests etc. and (2) immaterial, intellectual resources like knowledge and ideas – the 'codes' of information society and the codes of life; the knowledge commons. While natural resources are rival, which means that they are not divisible in use and consummation (they will be consumed or degraded), knowledge commons are – like public goods – non-rival. A software or a recipe can simultaneously be used by an arbitrary amount of people – they won't be exhausted.

Thus, in the current debate the term commons not only refers to the gifts of nature, but also to cultural resources and immaterial goods, as far as they are in shared property of local or global communities or should, for normative reasons, be held in common.[111]

In addition, David Bollier points out that 'the commons is not [simply] a resource. It is a resource plus a defined community and the protocols, values and norms devised by the community to manage needed resources.' For this reason he adds: 'Many resources – such as the atmosphere, oceans, genetic knowledge and biodiversity – urgently need to be managed as commons.' (Bollier 2014, p. 176)

Definition of the commons and common principles

The Commons are systems of natural and social resources (Ostrom 1990, pp. 30-33). In these systems, social goods are created that people need for a successful life. These goods must be reproduced and developed. The access of all members of a community to these goods must be secured. In principle, social goods can be distinguished in two ways – (1) the amount of costs incurred by excluding others from the use of the goods (exclusion costs) and (2) the amount of profits that can be made from the participation of

[109] https://en.wikipedia.org/wiki/Commons (last accessed 22.08.2019)

[110] https://commons.blog/ (last accessed 22.08.2019)

[111] Cf. https://commons.blog/was-sind-commons/ (last accessed 22.08.2019)

others in the use of the goods (inclusion gains). These costs and benefits depend both on the social framework (culture, institutional environment, etc.) and existing technologies. Such a classification makes it possible to assume the existence of four types of goods: (1) public goods, (2) common pool goods, (3) individual goods and finally (4) associated goods (see quite similar Ostrom 2005, p. 24).

Public goods are those goods from whose use others can only be excluded at high cost (high exclusion costs) and whose open social use increases the value of the goods (high inclusion profits). The classic example of a public good is knowledge. *Common goods* are marked by the combination of high exclusion costs and high inclusion losses. Access to their use is therefore a problem: the more these goods are used, the more they are consumed. Health facilities are one example. Societies which exclude their members from using these facilities for reasons of lack of solvency, ethnicity, citizenship, etc. accept that basic human rights will not be respected. This results in high social exclusion costs. The term *individual goods* describes those resources from whose use others can be excluded with little effort and whose use by others greatly reduces their value (high inclusion losses). The majority of objects of individual consumption have this characteristic. A fourth category of goods are those to be referred to as *associated goods*. Their use in common by defined groups enhances the abilities of all members together. But it has to be mentioned: All goods are the results of humans living and acting in a limited world of common pool resources which need nurturing and shared responsibility.

From the point of view of use, those actors who have the greatest interest in exploiting their inherent potential should own the aforementioned goods. Public goods should be open to free use by as many people as possible, as their free and unlimited use increases the benefit for society. They require comprehensive public support. Community property must be owned by those who, on the one hand, ensure that nobody is excluded from access who is entitled to it and, at the same time, ensure that it is not overused and that the property is constantly being renewed. They should be in administration of clearly defined communities. And while individual goods should remain in individual ownership, a clear regulation is needed on what conditions, for example, state, collective or private entrepreneurs can combine labour, finance (in the form of loans), real estate (by lease) and knowledge (including through licenses) in the form of associated ownership of the company by those who have a stake in it.

A commons based society has rich systems of common pool resources as its basis, which are produced, developed and reproduced in polycentric systems of a multiplicity of associations of public, community, cooperative and also private-legal form. To secure these systems, a supporting and service-providing state and a corresponding legal system as a 'superstructure' are required. In addition to human and civil rights, the constitutions of societies must guarantee the protection of the commons and the guaranteed access of everyone to the common-based freedom goods as a legally enforceable right. David Bollier .(Bollier 2014, p. 179) summarizes the principles of the Commons paradigm in contrast to the profit paradigm on the following table.

	The For-Profit Paradigm	**The Commons Paradigm**
Resources	*Scarcity is given or created (through barriers and exclusions).*	*For rivalrous resources, there is enough for all through sharing. For non-rivalrous resources, there is abundance.*
Strategy	*"efficient" resource allocation.*	*strengthening social relations is decisive for assuring fair shares and sustainable use of resources.*
Idea of the individual	*Individuals maximize benefits for themselves (Homo economicus).*	*Humans are primarily cooperative social beings.*
Relationships to nature and people	*Separation •Either/or •Individualism vs. collectivism •Human society vs. nature*	*Interrelationality •Individuals and the collective are nested within each other and mutually reinforcing.*
Change agents	*Powerful political lobbies, interest groups and institutionalized politics focused on government.*	*Diverse communities working as distributed networks, with solutions Coming from the margins.*
Focus	*Market exchange and growth (GDP) achieved through individual initiative, innovation and "efficiency".*	*Use-value, common wealth, sustainable livelihoods and complementarity of enterprise.*
Core questions	*What can be sold and bought?*	*What do I/we need to live?*

While we share the hitherto mentioned definitions and descriptions, our traditions differ in their respective approaches to the issue of commons.

In order to better understand each other, in the next step these diverging approaches will be made explicit.

Commons in the Christian / Catholic tradition

In the Christian tradition, we can basically identify *three interrelated roots* for the notion of commons: Biblical roots, the principle of the common good, and the universal destination of goods.

Biblical roots

Let us first turn to the Old Testament. At its very beginning we find a metaphorical narration about the earth as God's creation, which is entrusted to the first human beings, who are called 'to have dominion over' (Gen 1:26) the other created beings. Unfortunately, this narration was sometimes interpreted in an exploitative sense. However, in the original biblical context, the divine mandate calls humans to stewardship and care for the created world, to being responsible for what is entrusted to them, like a good king is responsible for the wellbeing of his people.

An exemplary story from the New Testament translates into practice, what this stewardship and care might actually look like in a concrete Christian community: It is the NT-account of the community of goods practice in the Jerusalem congregation in Acts 4:32-35.

32 Now the full number of those who believed were of one heart and soul, and no one said that any of the things that belonged to him was his own, but they had everything in common. 33 And with great power the apostles were giving their testimony to the resurrection of the Lord Jesus, and great grace was upon them all. 34 There was not a needy person among them, for as many as were owners of lands or houses sold them and brought the proceeds of what was sold 35 and laid it at the apostles' feet, and it was distributed to each as any had need.

This text has spurred vivid theological debates: Does it imply that anyone who wants to follow Christ must sell all their possessions like did these first Christians? Kari-Shane Davis Zimmerman explains that this text passage is not necessarily designed to be a *general* model that must be followed by all Christian communities. What is important, is that it describes a *practice that goes beyond the Greek ideal of friendship among equals*. It addresses *friendship between socially unequal persons* and a new motivational guide for social relations: *concern for those most in need*. According to Davis Zimmerman the latter provides the key to understanding the community of goods practice of the Jerusalem community, while also taking into account that the community of goods practice is in tension to some other passages in Luke, which commend wandering destitution, almsgiving, or hospitality. Ultimately, argues Davis Zimmerman, *all of these practices coincide in one thing*: they aim at meeting the needs all and especially of the poor and keeping them at the center of attention.[112]

The principle of the common good

A second root for understanding the commons in the Christian theological and philosophical tradition can be found in the so-called *principle of the common good*. (Cf. Compendium 2004, 164-170)

As to the *historical background* it can be said that the common good was already discussed in the political philosophies of the ancient world. Here, the common good was understood as the function as well as the aim of political communities. While Plato's understanding represents a more *normative-apriori* concept of the common good, Aristotle provides a more *empirically interested aposteriori* concept. In the 13th century, the influential theologian Thomas Aquinas took up an Aristotelian concept of the common good and connected it to the medieval concept of the *Ordo*, i.e. the teaching about the God-given order and hierarchy of things – in contrast to man-made norms and laws. In consequence, for Thomas Aquinas the common good is not restricted to the political community and the immanent world alone. Rather, he understands humans as beings striving for the highest good, the *summum bonum*, which ultimately is God. Therefore, the common good as well as the individual good point towards the transcendent origin and final destination of creation.

Thomas Aquinas' understanding of the common good subsequently became *one of the fundamental principles*[113] of Catholic Social Teaching and

---

[112] 'Luke describes different ways in which Christians can form new social relationships between each other and keep the needs of the poor a priority. Although the forms vary, this underlying concern can find fulfillment [...] in the practice of community of goods.' (Zimmerman, K. D. 2012, p. 784)

[113] Even though globally the list of key principles differs depending on their commentators

the academic discipline of Social Ethics, which were both explicitly developed from the end of the 19th century in view of the new issues and challenges European societies were facing as a result of the Industrial Revolution and the social transformation this brought about.[114] In the 1960s the Second Vatican Council in its pastoral constitution *Gaudium et spes* (GS) defined the common good as 'the sum of those conditions of social life which allow social groups and their individual members relatively thorough and ready access to their own fulfillment' (GS 26).

In the context of social ethical theory building, usually two components of the common good are distinguished: the formal/organizational and the material dimension. *Formally*, the *common good* (Gemein*wohl*) refers to the functional organization of society and its institutions, which 'must take account of all those social conditions which favor the full development of human personality' (MM 65), especially safeguarding the rights and duties of the human person. The common good is realized by the legal and welfare systems on national, European and international scale, which are to be judged by their ability to bring about the best possible conditions for the development of the human person and for a responsible conduct of life. Therefore, the common good asks for the continuous improvement of social structures according to the requirements of the respective situation. *Materially*, the *common good* (Gemein*gut*) refers to aims and values, which are supposed to guide politics in terms of notions of social justice and personal development, thus forming future structures. Both dimensions of the common good are related to each other, as existing institutional arrangements are the result of previous political value options, which form the basis of future standards of justice.

In *democracies*, citizens we are involved in the material specification of the common good as the highest guiding principle for politics. By contributing our value options, we also determine the future shape of the com-

---

and local contexts, in the German speaking academic discourse a 'canon' of five social principles has been established. Apart from the common good they are the principle of personhood, the principle of solidarity, the principle of subsidiarity and – lately – the principle of sustainability.

114 The Encyclical Letter *Rerum Novarum* (RN) issued by Pope Leo XIII was the first papal text directly and systematically dealing with these social concerns. As the Christian response to the 'labor problems' of this time, it was also directed against the atheist strands of the socialist movements.

munity. These value options are on the one hand defined by the specific interests of individuals and groups, on the other hand by basic political values such as peace, justice, solidarity and freedom, which – obviously – can be conflicting: How much individual freedom can be tolerated and guaranteed by a society, even at the expense of solidarity? Are there limits to tolerance when it comes to safeguarding a peaceful and ordered living together? Such questions show the importance of an ongoing discourse about the European common good and thus the finality of the Union.

The universal destination of goods

A third root for understanding commons from a Christian perspective, which is intrinsically connected to the two roots mentioned before, is the 'universal destination of goods.' (Cf. Compendium 2004, 171-184) According to the *Compendium of the Social Doctrine of the Church*[115] it is based on the fact that

God gave the earth to the whole human race for the sustenance of all its members, without excluding or favouring anyone. (171)

From this follows, that 'each person must have access to the level of well-being necessary for his full development' and that 'the right to the common use of goods is the "first principle of the whole ethical and social order" [363] and "the characteristic principle of Christian social doctrine' [364]. This right is understood as 'a natural right, inscribed in human nature and not merely a positive right connected with changing historical circumstances'. Moreover, it is seen as 'an inherent' [365] right. It is innate in individual persons, in every person, and has priority with regard to any human intervention concerning goods, to any legal system concerning the same, to any economic or social system or method: 'All other rights, whatever they are, including property rights and the right of free trade must be subordinated to this norm [the universal destination of goods]; they must not hinder it, but must rather expedite its application.' (172)

Thus, the principle of the universal destination of goods is an invitation to develop an economic vision inspired by moral values that permit people

[115] The Compendium was published in 2004 by the Pontifical Council for Justice and Peace at the request of John Paul II – in order to present 'a precise but complete over-view' of the social teaching of the Catholic Church. In the following paragraphs the respective numbers will be given in brackets after each quote.

not to lose sight of the origin or purpose of these goods, so as to bring about a world of fairness and solidarity, in which the creation of wealth can take on a positive function. (174)

The universal destination of goods does not outrule private property, as 'private property and other forms of private ownership of goods "assure a person a highly necessary sphere for the exercise of his personal and family autonomy and ought to be considered as an extension of human freedom. … stimulating exercise of responsibility".' (175) However, 'the Church's social doctrine requires that ownership of goods be equally accessible to all' (176) and ultimately, private property 'is in its essence only an instrument for respecting the principle of the universal destination of goods; in the final analysis, therefore, it is not an end but a means.' (177) Consequently, 'the principle of the universal destination of goods requires that the poor, the marginalized and in all cases those whose living conditions interfere with their proper growth should be the focus of particular concern'. (182)

The universal destination of goods implies that the *environment is a collective good* and the 'care for the environment […] a challenge for all of humanity. It is a matter of a common and universal duty' (466), a responsibility that does not only extend to present needs but also includes the needs of *future generations* (467). In order to live up to this responsibility, the Compendium asks for an adequate expression of this responsibility on a *juridical level* (468).

Moreover, the Compendium calls 'for an effective change of mentality leading to the adoption of new lifestyles, [1012] 'in which the quest for truth, beauty, goodness and communion with others for the sake of the common good are the factors that determine consumer choices, savings and investments"' (486), a *lifestyle that breaks with the logic of mere consumption* – a lifestyle based on *gratitude and appreciation* of a world that reveals the mystery of its Creator and Sustainer. (487) Thus, the Compendium already anticipates some of the main topics of Pope Francis's Encyclical *Laudato Si*.

Short summary

Concluding this part, it can be summarized that the biblical accounts of creation and of the early Christian community in Jerusalem, the notion of the common good, and the notion of the universal destination of goods are the foundations for understanding and establishing a commons culture from a Christian / Catholic point of view.

Commons in the Socialist Tradition

Historical background

The modern socialist movements originated at the end of the 18th century. The background was the combination of European intellectual revolution (of the Enlightenment), French political revolution and English industrial revolution. These movements have their precursors in the broad popular movements since the 12th century, which had linked claims to freedom and collective self-determination with the defence of the traditional common good and its collective management and administration. Reference was made to the Old Testament. God has given the earth and its fruits to all as a common good and the earth is our common table where all can be fed, as posed by the French social philosopher and communist (Morelly 1964, pp. 92f.). The community of property of the early Jerusalem congregation in which distribution was made 'unto every man according as he had need' (Acts 4:32) was regarded as a model and practised. In the Great French Revolution and the revolutions against slavery and colonialism, racism and patriarchal oppression inspired by it, the contrast between proclaimed human and civil rights and old and new conditions of oppression, exploitation and degradation came to the fore. Against the background of the new economic, social, political and cultural possibilities, the associated inequality no longer seemed legitimate and particularly intolerable. On this basis, the inviolability of private property was called into question, demands were made for the provision of essential public goods (labour, social security, health care, education) and a balanced distribution of property. New communist projects of common production, democratic self-government and common life emerged.

Basic historical reference

In early socialism and communism after the Great French Revolution, very different approaches were experimented with in order to deal with the contradiction between freedom, equality and solidarity. First, there were strictly communist responses to the creation of a society based on indivisible common property, which regulates production according to a uniform plan and organizes the distribution according to needs (the school in the tradition of Morelly and Babeuf). Secondly, plans for a scientific reorganization and management of society as a society of workers were developed according to the performance principle (the school of Saint-Simon). Third, demands for a social state and democratic reorganization of the societies shaped by the capitalist market economy (Robert Owen and the British Chartist movement) were formed. Fourthly, many communist or communitarian experiments (mainly under the influence of Owen, Fourier and Cabet) and forms of cooperatives emerged. Fifthly, anarchist approaches developed which sought to build a federalist society of free associations from the free and constantly revisable agreement of individuals from below (Proudhon). Marx tried to link the different approaches organically on the basis of a 'critical communism'.

The 20th century saw a whole series of attempts to put these approaches into practice – in the form of the social democratic projects of the democratic welfare state and a socially regulated market economy, the state-socialist projects of planned economy under party-communist leadership but also of worker's self-government in Yugoslavia or of communes in China, anarcho-syndicalism and its projects of self-government of enterprises by the workers and the Jewish kibbutz movement, among others.

A common challenge: the endangerment of the commons

As we have seen, the preconditions of our respective understanding differ, but some commonalities have become visible as well, particularly the biblical references to the OT creation accounts and the NT community of goods practice in the Jerusalem congregation, as well as the pressing social challenges in the wake of the Industrial Revolution igniting and spurring the sociopolitical commitment on both sides. Knowing about and building on these commonalities, we now want to briefly look at a common challenge of our days: our jeopardized commons. As we all know, today commons like the climate, clean drinking water, fish stock etc. are widely endangered. One of the big challenges commons are facing was – as mentioned before – described by microbiologist and ecologist Garett Hardin in the magazine *Science* in 1968. (Cf. Hardin 1968)

The looming tragedy of the commons

Hardin argues that as soon as a depletable resource t for example pastures, fish in open sea, water or fresh, unpolluted air t is unrestrictedly available to all people, every individual or company will try to gain as much profit for him/herself. This works, as long as the resource is not depleted. However, if the number of the users rises over a certain level, they are trapped in the tragedy of the commons: Everyone still tries to maximize their profits, but the resource doesn't suffice for all. In consequence it is slowly used up. The costs produced by the overexploitation are distributed on the community, while for the single overuser the momentary profit is still higher than the long-term costs. The tragedy mentioned by Hardin is that finally, everyone contributes to their own ruin as well to that of the community.[116] Hardin's summary: 'Freedom in a commons brings ruin to all.' (Hardin 1968, 1244) But is this tragedy really inevitable?

Elinor Ostrom's approach: Why and when commons are not doomed to fail

Nobel Prize Laureate for Economic Sciences Elinor Ostrom challenged Hardin's approach arguing that there are more possibilities than top-down government/centralization or free market/privatization solutions. In her Nobel-Prize-Lecture Ostrom explained under which conditions commons can be successfully managed by a community. In her research she 'tried to understand the broader institutional regularities among the systems that were sustained over a long period of time and were absent in the failed systems.' She explains:

I used the term 'design principle' to characterize these regularities. I did not mean that the fishers, irrigators, pastoralists, and others overtly had these principles in their minds when they developed systems that survived for long periods of time. My effort was to identify a set of core underlying lessons that characterized the long sustained regimes as contrasted to the cases of failure. (Ostrom 2009, p. 422)

And she offers the following list of principles:

1A. User Boundaries: Clear and locally understood boundaries between legitimate users and nonusers are present.

[116] Cf. https://www.youtube.com/watch?v=CxC161GvMPc (last accessed 22.08.2019)

1B. Resource Boundaries: Clear boundaries that separate a specific common-pool resource from a larger social-ecological system are present.
2A. Congruence with Local Conditions: Appropriation and provision rules are congruent with local social and environmental conditions.
2B. Appropriation and Provision: Appropriation rules are congruent with provision rules; the distribution of costs is proportional to the distribution of benefits.
3. Collective-Choice Arrangements: Most individuals affected by a resource regime are authorized to participate in making and modifying its rules.
4A. Monitoring Users: Individuals who are accountable to or are the users monitor the appropriation and provision levels of the users.
4B. Monitoring the Resource: Individuals who are accountable to or are the users monitor the condition of the resource.
5. Graduated Sanctions: Sanctions for rule violations start very low but become stronger if a user repeatedly violates a rule.
6. Conflict-Resolution Mechanisms: Rapid, low-cost, local arenas exist for resolving conflicts among users or with officials.
7. Minimal Recognition of Rights: The rights of local users to make their own rules are recognized by the government.
8. Nested Enterprises: When a common-pool resource is closely connected to a larger social-ecological system, governance activities are organized in multiple nested layers. (Ostrom 2009, p. 422)

On the Commons (OTC), a commons movement strategy center founded in 2001, breaks down Ostrom's design principles into eight basic recommendations or guidelines to be followed when dealing with commons:

1. Define clear group boundaries.
2. Match rules governing use of common goods to local needs and conditions.
3. Ensure that those affected by the rules can participate in modifying the rules.
4. Make sure the rule-making rights of community members are respected by outside authorities.
5. Develop a system, carried out by community members, for monitoring members' behavior.

6. Use graduated sanctions for rule violators.
7. Provide accessible, low-cost means for dispute resolution.
8. Build responsibility for governing the common resource in nested tiers from the lowest level up to the entire interconnected system.[117]

Aware of the challenge of the multifaceted endangerment of commons in our global society as well as the findings of Ostrom's research, we now want to turn back to our respective approaches, in order to carve out, how they might contribute to a better understanding of as well as possible solutions to the mentioned problems. Thereby we agreed to focus on our underlying anthropological foundations as well as our respective visions and strategies to bring about change.

Contemporary approaches to commons from a Socialist perspective

The socialist tradition can refer to Marx's categorical imperative and his understanding of radical criticism:

> 'To be radical is to grasp the root of the matter. But for man the root is man himself. […] The criticism of religion ends with the teaching that man is the highest being for man, hence with the categorical imperative to overthrow all relations in which man is a debased, enslaved, forsaken, despicable being.' (Marx 1844, p. 182)

Anthropological foundation

In the Marxist tradition, man is understood as a being who can develop his/her physical and spiritual potencies only in successful social conditions, or as Marx put it: '… the essence of man is no abstraction inherent in each single individual. In its reality it is the ensemble of the social relations.' (Marx 1976, p. 4) The search for a fixed human nature ('good' or 'evil', selfish or altruistic, etc.) is misleading. Humans are open-minded and hidden beings, who always transcend every boundary. There is therefore no ideal social form that would correspond to human nature. It requires plural forms within which people can move – supported in solidarity and self-

[117] http://www.onthecommons.org/work/8-principles-managing-commmons{#}sthash.mO9VUgCG.dpbs (accessed August 22, 2019)

confidently free. Reference can be made to the cooperative orientation of humans (Bauer 2010).

The vision of a society of free and equal human beings

In the *Communist Manifesto* the above mentioned categorical imperative was reformulated into the positive vision to struggle for 'an association, in which the free development of each is the condition for the free development of all' (Marx and Engels 1976, p. 506). Marx saw the capitalist mode of production as most destructive because it destroys according to him the common foundations of human civilization which would fall into barbarism if no transformation toward a higher – socialist – stage of development occured. He wrote: 'Even a whole society, a nation, or even all simultaneously existing societies taken together, are not the owners of the globe. They are only its possessors, its usufructuaries, and, like *boni patres familias,* they must hand it down to succeeding generations in an improved condition.' The common ground of human development – the means of production, transport and communication, the natural resources – should be brought under the common control of the common people and then transformed into the 'organic social body' of the associated individuals to secure and enhance freedom, equality and solidarity of each and everybody. For Marx, a post-capitalist society should be characterised by the fact that individual property is restored on the basis of his own work, but not as private property of small craftsmen or peasant families, but rather as 'individual property based on the acquisitions of the capitalist era: i.e., on co-operation and the possession in common of the land and of the means of production' (Marx 1996, p. 751).

A tension between individual property (understood as appropriation) and social disposal of social means of production is opened up without discussing the associated institutional problems in more detail. The long-term goal of a comprehensive transformation is described:

> 'In a higher phase of communist society, after the enslaving subordination of the individual to the division of labour, and thereby also the antithesis between mental and physical labour, has vanished; after labour has become not only a means of life but life's prime want; after the productive forces have also increased with the all-round development of the individual, and all the springs of common wealth flow more abundantly – only then can the narrow horizon of bourgeois right be crossed in its entirety and society inscribe on its banners:

> From each according to his abilities, to each according to his needs!' (Marx 1989, p. 87)

Based on the experiences of the 20th century and drawing on partially repressed traditions, this guiding vision was enriched and reformed in the more recent discussion. Three related items are worth mentioning.

First, the concept of conviviality was developed. This term goes back to the Austro-American philosopher and theologian Ivan Illich (Illich 1975, p. 23). It understands the worlds humans live in as a being with people and other creatures of nature, from which alone a rich life of needy people can grow in rich relationships of work, care, play and leisure. Against the vision of a uniform world of abstract equality, the Zapatistas have developed the vision: 'In the world we want many worlds to fit.' (EZLN 1994).

Second: In the field of the commons research, the vision of a polycentric society has been developed by the group around the Nobel Prize winner for economics, Elinor Ostrom, and her husband, Vincent Ostrom. Their elementary cells are free communities that maintain, develop, use and manage the natural, social and cultural common pool resources largely independently, integrating them into cooperative horizontal and supportive vertical networks. It is not a centralist state or so-called free markets that should form the dominant principle of order, but rather common-based cooperation in networked polycentric contexts (Ostrom 2005, p. 255).

Thirdly: The liberation theologians Ulrich Duchrow and Franz Hinkelammert formulate the criterion of human rights obligation for an alternative order of property: 'Every concrete proposal of alternative institutions and actions must then be examined and assessed as to whether it actually benefits concrete life and whether nobody is excluded in its elaboration and in view of its consequences.' (Duchrow and Hinkelammert 2002, p. 193) This can only be judged from the perspective of the humiliated, the downtrodden, the abandoned, the despised: The perspective of the common good, according to Duchrow and Hinkelammert, is 'basically determined by the weakest and most vulnerable members of the community. If they can live, everyone can live.' (ibid., p. 188)

Access to the basic goods of a free life is a decisive condition for property subject to human rights. The goal of capitalist production is the production of surplus value, the goal of socialist production is the creation of conditions of free individuality or true wealth in a rich world. Goods have a socialist 'value' when they are freedom goods, goods on which the free development of the individual depends – good and self-determined work, democratic co-determination, education, knowledge, health, an environment worth living in, and so on (Klein 2003). There is a proposal for a Universal Declaration of the Common Good .(see Houtart 2012).

Strategies

Obstacles to overcome

Today's societies are characterised by a multitude of overlapping power relations that stand in the way of solidarity-based emancipation. The experiences of Soviet state socialism and fascism must also be taken into account. With the new communication, information and biotechnologies, new forms of domination are emerging. The ecological destruction and global social polarization are going on. Fundamentalisms of the market and of religions and ideologies as well as racism, imperialism and patriarchalism are gaining influence. This is combined with the tremendous dynamism and innovative power of capitalist-shaped societies.

The Way: Transformation in Capitalism and beyond

Capitalism transforms the basic goods of the production of life and exchange – labour, nature, money, culture – into commodities and subjects the economy and society to capital accumulation. From this Marxian and Polanyian perspective, capitalism is incompatible with emancipation and democratic self-determination. The common foundations of a free life are being privatized, and the imperatives of a capitalist market society are in direct contradiction to social and ecological democracy. The flip side of this transformation of the basic goods of life is the possibility of constantly combining the conditions of production and reproduction anew, constantly revolutionizing society and initiating an infinite process of innovation. Paraphrasing Joseph Schumpeter one could speak of destructive creation. The dictum of Marx and Engels from the 'Manifesto of the Communist Party' still applies today:

'The bourgeoisie, by the rapid improvement of all instruments of production, by the immensely facilitated means of communication, draws all, even the most barbarian, nations into civilisation. The cheap prices of its commodities are the heavy artillery with which it batters down all Chinese walls, with which it forces the barbarians' intensely obstinate hatred of foreigners to capitulate. It compels all nations, on pain of extinction, to adopt the bourgeois mode of production; it compels them to introduce what it calls civilisation into their midst, i.e., to become bourgeois themselves. In one word, it creates a world after its own image.' (Marx and Engels 1976, p. 488)

From this ambivalence of capitalism arises the task of a double transformation. On the one hand, it has the task of overcoming the exploitative, oppressive and destructive character of today's capitalist society and, at the same time, of producing forms that keep the innovative capacity of modern societies in a solidary, democratic, ecological form. On the other hand, it is a double transformation, since in view of the real possibilities it is transformation inside capitalism and beyond it at the same time. It is about the connection of 'transformation to a socially and ecologically regulated capitalism with the beginning of a second great transformation beyond capitalism' (Klein 2013, p. 15). Erik O. Wright adds:

> 'The optimistic view is that we don't know what system challenges and transformation possibilities there will be in the future: interstitial strategies today can strengthen popular understanding that another world is possible and contribute to moving along some of the pathways of social empowerment; symbiotic strategies can potentially open up greater spaces for interstitial strategies to work; and the cumulative effect of such institution-building around expanded forms of social empowerment could be render ruptural transformations possible under unexpected future historical conditions.' (Wright 2010).

Contemporary approaches to commons from a Christian perspective

Anthropological Foundations: Created in the image and likeness of God, but affected by original sin

As above explained for the Socialist tradition, also in a Christian understanding, human beings are neither seen as only good and altruistic nor bad and selfish. In the Christian context, the key to understanding human beings, lies in two aspects, which – again – were metaphorically described already in the OT creation story: One aspect is that they are created 'in

God's image and likeness', from which derives their inherent, nonvolatile dignity, which also accounts for a Christian understanding of unalienable human rights. The second aspect is introduced shortly after the creation account and is – in the theological tradition – known as (original) sin. (Cf. Wandinger 2003) As this is a difficult and easily mistakeable concept, we have to understand how the notion of 'original sin' could be understood today by modern, scientifically trained people and why it is important with regard to commons.

I will, for this purpose, draw on Mimetic Theory, which was developed by the anthropologist and cultural scientist René Girard and was called 'a scientific version of the doctrine of original sin' (Sloterdijk 2002, 250; translated by PSP) by German philosopher Peter Sloterdijk. In a nutshell, Girard argues that human beings are characterized by their mimetic desire. This mimetic desire 'is responsible for the best and the worst in us, for what lowers us below the animal level as well as what elevates us above.' (Girard 2001, p. 6) Girard gives the following description, of the triangular mimetic structure of human desire:

> 'Once his basic needs are satisfied (indeed, sometimes even before), man is subject to intense desires, though he may not know precisely for what. The reason is that he desires being, something he himself lacks and which some other person seems to possess. The subject thus looks to that other person to inform him of what he should desire in order to acquire that being.' (Girard 1977, p. 146)

Thus, the fundamental desire, which unthematically aims at being or – theologically speaking – at transcendence, is immediately interlinked with the mimetic nature of the human person. It is mimetic desire that distinguishes the human person from instinct-determined animals, it is mimetic desire that makes a person receptive to her/his fellow human beings as well as to the divine. Their mimetic ability allows human beings to learn as quick and efficient as no other animal (think, for example, of language skills). On the other hand, mimetic desire has a dark flip side: Especially, when persons desire the same, finite object, conflicts arise, which through mimetic contagion easily contaminate whole groups and societies. In archaic societies lacking social institutions to keep the rising violence in check, this would have led to the extinction of whole populations, had there not been another mechanism, also fueled by mimetic capacities, which Girard calls the scapegoat mechanism. We don't have the time to go into detail here, because Girard develops a whole theory of culture based on this scapegoat mechanism.

For our topic suffice it to say that human beings, as long as their desire doesn't find its ultimate destination in the transcendent, are constantly comparing themselves to others and orienting their desires according to the desires of others, thus getting time and again caught up in mimetic rivalries and conflicts. Already Augustine of Hippo declared in a prayer in his *Confessions* (book I, chapter 1): 'our hearts are restless until they rest in You.'

For the economic sphere this implies that in our decisions as human beings we are not only driven by reasonable arguments and rational strategies, but often by competition, by implicit or explicit rivalries, by the wish to distinguish ourselves etc. The notion of the *homo oeconomicus*, the rationally calculating, profit maximizing man, is therefore challenged by sociologists drawing on mimetic theory. And current empirical economics provides some obvious examples for that seemingly irrational behavior: E.g. confronted with the question, whether they would prefer to have a smaller absolute amount of money while being richer than their peers or having a larger absolute amount while being poorer than their friends and neighbors, the majority prefers the first option.

Related to this is our lacking willingness to downsize and to consume less. Classical economic theory assumed that since goods and services are scarce, since they are not available in the amounts that would be necessary to meet the existing human needs, production has to be increased to meet the needs of everyone. Thus, it reasoned, conflictive scarcity could be abolished and the way paved to peace and satisfaction.

In contrast, mimetic philosophers Paul Dumouchel and Jean-Pierre Dupuy explain why in the current economic system and mindset scarcity will never be overcome but is perpetually regenerated. The key here is the phenomenon of *social scarcity*, argues Dumouchel. He points out that especially in those societies where traditional hierarchies and differences are diminishing, positional goods and status symbols constantly introduce new differences. In the mimetic struggle for the best positions marked by prestige goods, the gap between human desires and available goods will never be bridged even if production rose to an infinite level. Thus, Dumouchel reveals the engine of the economic growth imperative. (Cf. Dumouchel 1999, pp. 175–308)

Remembering what we heard from Elinor Ostrom about managing the commons, this human tendency must be considered, if we don't want to fall prey to a naïve rationalism. Not always do human beings act in the way that would rationally be the best for the whole community and also for themselves, but sometimes our decisions are just about having more, being more famous, more respected than our peers. And that is rooted in our deep anxious desire for being.

Against this background it becomes evident why good arguments and rational strategies are less successful in reducing the ecological collateral damage of our economic system than we would hope. Bruno Latour and Ulrich Beck state a 'great abyss between the dimension of the phenomenon [of global warming] and the change of thought and action that would be necessary to come to terms with the crisis.' (Selchow 2014, translated by PSP) And – as we just heard before – also Elinor Ostrom talks about the necessity of a major change in our thoughts and actions.

Visions and Strategies for Societies

What can bring about this change? How is it possible? Let us finally turn to visions and strategies for societies.

Understanding the significance of the spiritual dimension

Based on the anthropological understanding presented before, such a major social transformation is not possible without a major transformation within human beings, regarding their (mimetic) desire. Social activist, writer, and mystic Thomas Merton explains:

> 'He [or she] who attempts to act and do things for others or for the world without deepening his own self-understanding, freedom, integrity and capacity to love will not have anything to give others. He will communicate to them nothing but the contagion of his own obsessions, his aggressiveness, his ego-centered ambitions, his delusions about ends and means, his doctrinaire prejudices and ideas. There is nothing more tragic in the modern world than the misuse of power and action.' (Merton 1992, p. 375)

For Merton, this is the reason, why action must be founded in contemplation, as 'the consistent practice of contemplation helps to uncover our essential Self, our connected Self, our True Self'. (Rohr 2018) Unlike the small ego self, who anxiously desires being without realizing that he/she already is in union with this being and with the rest of creation, this essentially connected Self lives in and draws upon the union with God.

The Franciscan and spiritual teacher Richard Rohr explains:

> 'Unfortunately, separateness is the chosen stance of the small self which has a hard time living in unity and love with the One, Ultimate Reality, and the diverse manifestations of this Reality (i.e., ourselves, other people, and everything else). […] The small self is still objectively in union with God, it just does not know it, enjoy it, or draw upon it.' (Rohr 2018)

Like Thomas Merton, Richard Rohr, and many others, also Pope Francis underlines the spiritual dimension of the necessary shift from separateness to unity. In his encyclical *Laudato si' , he advances the same argument writing:*

> *'We lack an awareness of our common origin, of our mutual belonging, and of a future to be shared with everyone. This basic awareness would enable the development of new convictions, attitudes and forms of life.' (LS 202)*

Treating the earth as our common home, for which we bear a common but differentiated responsibility

Even if there are adequate legal regulations (which are undoubtedly necessary as well), this shift in awareness of individuals and a notion of 'ecological citizenship' (LS 211) are indispensable. For

> 'the existence of laws and regulations is insufficient in the long run to curb bad conduct, even when effective means of enforcement are present. If the laws are to bring about significant, long-lasting effects, the majority of the members of society must be adequately motivated to accept them, and personally transformed to respond. [If they are not, they will undermine legal regulations. PSP] Only by cultivating sound virtues will people be able to make a selfless ecological commitment.' (LS 211)

And then Pope Francis gives very concrete and practical examples of how little lifestyle changes could look like and how education in environmental responsibility can bring about these positive changes.

> 'A person who could afford to spend and consume more but regularly uses less heating and wears warmer clothes, shows the kind of convictions and attitudes which help to protect the environment. There is a nobility in the duty to

> care for creation through little daily actions, and it is wonderful how education can bring about real changes in lifestyle. Education in environmental responsibility can encourage ways of acting which directly and significantly affect the world around us, such as avoiding the use of plastic and paper, reducing water consumption, separating refuse, cooking only what can reasonably be consumed, showing care for other living beings, using public transport or car-pooling, planting trees, turning off unnecessary lights, or any number of other practices.' (LS 211)

Altogether, the encyclical formulates the framework of 'house rules' for our common home concerning the solidary handling of global resources. (Cf. Vogt 2015) It especially addresses the climate as 'common good' (LS 23-26), for which we bear 'common and differentiated responsibilities' (LS 170). Since the rich countries 'have benefited from a high degree of industrialization, at the cost of enormous emissions of greenhouse gases' the encyclical attributes to them a 'greater responsibility for providing a solution'. (LS 170)

Collaborating with people from all kinds of religious and ideological backgrounds to face the global social and ecological challenges

Unlike prior encyclicals which addressed either only the clerics or only members of the Church, the encyclical *Laudato sí*, explicitly addresses 'every person living on this planet' (LS 3). It is the outspoken aim of Pope Francis 'to enter into dialogue with all people about our common home' (LS 3), as we are united by the same concern. Starting a transversal dialogue between Socialists and Catholics about our common home and the role of commons in a globalized world was the intention of the DIALOP summer school as well as this article. A first step has been made – others have to follow, as we are well aware that with these considerations we have only scratched the surface.

All those, who have nevertheless been inspired by our dialogue and are, asking themselves: 'How can I become more "commonable"?' we would like to encourage with the words of David Bollier: 'start with your passion and where you live' and then 'find others to help push the idea forward, however small the effort may seem at first', trusting 'the famous line by Margaret Mead': 'Never doubt that a small group of thoughtful, committed citizens can change the world; indeed, it's the only thing that ever has.' (Bollier 2014, p. 167)

Manifesto of Hermoupolis

The students of the Syros Summer School 2018

'Politics is one of the highest forms of charity, of love', Pope Francis We the participants of the Christian-Marxist DIALOP Summer School, considering the cultural complexity of Europe and its challenges (the lack of democratic participation in the decision-making process, the marketisation of social interactions and of human beings, the incapacity to welcome refugees, and the growing individualism and consumerism), see an urgent need for fundamental changes in Europe's social and institutional structure. For this reason, we are addressing the present Manifesto to the people in Europe.

We believe that Europe has to be more than an economy; it has to be a social common. We want an economy that serves social equality, justice, and ecological sustainability.

We believe in *solidarity*.

We believe in *human rights*.

We believe in *democracy* and the *respect of diversity*.

We realise that every concept must be concretely applicable and not consist of empty words. We need to take care of each other as we would ourselves. We need to act together for a shared purpose. We want to explain to every single citizen that solidarity means not following self-interest but searching for the common good. Solidarity is the opposite of competitiveness and greed. Solidarity is a reciprocal engagement, a reciprocal action on the level of the community to achieve the common good. It is an identity of interest that we expand together. Solidarity is the basis on which to fully realise freedom and equality.

We affirm the Universal Declaration of Human Rights of 1948 and the value of the European Charter of Fundamental Rights, as having established the highest level up to now of social and political rights in the Union, but, nonetheless, we cannot consider these to be fulfilled. Every person's duty is to declare them, defend them in the face of the institutions, and remind policy-makers of them.

How can we *transform* the problems into solutions?

We are convinced that everyone has the duty to act in co-responsibility (through involvement in movements, collectives, popular associations, think-tanks, etc.) in order to build networks at all levels – local, national, and transnational, for example in the form of Solidary Cities, deliberative processes, or the DIALOP Project, with diverse forms of political organisation.

The Pope indeed calls on us 'to create new forms of participation'[118], through our 'ability to organise and carry out creative alternatives'.[119]

For all these reasons, we propose different responses at various levels: right now, and in the medium, and long-term. Among the many problems we should face, the following issues urgently need to be addressed in order to promote a *universal culture of peace* based on fraternity and sisterhood and the active practice of dialogue:

1. stop military production and arms sales to countries at war;
2. stop climate change – strongly implement the Paris agreement;
3. stop unfair EU trade agreements;
4. stop modern slavery;
5. promote gender equality and stop every kind of abuse and violence (sexual, psychological, and social) against women.

We committed ourselves to these imperatives, encouraging all the participants to do so.

Hermoupolis, 7 September AD 2019

[118] First World Meeting of Popular Movements, 2014.
[119] Second World Meeting of Popular Movements, 2015.

What does it Mean to Govern in the Times of Covid-19?

A reflected experience from Colombia

Javier Andrés Baquero Maldonado[120]

Every morning you open your eyes to face the pain of death, disease and poverty. You are aware that the lives of 7 million people may depend on your actions and decisions. You visualize each person who loses their relatives over two weeks due to COVID-19 without even managing to say goodbye; you are aware of each citizen who does not have the resources to pay for a home during the quarantine and their children go hungry; you are aware of the people who lost their jobs due to the economic crisis, the company that closed. The days pass between hopelessness and faith for every member of the government working on the solutions in a city in crisis.

The world has faced the first truly global crisis and has demanded that governments and leaders take the lead to face it. However, this process is highly complex and has different impacts in each society. In this article I present an analysis of the experience of the Bogotá government from a particular perspective since I found myself part of the government team in the city. Firstly, I present the context, and secondly, I share some dilemmas regarding policy prioritization. Thirdly, I analyze the forms of administration. Finally, I consider the role of people and their relationships in this process.

---

[120] Public policy advisor to the Housing Secretariat of the Bogotá Mayor's Office, university professor of public policy, director of the Colombian Observatory of Public Policy and Secretary General of the International Political Movement for Unity.

Brief Context of the Bogotá - Colombia Case

Colombia is a country with a considerably new democracy compared to Europe. Since 1810 it has been a democratic state, consolidated after more than 300 years of colonization. This young democracy has the peculiarity of being immersed in various internal wars, initially due to differences on matters of the organization of the nation-state, then due to partisan divisions. Since the 1960s a guerrilla war was fought by far-right militias and the state military force. All this together left more than 8 million internally displaced people and more than 200 thousand dead, to which was then added the violence produced by the production and trafficking of drugs since the 80's.

In this context, Bogotá in particular, has not suffered directly or on a large scale from the violence of the country beyond some terrorist attacks and the fact that this city is receiving the highest amount of population displaced by violence (near 700 thousand people). The capital city has an institutional stability that has allowed it to have alternative center-left governments.

In the last 2019 elections, the Green Party made up of center and center-left politicians decided to nominate a woman for mayor of Bogotá, a member of the LGTB community, who had been an academic and a congresswoman. She has faced and uncovered major corruption cases in the country, particularly, the connection between Congress and right-wing armed groups allied to win elections and retain political control over certain regions through the use of violence.

The Green Party won the elections in alliance with one of the longest standing left parties running the country and began its administration on January 1, 2020. She was the first woman elected to the second highest office in the country (after the presidency).

Bogotá is a city of more than 7 million inhabitants. However ' with the metropolitan area the population increases considerably. Before the pandemic crisis 2.5% were under the extreme monetary poverty line (4.3% based in multidimensional poverty) and the 12% below the monetary poverty and a Gini coefficient of 0.504.

This reality was exacerbated by COVID 19 as many companies had to close thereby generating an increase in unemployment from 10.5% in December 2019 to 21.4% in July 2020. The situation is even more complicated due to the higher percentage of informal jobs which are particularly vulnerable to the crisis.

Care at the Center of the Government's Agenda and Its Dilemmas.

To govern is to choose to solve problems including finding the way to do it. It is a process that is dynamic in time and determined by multiple factors, which generates dilemmas among various social issues, objectives and conflicts between actors. Its fundamental legitimacy lies in the concept of *res publica or* public affairs. In a more emphatic way, it is often referred to as a public good, collective interest or public happiness (Donolo, 2012, p. 10).

The priorities of a government and a city are reflected in the government agenda specified in many political instruments such as the development of a government plan and budget. Time also reflects the prioritization in the framework of the dedication of institutional efforts, media attention and public debate. Given the scarce economic, organizational, political and media resources available, priority must be given to the issues that truly matter. This is what Schattschneider evidenced when referring back to the scheduling process in 1960.

> 'All forms of political organization are biased in favor of the exploitation of certain types of conflicts and the overcoming of others, since organization means mobilization of biases. Some issues are organized within a political context while others are organized outside of it [. . .] There is no more certain way to destroy the meaning of politics than to treat all matters as if they were free and equal. The inequality of the issues simplifies the interpretation of the policy. Politics makes sense when we are clear about our priorities.' (71-73)[121]

It does not seem to be a permanent dilemma on the governments' agenda: 'life or economy'. But it is often evident that the achievement of macroeconomic stability, growth and productivity have largely determined the agenda of governments, along with taking care of human life and the planet in general. This is how human beings die from hunger in the world or society although there are food and resources to solve this problem, with-

---

[121] All quotations are free translations from the original texts in Spanish and Italian.

out mentioning wars and the impact on lives of all illegal economic activity. Pope Francis exhorted in Evangelii Gaudium number 53 in this regard:

> 'Just as the commandment "Thou shalt not kill" sets a clear limit in order to safeguard the value of human life, today we also have to say "thou shalt not" to an economy of exclusion and inequality. Such an economy kills. How can it be that it is not a news item when an elderly homeless person dies of exposure, but it is news when the stock market loses two points? This is a case of exclusion. Can we continue to stand by when food is thrown away while people are starving? This is a case of inequality. Today everything comes under the laws of competition and the survival of the fittest, where the powerful feed upon the powerless. As a consequence, masses of people find themselves excluded and marginalized: without work, without possibilities, without any means of escape.
>
> Human beings are themselves considered consumer goods to be used and then discarded. We have created a "throw away" culture which is now spreading. It is no longer simply about exploitation and oppression, but something new. Exclusion ultimately has to do with what it means to be a part of the society in which we live; those excluded are no longer society's underside or its fringes or its disenfranchised – they are no longer even a part of it. The excluded are not the "exploited" but the outcast, the "leftovers".'

This has not been an exception in our context given that social distancing is the only effective way to prevent the impact of COVID-19 on health, which brings into evidence the dilemma of whether to stop the economy to go to quarantine. In Colombia, this trade-off between economic stability and public health has been a subject of an ongoing debate between the national government and the city government, since the national government has prioritized the economic effects of the quarantine and the government of Bogotá the effects on public health. In this context, Löwy recognizes 'different types' of problems will give rise to 'different types of politics' (Parsons, 1995, p. 118).

Faced with economic problems and giving priority to economic reactivation, the national government has promoted measures such as decreeing some days off from the consumer tax, encouraging massive purchases in public establishments, which generated large crowds in the most important stores. In the same way, the national government issued decrees to reactivate certain sectors of the economy for the entire country which has impacted large cities since the use of public transportation and shopping have considerably increased the rate of contagion, and therefore deaths. Finally, the economic measures that have been taken to a large extent have focused on the stability of the financial sector and the most relevant and formal economic sectors.

The city government has been cautious in its measures to reactivate the economy, prioritizing the care of citizens, quarantine measures, distancing and supporting the health system to prevent its collapse. Although the district government initially had transportation, education, reduction of poverty and gender as its priorities; the COVID emergency changed the agenda to *care.* As Toro affirmed in 2014 'Within the current global context of the planet and of societies, care is and will be the new organizing and guiding paradigm for politics, science, economics, business, aesthetics, everyday life. ... ' (p. 4). This recalls L. Boff's arguments:

> 'When we love we care and when we care we love. Care constitutes the central category of the new paradigm of civilization that seems to emerge throughout the world. Care takes on the dual role of preventing future damage and regenerating past damage.'

Likewise, decisions had been made affecting the economy at first due to the lack of the health system's capacity. Several total and partial quarantine measures were declared. For instance, the national government was asked to close the airport and the roads to avoid the increase of contagion rates.

This has involved great challenges to guarantee the basic needs of the most vulnerable population. Efforts have been made to identify this poorest population and the *Bogotá Solidaria en Casa* strategy was implemented to promote the care of vulnerable households through cash transfers providing a basic income for more than 550 thousand households; other measures implemented were the distribution of about 1 million food baskets, the allocation of 30 thousand grants for rent payment, discounts in public services, universal health care regardless of the particular health insurance system; and finally subsidies for the cremation of COVID-19 corpses.

The quarantine has drastically increased domestic violence against women. Therefore, women's housing and rental subsidies were set up. Poor people have been infected and have died at a higher rate given their need to generate income leading them to expose themselves. Besides they live in more overcrowded homes, with limited resources for care. So new alternatives for distancing had to be considered.

Despite the efforts of the government of Bogotá, these measures would not have been enough to help the number of vulnerable households in the city in a sustainable way. These measures recognize the difficulties that the quarantines have generated, but they also make more evident the high vulnerability in which the current economic system places a large part of the population as a result of the high poverty and inequality prevailing in the country.

Co-governance to Overcome the Crisis

Given the context described above, it is very complex to govern a city the size of Bogotá, affected by a pandemic. This is even more so given the uncertainty of a crisis where every decision is an act of acupuncture so delicate that each decision can activate or deactivate a nerve to the point of determining reactions in the system.

The liberal reforms in Latin-American gave a reduced role to governments in managing public affairs, leading to the dismantling of the state apparatus with the idea that they are very costly, inefficient and large. So many of the services provided by the state before 1980 have been privatized. This is the case with health, education and housing, promoting a governance system that delegates many public issues to the market, with the thought that it would be more efficient and effective.

The emergency situation produced by the coronavirus has shown the important role that politics, the state and governments have to play in the direct coordination and management of public problems. Politics plays a central role in guaranteeing the common good, which is why not everything can be delegated to the market, to the logic of supply, demand, economic efficiency, profitability and the capacity to pay.

Despite the fact that a good part of the health services are provided by private companies in Colombia, in the face of the emergency the State regained control of the entire health system to guarantee universal care for all citizens. Likewise, it defined and provided mechanisms for direct marketing of products between farmers and consumers in the city, for systems managed directly by public bodies, to ensure the food security and fair payments to farmers.

Additionally, the State restricted free movement, as well as free production and commercialization, generating controls and conditions so that companies could start activities with a level of control over compliance with biosecurity protocols.

However, since the government has failed to respond fully effectively to all the problems, the population suffers the consequences of the pandemic and the costs of bureaucratic inefficiency. Even though the government is monitoring the effects in real time, aid arrives with some delay which could be frustrating for decision-makers.

To be part of the government team implies being aware of people's pain and our inability as rulers to completely solve these problems. In particular, I had the opportunity to meet the citizens most affected by the quarantine, who take to the streets to protest because they find it difficult to obtain food or pay rent. I am aware of the Government's inability to respond to so many needs effectively and promptly. And although we have not caused the pandemic, we do become those responsible for the inefficiency in achieving results despite the best political will to face the emergency. There has been a learning curve to operate new services and functions due to the pandemic; the government especially did not have the operational capacity to respond; it has had to acquire this capacity in the process.

However, this *emergency government* model is politically, economically and socially unsustainable, which is why the proposal for collaborative governance or co-governance has taken on greater force. We are all co-responsible for our present and future with a central role for civic culture. But this requires the commitment of the private sector and academia in coordination with the state. In a particular way, Prats describes this new way of governing

> 'as relational government or networks for public-private-civil interaction along the local/global axis… The interactive, relational nature of the new way of governing is conceptualized as 'network management', with the observation that the government is not just another actor in the network, given that it is the only participant that has the characteristic of representation and democratic authority for its society, but its incorporation requires specific networks of public interest and a more complex managerial role of entrepreneur, facilitator, mediator, negotiator, arbitrator and formulator depending on the circumstances … ' (2004, p. 31).

Civic culture is referred as the,

> '... background of meaning that regulates citizen behavior, to the extent that it establishes minimum standards that make citizens' relationships with each other and with their environment possible, as well as the production, circulation, recognition, appropriation and reception of this universe of meaning by them, including the civil servants' (Barbero 1987, p. 227).

Thus, the civic culture of care refers to the sense that I give to mutual responsibility for care, in which I am responsible not only for whether I am infected, but also for infecting others, our loved ones. Therefore, we must self-restrict encounters, keep distances, always use elements for protection appropriately, in such a way that care depends on the way each and every citizen behaves.

Besides, we find co-responsibility among the various governments: Bogotá, the metropolitan area and the central government. It is important to state that the political parties in these areas could be in disagreement. There has been effective coordination between the government of Bogotá and the governments of neighboring cities, which has made it possible to restrict and control mobility, universalize the right to health and promote economic exchange.

Taking into consideration the warning made by Ropelato that governance 'grafts itself in the search for new forms of regulation in the network, in a position to manage increasingly decentralized, fragmented and complex political scenarios' (Ropelato, D. 2006, p. 194), it is also understood that coordination and harmonization of decisions is critical in this time of crisis. In practice this work has not been easy overall between the local government of the city and the national government. Conflicting decisions have been made between the two governments and dialogue failed to avoid major mistakes in handling the crisis. This has shown the high cost of resolving political conflicts with partial criteria and not with a comprehensive, complete vision of the common good.

Finally, there has been a virtuous collaboration with the private sector and the academy. Despite the high economic costs, the city's entrepreneurs have been aware of the situation in which the city finds itself. Firms have accepted most quarantines, acknowledging that economic recovery requires them to make efforts to implement biosecurity protocols. Additionally, several businesses have assumed the costs of keeping their workers' jobs even with operations stopped, but what has surprised the city the most is the solidarity they have shown in the substantial donations they have made to generate hospital emergency care and social assistance.

Meanwhile, citizens have maintained a responsible tax culture, making their tax payments and helping to maintain the city's budget.

In this sense, liberal governance has not made it possible to overcome the crisis, but it is clear that a governance model dependent solely on the ability of the state to solve all the problems is inadequate to deal with the complexity of the COVID crisis. Thus, collaborative governance is the model that allows effective results, sustainability and responsibility, so that each one is part of the solution. Nevertheless, it is important that government generates trust, legitimacy, dialogue, openness and respect for each of the actors, not putting the government network at risk as a consequence.

People and Relationships Are the Key

Structural and institutional factors have been given great weight historically in the strategies or methods to build and promote social change. Therefore, all faith has been put in institutional systems and arrangements since this is a particular vision of economists, politicians, lawyers and bureaucrats.

However, the management of this pandemic has shown that it is people and their relationships that determine the outcome of governments, since it depends on the ethics and responsibility of decision-makers and the behavior of the leaders and of the various actors.

This is very evident in certain countries guided by 'maternal governments' as described by Del Percio in his article of June 14, 2020 in the newspaper El Perfil de Argentina. Leaders such as Merkel, Ardern, Marin or Tsai have put care at the center, in contrast with compulsive males like Donald Trump, Boris Johnson or Bolsonaro. This is only a small indicator of the importance of the people who are in decision-making spaces and who are highly responsible for their actions.

However, as the tasks not only depend on the leaders but on all people who are part of the government, it is an unusual challenge, particularly in Bogota, to ensure that all public servants feel the pain of every person and seek the best solutions. Every public servant needs to develop the ability to be empathetic, to be able to see through a citizen's eyes with the love that he sees his children, to act towards their well-being, without fostering dependency, but maturity and freedom, and always with dignity.

Change cannot be brought about if those governing cannot experience the feeling of complete abandonment in all its dimensions and expressions; this is the pain of those who suffer because of injustice, of those who lost a certain quality of life or have never had it. If it is not possible to live the experience of abandonment and thus experience the inability of a government that finds it difficult to respond to the challenges of each moment, there is not enough motivation to govern for the common good and cooperate socially.

It is so that people who are behind a desk deciding matters, who must have the integrity and ability to feel this in order to verify a government's representativeness. For example, silencing a social protest that demands a better quality of life using police force is an act of ignorance of otherness and the pain of those who are on the street demanding their rights. Social dialogue must overcome the vision of enmity between the state and social movements, because a government has the responsibility not only to decide and act, but to listen, dialogue and agree, even in times of crisis.

In Bogotá we have not been able to resolve all the pain, but by embracing the pain of citizens with empathy, by apologizing for the lack of effective responses, it has allowed us to experience something more than that pain. Little by little, some communities which protested earlier have also identified the limitations of the government as a result of the dialogue; they have understood the efforts and have contributed to solving the problems.

Finally, it is equally important to recognize that the rulers are also under high political, media, social and judicial pressure, which leads to high levels of stress, frustration and exhaustion. This also requires a degree of reciprocity on the part of the citizenry. It is evident that interpersonal relationships among members of the government give strength. They are fundamentally important in times of crisis.

We must identify new political categories as Edgar Morin does in the text 'Introduction to a Politics of Man' when saying that:

> 'Love... must irrigate humanity's goal and path in the world. Man must return to the great mysterious, cosmic spring to start his journey again, like a

> Nile that fertilizes human work... ... this duty has never ceased to sprout from hope, from human hope.' (Morin., E. 2002, p. 45)

Conclusion

In Bogotá, even with all these sufferings, despite the increase in COVID-19 infections and deaths, the care of people has been at the center of decisions over the economic consequences. However, the most important thing we achieved is to partly disinfect society of selfishness and recognize that we are co- responsible for taking care of each other, recognizing that rulers aren't solely responsible, that we are all responsible for everyone. We all become politicians when we leave ourselves to embrace the pain in the other (person or people).

Thus, a government that feels and takes charge of the suffering of its people is capable of making love a daily political practice; taking care of the city, the country, humanity, the planet; losing everything to go out to meet others even in the midst of the experience of hopelessness.

To conclude, it is worth remembering the following words from Chiara Lubich at the '1000 Cities for Europe' European Congress in Innsbruck (Austria), on November 9, 2001, widening our political vision to a universal horizon:

> '... The idea of the "human family" made possible by universal brotherhood in action. Consequently, he destroyed the walls that separate those who are "the same" from those who are "different," friends from enemies, walls that isolate one city from another. And he loosened the bonds that imprison people in so many ways, from the thousands of forms of suppression and slavery, from every unjust relationship. In this way he brought about an authentic existential, cultural and political revolution.'

Three
Challenges to Deepen the Dialogue

Prospects of the RESET Project

José Manuel Pureza[122]

Perhaps exclusion is the most striking feature of the time we are living in. In Europe and the world, the striving for a social peace that resulted in political peace – in which a broad social contract, based on the recognition of social rights and the provision of universal public services, played a fundamental role – has given way to aggressive social Darwinist policies, especially affecting the poorest and most socially vulnerable.

For a long time, the Church's Social Doctrine, through the luminous texts of successive Popes, has underlined the existence of structures of sin that determine a profound social disruption. These texts evidence an unmistakably critical view of the individualist and materialist anthropology that endorses competition, while slighting an ethic of brotherhood and a seriously demanding spirituality. These pronouncements of the Church, so often ignored inside and outside it, have never ceased to criticize two negative dynamics brought about by the functioning of the capitalist economy: on the one hand, a devaluation of labor and associated direct and indirect rights, and the indulgence of capital and its prerogatives on the other hand, a growing irresponsibility in the administration of goods, breaching the fundamental principle of the universal destiny of goods and paving the way to the collapse of our Common Home by way of an unprecedented environmental crisis and unpredictable future.

[122] Professor of the University of Coimbra, Portugal. Member of the Portuguese parliament.

By stating loudly and clearly that 'this economy kills' and that the priority of our time is 'to hear [. . .] the cry of the poor', Pope Francis calls upon all humanity to radically change mode of life and social and economic organization. He does so clearly and with an unprecedented call for inclusion. If several previous Popes' encyclicals were addressed 'to all men and women of good will', the texts of Francis do so in a particularly pronounced way. All those who realize that the pillaging of land and of the poor, fueled by an economic system that exploits people and resources, are the main affront to people's dignity are called upon to come together around a different ethic that encourages a different policy.

The dialogue between Christians and Marxists is a fitting response to this call. Faced with social Darwinism and ecological irresponsibility, Christians and Marxists are called on to nourish public discourse and policies with substantial arguments for solidarity, justice, and common responsibility. This is a huge challenge, and it is why the first DIALOP summer course in Syros has been a landmark in the common search for bridges and complementarities between Christians and Marxists on very concrete issues like democracy, the commons, or the European project. The texts gathered in this book show how fruitful the building of bridges between Christians and Marxists experienced in that beautiful Greek island was and how it opened so many windows for further reflection and common action in favor of the poor who cry out to us. It is clear, that in valuing commons as goods and resources that require common management aimed at the common good, in critically assessing the path taken by the European project, and in the awareness that the prevailing policies of competitiveness and exclusion destroy any horizon of peace and progress for Europe, or even in the understanding that democracy, to be sturdy, requires resolute policies that valorize work, struggle against poverty, and aim at the inclusion of all peripheries – in all this we were able to see a concrete space of convergence and complementarity between concerns and hopes, but also between conceptions of politics, those of Christian and Marxist.

After this first step at Syros, the search for convergences and this project of common presence in public space animated by transversal ethics has to be deepened. I believe this project's next step must be to propose a corpus of transversal ethics able to influence the public discussion around individual and collective liberation, around different types of obstacles to it, and convergent changes that enable it. I will very briefly indicate three obstacles and three changes.

The first obstacle is alienation. For Marxism, one of the consequences of the capitalist mode of production is how it deprives the worker of the ability to think of himself as directing his own actions. Alienation is the result of the lack of working class consciousness, itself expressing the transformation of workers from people into objects of production. Central to the Marxist concept of alienation is, therefore, the distortion of self-awareness and reality caused by devices of representation of this reality that serve the interests of the ruling class. Among these devices, perhaps the most important is fetishization, that is, the idolatry of goods and money. As well in the Church's social Teaching as in broader Christian thought, the idolatry of money and goods is referred to as a departure from the kind of life committed to the building of the Kingdom of God. 'Only if we discover, that our true wealth is relations and not merely material goods will we find alternative ways to live and inhabit a society that is not governed by the god of money, an idol that deludes and leaves it increasingly inhuman and unjust, and also, I would say, poorer', Pope Francis said in an audience with members of the Confederation of Italian Cooperatives.

The answer to this obstacle to liberation is the adoption of critical thinking that refocuses each person on the essentials of personal and collective existence. Christians have a word for this refocusing: metanoia, conversion. It supposes a profound inner change, something Leonardo Boff epitomised with particular felicitousness in this expression: 'a new optic for a new ethic'. He writes: 'The current ethic is predatory, irresponsible, individualistic, perverse towards others, treated with dissymmetry and injustice in the processes of production, distribution and compensation. It is cruel and merciless to the vast majority of living beings, human and nonhuman. Finally, it threatens the future of the biosphere and the human project. To overcome this highly destructive ethics of the future of humanity and planet Earth, we must start from another perspective. Only a new optic can generate a new ethic" (Boff, L. 2013). It is essentially this change of optic toward a new ethic, which is intended by critical Marxist thinking. In the elaborations of the Frankfurt School, above all, the rescue of the modern ideal of emancipation appears articulated with the notion that there is no neutral knowledge and that the subjective optics of each person is determining for his/her knowledge of reality. From a knowledge made of a worship of the facts one must move, from the Marxist perspective, to a knowledge committed to the transformation of facts. A new optic, thus, for a new ethic.

The second obstacle to liberation is the hegemony of individualism. The ethos of individualism and competitiveness is, for Marxist thinking, inherent in capitalism's 'way of life'. A mystified individualism prevails in the case of the ruling class because the self-made entrepreneur is, after all, someone whose triumph is the result of the consolidation of relations of exploitation vis-à-vis many others. A mystified individualism prevails also in the case of workers, because in capitalist society everything (including one's identity) is deeply conditioned by exchange relations that distort human relations and transform them into mere market relations.

This individualistic ethos is also viewed critically by the Church's social Teaching. It is true that this critical pronouncement at times has the mark of nostalgia for premodern communitarianism. Yet in Pope Francis, for example, the critique of individualism is not confused with a reactive bitterness against modernity. Since brotherhood is the existential and social condition of the Christian, Francis sees the reigning individualism as a factor in disrupting these fundamental relations: 'The individualism of our postmodern and globalized era favors a lifestyle which weakens the development and stability of personal relationships and distorts family bonds' (EG 67). The existential emptiness that results from this isolation feeds the consumerist fetishism with which the self-referential individual intends to fill the absence of relational meaning in his life. 'When people become self-centered and self-enclosed, their greed increases. The emptier a person's heart is, the more he or she needs things to buy, own and consume. It becomes almost impossible to accept the limits imposed by reality. In this horizon, a genuine sense of the common good also disappears' (LS 204).

Against this culture of exclusionary and proprietary individualism, Marxists and Christians affirm the primacy of solidarity and collective action. Francis writes: 'Disinterested concern for others, and the rejection of every form of self-centeredness and self-absorption, are essential if we truly wish to care for our brothers and sisters and for the natural environment. These attitudes also attune us to the moral imperative of assessing the impact of our every action and personal decision on the world around us. If we can overcome individualism, we will truly be able to develop a different lifestyle and bring about significant changes in society'(LS 208). The same requirement to break with isolated egocentrism is affirmed by Marxist thought. Solidarity is the fundamental ethic of the workers' movement, according to which workers are supposed to support the struggles of all other oppressed. This was reflected in the justification of the creation of the International: 'All efforts aiming at the great end hitherto failed from the want of solidarity between the manifold divisions of labor in each country, and from the absence of a fraternal bond of union between the working classes of different countries; [. . .] For these reasons – The International Working Men's Association has been founded'. (Marx, K. 1988, pp. 3-4). Solidarity among workers has its most singular expression in internationalism, and it transposes the critique of individualism to a higher level, that of the critique of national rivalries. International solidarity appears in Marxism not as an expression of an idealistic conception of justice, selflessness, or humanitarianism which results in 'being a good person', but rather as the recognition that each worker has a stake in the outcome of each other's struggle.

Finally, the third obstacle to individual and collective liberation I want to refer to is poor spirituality. I believe that poor spirituality was at the heart of the well-known Marxist accusation that religion is the opium of the people. Marx referred to a religion not only detached from concrete struggles for concrete dignity, but moreover, discouraging all the energies that lead to those struggles. Awareness of the alienating nature of such a religion leads Pope Francis to criticize 'the spiritual life [which] comes to be identified with a few religious exercises which can offer a certain comfort, but which do not encourage encounter with others, engagement with the world or a passion for evangelization' (EG, 78). It moves away from lived religion by becoming a 'form of a spiritual consumerism tailored to one's own unhealthy individualism' (EG, 89).

In contrast to this alienating spirituality, individual and collective emancipation requires a spirituality embodied in history, which considers the spirit within its structural conditioning. In Claudio Perani's words, '[t]raditionally the spirit was related to the 'heart' of man and not to the structures of society, considered as a mere setting of human actions; today it is recognized that everything that has to do with the spirit is closely related to the present social situation, the mode of economic production, the political regime [. . .]. If such structural and ideological mechanisms are not understood, rather than reflecting the word of God, one runs the risk of being an unconscious mouthpiece of the ruling class's ideas [. . .]. The new spirituality appears as the ability to make the contribution of scientific reflection and theological reflection converge in an existential unity, where economic and political contents are considered as crucial' (Perani, C. 1980, pp. 62-72).

These three obstacles to individual and collective liberation – alienation, individualism, and poor spirituality – and the answers to them – critical thinking, solidarity, and liberating spirituality – are undeniable challenges to the new stage of dialogue between Marxists and Christians. What is required of them is that they realize that the bridges between their ways of thinking and acting are crucial to transforming the concrete lives of men and women. And that their complementarity is much more important and useful than the differences that set them apart.

The Preferential Option for the Poor

A Key Criterion of Christian Authenticity

Pope Francis

General Audience, August 19th, 2020

Dear brothers and sisters, good day!

The pandemic has exposed the plight of the poor and the great inequality that reigns in the world. And the virus, while it does not distinguish between people, has found, in its devastating path, great inequalities and discrimination. And it has exacerbated them!

The response to the pandemic is therefore dual. On the one hand, it is essential to find a cure for this small but terrible virus, which has brought the whole world to its knees. On the other, we must also cure a larger virus, that of social injustice, inequality of opportunity, marginalisation, and the lack of protection for the weakest. In this dual response for healing there is a choice that, according to the Gospel, cannot be lacking: the preferential option for the poor (see EG, 195). And this is not a political option; nor is it an ideological option, a party option… no. The preferential option for the poor is at the centre of the Gospel. And the first to do this was Jesus; we heard this in the reading from the Letter to the Corinthians which was read at the beginning. Since He was rich, He made Himself poor to enrich us. He made Himself one of us and for this reason, at the centre of the Gospel, there is this option, at the centre of Jesus' proclamation.

Christ Himself, Who is God, despoiled Himself, making Himself similar to men; and he chose not a life of privilege, but he chose the condition of a servant (cf. Phil 2:6-7). He annihilated Himself by making Himself a servant. He was born into a humble family and worked as a craftsman. At the beginning of His preaching, He announced that in the Kingdom of God the poor are blessed (cf. Mt 5:3; Lk 6:20; EG, 197). He stood among the sick, the poor, the excluded, showing them God's merciful love (cf. CCC, 2444). And many times He was judged an impure man because He went to the sick, to lepers ... and this made people impure, according to the law of the age. And He took risks to be near to the poor.

Therefore, Jesus' followers recognise themselves by their closeness to the poor, the little ones, the sick and the imprisoned, the excluded and the forgotten, those without food and clothing (cf. Mt 25:31-36; CCC, 2443). We can read that famous protocol by which we will all be judged, we will all be judged. It is Matthew, chapter 25. This is a key criterion of Christian authenticity (cf. Gal 2:10; EG 195). Some mistakenly think that this preferential love for the poor is a task for the few, but in reality it is the mission of the Church as a whole, as Saint John Paul II said. (cf. SRS 42). 'Each individual Christian and every community is called to be an instrument of God for the liberation and promotion of the poor society'. (EG 187).

Faith, hope and love necessarily push us towards this preference for those most in need,[123] which goes beyond necessary assistance (cf. EG 198). Indeed it implies walking together, letting ourselves be evangelised by them, who know the suffering Christ well, letting ourselves be 'infected' by their experience of salvation, by their wisdom and by their creativity (see ibid.).

Sharing with the poor means mutual enrichment. And, if there are unhealthy social structures that prevent them from dreaming of the future, we must work together to heal them, to change them (see ibid, 195). And we are led to this by the love of Christ, Who loved us to the extreme (see Jn 13:1), and reaches the boundaries, the margins, the existential frontiers. Bringing the peripheries to the centre means focusing our life on Christ, Who 'made Himself poor' for us, to enrich us 'by His poverty' (2 Cor 8:9),[124]Benedict XVI, Address at the Inaugural Session of the Fifth General Conference of the Bishops of Latin America and the Caribbean (13 May 2007). as we have heard.

---

[123] See Congregation for the Doctrine of the Faith, Instruction on some aspects of 'Liberation Theology', (1984), chap. V.

[124]

We are all worried about the social consequences of the pandemic. All of us. Many people want to return to normality and resume economic activities. Certainly, but this 'normality' should not include social injustices and the degradation of the environment. The pandemic is a crisis, and we do not emerge from a crisis the same as before: either we come out of it better, or we come out of it worse. We must come out of it better, to counter social injustice and environmental damage.

Today we have an opportunity to build something different. For example, we can nurture an economy of the integral development of the poor, and not of providing assistance. By this I do not wish to condemn assistance: aid is important. I am thinking of the voluntary sector, which is one of the best structures of the Italian Church. Yes, aid does this, but we must go beyond this, to resolve the problems that lead us to provide aid. An economy that does not resort to remedies that in fact poison society, such as profits not linked to the creation of dignified jobs (see EG 204). This type of profit is dissociated from the real economy, that which should bring benefits to the common people (see Encyclical Laudato si' [LS] 109), and in addition is at times indifferent to the damage inflicted to our common home. The preferential option for the poor, this ethical-social need that comes from God's love (cf. LS 158), inspires us to conceive of and design an economy where people, and especially the poorest, are at the centre. And it also encourages us to plan the treatment of viruses by prioritising those who are most in need. It would be sad if, for the vaccine for Covid-19, priority were to be given to the richest! It would be sad if this vaccine were to become the property of this nation or another, rather than universal and for all. And what a scandal it would be if all the economic assistance we are observing – most of it with public money – were to focus on rescuing those industries that do not contribute to the inclusion of the excluded, the promotion of the least, the common good or the care of creation (ibid.). There are criteria for choosing which industries should be helped: those which contribute to the inclusion of the excluded, to the promotion of the last, to the common good and the care of creation. Four criteria.

If the virus were to intensify again in a world that is unjust to the poor and vulnerable, then we must change this world. Following the example of Jesus, the doctor of integral divine love, that is, of physical, social and spiritual healing (cf. Jn 5:6-9) – like the healing worked by Jesus – we must act now, to heal the epidemics caused by small, invisible viruses, and to heal those caused by the great and visible social injustices. I propose that this be done by starting from the love of God, placing the peripheries at the centre and the last in first place. Do not forget that protocol by which we will be judged, Matthew, chapter 25. Let us put it into practice in this recovery from the epidemic. And starting from this tangible love – as the Gospel says, there – anchored in hope and founded in faith, a healthier world will be possible. Otherwise, we will come out of the crisis worse. May the Lord help us and give us the strength to come out of it better, responding to the needs of today's world. Thank you.

Bibliography

Abbreviations for papal documents:

CA: St. John Paul II, Centesimus annus
CCC: Catechism of the Catholic Church
CDSC: Compendium of the Social Doctrine of the Church
CIV: Pope Benedict XVI., Caritas in veritate
EG: Pope Francis Apostolic Exhortation Evangelii gaudium,
EV: St. John Paul II, Evangelium vitae
GE: Pope Francis, Gaudete et exsultate
GS: II.Vatican Council, Gaudium et spes,
LE: St. John Paul II, Laborem exercens
LF: Pope Francis, Lumen fidei
MM: St. John XXIII., Mater et Magistra
PT: St. John XXIII., Pacem in terris
RN: Pope Leon XIII, Rerum Novarum
SRS: St. John Paul II, Sollicitudo rei socialis
VG: Pope Francis. Veritatis gaudium
VS: St. John Paul II, Veritatis splendor

Alston, W. (2000). *Illocutionary Acts and Sentence Meaning,* Ithaca and London: Cornell University Press.

Altvater, E. (2013). *Wachstum, Globalisierung, Anthropozän. Steigerungsformen einer zerstörerischen Wirtschaftsweise*, retrieved from: http://www.emanzipation.org/?q=ema_3-1

An-Na'im, A.A. (2008). *Islam and the Secular State: Negotiating the Future of Shari'a,* Cambridge: Harvard University Press.

An-Na'im, A.A. (2009). *Islam and the Secular State: Framework for Christian-Muslim Relations*. In: PISAI Islamochristiana n. 35.

Anderson, B. (2006). (Revised edition). *Imagined Communities: Reflections on the Origin and Spread of Nationalism*, London, NY: Verso.

Anderson, P. (2011). *Le Nouveau Vieux Monde,* Marseille: Agone.

Augustinus, (2019). *Confessions*, retrieved from: http://www.newadvent.org/fathers/110101.htm

Austin, J. L. (1962). *How to Do Things with Words*, Cambridge MA.

Baggio, A.M. (1980). *Da Marx a Cristo: L'itinerario intellettuale di un marxista*, Roma: Città Nuova.

Baier, W. and Muhri, F. (Eds.). (2001). *Stalinismus und die Rehabilitierung österreichischer Opfer*, Vienna: Globus Verlag.

Baier, W., Sello, L. (Eds.) (2018). *Europe as a common – let's think about it. Textbook for the Syros Summer School 2018*, DIALOP.

Bauer, J. (2010). *Das kooperative Gen. Evolution als kreativer Prozess,* München: Heyne Verlag.

Bauman, Z. (2008). *Does Ethics Have a Chance in a World of Consumers?*, Harvard University Press, Bildungsteam Berlin-Brandenburg e.V., retrieved from: http://www.baustein.dgb-bwt.de/PDF/C1-BilderImKopf.pdf (accessed: 02.09.2019), Cambridge, London.

Beck, U. (2016). *The Metamorphosis of the World: How Climate Change is Transforming Our Concept of the World*, Cambridge: Polity Press.

Bekemans, L. (2012). *Education for European Citizenship-building.* In: Globalisation vs Europeanisation. A Human-centric Interaction, Brussels: P.I.E. Peter Lang.

Bekemans, L. (2013a). *Globalisation vs Europeanisation: A Human-centric Interaction*, Brussel, Bern, Berlin, New York: P.I.E. Peter Lang.

Bekemans, L. (2013b). *Building Urban Civitas in intercultural dialogue and spiritual spaces.* In: Globalisation vs. Europeanisation: A Human-centric Interaction, International Academic, Brussels, Berlin, Bern: P.I.E. Peter Lang

Bekemans, L. (2018a). *Citizens' Participation and Participatory Governance in the EU*. In: Studies in European Affairs, Rok 22, Number 4.

Bekemans, L. (2018b). *The Future of Education, in a (drastically) changing Europe*. In: Foreign Policy Review, Institute for Foreign Affairs and Trade.

Bekemans, L. and de la Torre, V. M. (2018c). *Schuman's concept of European Community: what lessons for Europe's future?*. In: Modelling the new Europe, No. 28.

Bertolini, R. (Ed.) (2012). *Allmende Vorarlberg. Von der Kraft des gemeinsamen Tuns*. Bregenz: Bertolini Verlag.

Bertoncini, Y. (2017). *Differentiated Integration and the EU: A Variable Geometry Legitimacy*. In: EU60, Re-founding Europe: The Responsibility to propose, Istituto Affari Internazionali: Rome.

Betz, H. D. (1994). *The Birth of Christianity as a Hellenistic Religion: Three Theories of Origin*, Journal of Religion 74, The University of Chicago: Press Journal.

Boff, L. (2013). *Como nasce a ética?*, retrieved from: https://www.ethos.org.br/cedoc/como-nasce-a-etica/#.Xez7Gej7SM8

Bohm, D. (1996). *On dialogue*, New York: L. Nichol

Bollier, D. (2014). *Think like a Commoner*, Gabriola Islands: New Society Publishers.

Bosworth, A.B. (1998). *Conquest and Empire, the Reign of Alexander the Great*, Cambridge: University Press.

Brady, T. A. (1935). *The Reception of the Egyptian Cults by the Greeks (130-30 B.C.)*, Columbia, Mass.

Brie M. and Thomasberger C. (Eds) (2018). *Karl* Polanyi's *Vision of a Socialist Transformation,* Montreal: Black Rose Books.

Buber, M. (1973). *Das dialogische Prinzip*, Heidelberg: Lambert Schneider.

Buber, M. (1982). *Das Problem des Menschen.* Heidelberg: Lambert Schneider.

Bulloch, A., Gruen, E. S., Long, A.A. & Stewart A. (Eds.) (1993). *Images and Ideologies: Self-Definition in the Hellenistic World,* Berkeley.

Butts, M. (1994). *The Macedonian: Scenes from the Life of Cleopatra*, Kingston, NY: McPherson & Company.

Callebaut, B. (2017). *La nascita dei Focolari: storia e sociologia di un carisma*, Roma: Città Nuova.

Cartledge, P. (2004). *Alexander the Great: The truth behind the myth*, Pan Mc. Millan.

Castellina, L. (2016). *Manuale Antiretorico dell'Unione Europea: Da dove viene (e dove va) quest'Europa*, Manifestolibri, Roma: La Talpa.

Coda, P. (2018). *For a Nonviolent Style of Thinking*. In: Transform Yearbook 2018.

Coda, P. (2017/1). *La trinità come pensiero: Un manifesto*. In: Sophia IX

Coda, P. (2017/1-2). *The Unity of reciprocal love: The charism of Chiara Lubich and the theology of Klaus Hemmerle*. In: International Journal of philosophy and Theology, Vol. 78. 155-171.

Coda, P. (2017). *Trinitarisches Denken benötigt trinitarisch geteiltes Leben*. In: M. Sellmann (Ed.), Gedanken Gänge. Klaus Hemmerles Theologie als Project beweglichen Denkens, Würzburg: Echter Verlag, 123-135.

Cohn, R. (1997). *Von der Psychoanalyse zur Themenzentrierten Interaktion,* Stuttgart.

Coleman, J. (1966). *Foundations for a Theory of Collective Decisions*. In: American Journal of Sociology, 615-627.

Compendium of the Social Doctrine of the Church, (2004), (accessed August 22, 2019) retrieved from: http://www.antoniano.org/carbajo/FST/Readings/Magisterium/EN_Compendium_CST.pdf

Coste, R. (1984). *Pas de pauvre chez toi. La pensée sociale de l'Église,* Paris: Nouvelle Cité.

Dahl, R.A. (1989). *Democracy and its Critics*, New Haven: Yale University.

Dahrendorf, R. (2006). *Homo Sociologicus. Ein Versuch zur Geschichte, Bedeutung und Kritik der Kategorie der sozialen Rolle*, Bd. 16, Wiesbaden.

Davies, G. (2002). *A history of money from ancient times to the present day,* 3rd ed., Cardiff: University of Wales Press.

Davis Zimmerman, Kari-Shane (2012). *Neither Social Revolution Nor Utopian Ideal: A Fresh Look at Luke's Community of Goods Practice for Christian Economic Reflection*. In: Acts 4:32-35. In: The Heythrop Journal 53, no. 5: 777–786. doi:10.1111/j.1468-2265.2010.00588.x.

De Beni, M. (Ed.) (2019). *Per una cultura dell'unità. I dieci primi anni dell'Istituto Universitario Sophia,* Quiedit Universitaria-Istituto Universitario Sophia, Verona – Incisa Valdarno.

Del Percio, E. (2020). *Chau, macho: del Estado patriarcal al Estado maternal,* retrieved from: https://www.perfil.com/noticias/elobservador/chau-macho-del-estado-patriarcal-al-estado-maternal.phtml?rd=1

Derrida, J., Dufourmantelle, A. & Bowlby, R. (2000). *Of hospitality. Cultural memory in the present,* Stanford University Press.

Donolo, C. (2012). *L'arte di governare.* Roma: Donzelli editore.

Duchrow, U. and Hinkelammert, F.J. (2002). *Leben ist mehr als Kapital. Alternativen zur globalen Diktatur des Eigentums.* Oberursel: Publik-Forum.

Dumouchel, P. (1999). *Die Ambivalenz der Knappheit.* In: Die Hölle der Dinge: René Girard und die Logik der Ökonomie, Edited by Erich Kitzmüller et al., 175–308. Beiträge zur Mimetischen Theorie 9. Wien: LIT.

European Commission, Going Climate-Neutral by 2050, (2019). *A Strategic Long-Term Vision for a Prosperous, Modern, Competitive and Climate-Neutral EU Economy*, retrieved from: https://op.europa.eu/en/publication-detail/-/publication/92f6d5bc-76bc-11e9-9f05-01aa75ed71a1

European Commission, (2017).*White Paper on the Future of Europe, Reflections and Scenarios for the EU27 by 2015,* retrieved from: https://ec.europa.eu/commission/sites/beta-political/files/witboek_over_de_toekomst_van_europa_nl.pdf

Evans, D. (1996) . *An Introductory Dictionary of Lacanian Psychoanalysis*, London: Copyrighted materials.

EZLN, (1994). *Fourth Declaration of the Lacandon Jungle*, Wikisource. (accessed August 26, 2019), retrieved from: https://en.wikisource.org/wiki/Fourth_Declaration_of_the_Lacandon_Jungle

Fauser, P. (1991). *Erfahrene Aufklärung. Zur Rationalität und Anthropologie der Schule als Institution*, Habilitationsschrift, Tübingen.

Fauser, P. (1996). *What is Practical Learning? Clarification of the term,* European Education, 28:4 6-24.

Fauser, P. (2003). *Lernen als innere Wirklichkeit*. In: Rentschler, I., Madelung, E. (Eds.), Bilder im Kopf. Beiträge zum imaginativen Lernen, Seelze, 242-286.

Ferstl, E. (1996). *Unter der Oberfläche*, Wien, Klosterneuburg. After: Broßmann, M., Mödinger, W. (2011). Praxisguide Wissensmanagement: Qualifizieren in Gegenwart und Zukunft. Planung, Umsetzung und Controlling in Unternehmen. Heidelberg e.a. 40.

Foster J.B. and McChesney, R. W. (2014). *Surveillance Capitalism: Monopoly-Finance Capital, the Military-Industrial Complex, and the Digital Age.* In: Monthly Review, July-August, retrieved from: https://monthlyreview.org/2014/07/01/surveillance-capitalism/

Foucault, M. (1972). *The Discourse on Language: Translation as appendix to the Archaeology of Knowledge*, New York, 215–37.

Fourastié, J. (1979). *Les trente glorieuses ou la revolution invisible de 1946 à 1975*, Paris: Fayard.

Freire, P. (2000). *Pedagogy of the Oppressed*, New York – London: Continuum, 87-89.

Frey C.B., Osborne, M. (2017). *The Future of Automatization: How susceptible are Jobs to Computerization,* Technological Forecasting and Social Change 114 254-280, retrieved from: https://www.oxfordmartin.ox.ac.uk/downloads/academic/The_Future_of_Employment.pdf

Fukuyama, F. (1992). *The End of History and the Last Man*, New York: Free Press.

Ricard-Nihoul, G. (2012). *Pour une Fédération européenne d'États-nations. La vision de Jacques Delors revisitée*, Bruxelles: Larcier.

Gafurof, B. and Tsimpoukidis, D. (1982). *Αλέξανδρος ο Μακεδών και η Ανατολή*, transl. by Γ. Στεργίου, εκδ. Παπαδήμας, Αθήνα.

Giordani, I. (1945). *Pionieri cristiani della democrazia*, Roma: SELI.

Girard, R… (1977). *Violence and the Sacred*. With the assistance of translated by Patrick Gregory, Baltimore MD: The Johns Hopkins University Press.

Girard, R. (2001). *I See Satan Fall Like Lightning*, Maryknoll NY: Orbis Books.

Gramsci, A. (1971). *Selections from the Prison Notebooks of Antonio Gramsci: Prison Notebooks, Notebook 3, §34.* In: Quintin Hoare and Geoffrey Nowell Smith (Eds and transl.), New York: International.

Gramsci, A. (1999). *Gefängnishefte,* Vol. 2, Hamburg.

Habermas, J. (1986). *The New Obscurity: The Crisis of the Welfare State and the Exhaustion of Utopian Energie*. In: Philosophy & Social Criticism, 11,2, 1–18, retrieved from https://doi.org/10.1177/019145378601100201

Habermas, J. (2005). *Justification and application. Remarks on discourse ethics*, Cambridge: Polity.

Habermas, J. (2014). *On the pragmatics of social interaction. Preliminary studies in the theory of communicative action*, Cambridge: Polity.

Habermas, J. (2015). *The theory of communicative action 1. Reason and the rationalization of society*, Cambridge: Polity.

Hahn, B., McFarland, J. et al. (Eds.). (2018). *Lesenotiz zu Hannah Arendt: The Modern Challenge to Tradition: Fragmente eines Buches*. Vol. 6, Göttingen, retrieved from: https://www.theorieblog.de/index.php/2018/12/lesenotiz-zu-hannah-arendts-the-modern-challenge-to-tradition

Hammond, M. (1948). *Ancient Imperialism: Contemporary Justifications*, Harvard Studies in Classical Philology, Vol. 58/59.

Hammond, N. (1991). *The Miracle that was Macedonia*, Singwick and Jackson great civilization series, London: St. Martin's Press.

Hammond, N. (1995). *Philip of Macedon,* Gerald Duckworth & Co. Ltd.

Hardin, G. (1968). *The Tragedy of the Commons*. In: Science 162, no. 3859: 1243–1248. doi:10.1126/science.162.3859.1243.

Haug W. F., Haug F. et al. (Eds) (1995). *Historisch Kritisches Wörterbuch des Marxismus*, vol. 2, Hamburg: Argument-Verlag.

Havel, V. (1992). *Meditations on Politics, Morality and Civilty in a Time of Transition,* London: Faber & Faber.

Heifetz, R. (2012). *Interview to* Απόστολος Μαγγηριάδης, *«P'ws* να γίνεις ηγέτης» (How to become a leader). In: BHMAgazino No. 662.

Helfrich, S. and Heinrich-Böll-Stiftung (Eds.) (2014). *Commons: Für eine neue Politik jenseits von Markt und Staat*. 2nd ed. Bielefeld: transcript.

Higgins, W. E. (1980). Aspects of Alexander's imperial administration: some modern methods and views reviewed, Athenaeum 58.

Hoeksma, J.A. (2018). *The Theory of democratic integration*, Oisterwijk: Wolf Legal Publishers.

Horrocks, G. (2001). *From Classical Greek to Koinē* (Από την Κλασική Ελληνική στην Κοινή, μτφ. I. Βλαχόπουλος, in A. Φ. Χριστίδης (Ed.) Ιστορία της Ελληνικής Γλώσσας. Από τις Αρχές έως την ῾Υστερη Αρχαιότητα, Κέντρο Ελληνικής Γλώσσας, Ινστιτούτο Νεοελληνικών Σπουδών (῾Ιδρυμα Μανώλη Τριανταφυλλίδη), Αθήνα.

Houtart, F. (2012). *From 'Common Goods' to the 'Common Good of Humanity'* In: A Post-Capitalist Paradigm. The Common Good of Humanity, ed. Birgit Daiber and Francois Houtart, Brüssel: Büro der Rosa-Luxemburg-Stiftung, 11–56.

Illich, I. (1975). *Tools for Conviviality*, Glasgow: William Collins Sons & Co.

ILO Monitor, (2020). *COVID-19 and the world of work,* 5th Ed., retrieved from: https://www.ilo.org/wcmsp5/groups/public/--dgreports/--dcomm/documents/briefingnote/wcms_749399.pdf

IPCC Intergovernmental Panel on Climate Change, (2018). *Global Warming of 1.5°C, Summary for Policy Makers*, retrieved from: https://www.ipcc.ch/sr15/

Kalmanovitz, S., López Rivera, E. (2003). *La Economía de Santafé de Bogotá En 1810*, DOI: https://doi.org/10.1017/S0212610912000031, Cambridge University Press: 2012.

Ketteler, W.E. (1873). *Die Katholiken im Deutschen Reiche*, Mainz: Verlag von Franz Kirchheim. Ed. by Mumbauer, J. (1924). *Wilhelm Emmanuel von Kettelers Schriften. Band II: Staatspolitische und Vaterländische Schriften.*

Kevenhörster, P. (2008). *Aggregation der Interessen.* In: Politikwissenschaft, Band 1: Entscheidungen und Strukturen der Politik. Wiesbaden, 265-316.

Khatab, S. (2009). *The Power of Sovereignty: the Political and Ideological Philosophy of Sayyid Qutb,* New York: Routledge.

Khatami M. (1999). *Religione, libertà e democrazia*,, Roma-Bari: Laterza.

Kitzmüller, E., Büchele, H., Dumouchel, P. and Dupuy J.P. (Eds.) (1999). *Die Hölle der Dinge: René Girard und die Logik der Ökonomie.* Beiträge zur Mimetischen Theorie 9. Wien: LIT.

Klein, D. (Ed.) (2003). *Leben statt gelebt zu werden. Selbstbestimmung und soziale Sicherheit,* Zukunftsbericht der Rosa-Luxemburg-Stiftung. Berlin: Dietz.

Klein, D. (Ed.) (2013). *Das Morgen tanzt im Heute. Transformation im Kapitalismus und über ihn hinaus*, Hamburg: VSA.

Klein, N. (2007). *The Shock Doctrine: The rise of disaster capitalism*, Metropolitan Books/Henry Holt and Company.

Klissenbauer, I., Gassner, F., Steinmair-Pösel, P. and Kirchschläger P. G. (Eds.) (2020). *Menschenrechte und Gerechtigkeit als bleibende Aufgabe. Beiträge aus Religion, Theologie, Ethik, Recht und Wirtschaft*, Vienna: Vienna University Press.

Koenen, L. (1982). *The Ptolemaic King a Religious Figure*, UC Press E-Books Collection, 1982-2004.

Kohlberg, L., Levine, C., Hewer, A. (1983). *Moral stages. A current formulation and a response to critics*, Basel, NY.

Kroll T. (2007). *Kommunistische Intellektuelle in Westeuropa Frankreich, Österreich Italien, und Großbritannien im Vergleich*, Cologne, Weimar, Vienna: Böhlau Verlag.

Kronreif, F. (2018). *Kenosis als Dienst an der Einheit*. In: Communio 47, 290-301.

Lacan, J. (1991). *The Seminar of Jacques Lacan*: Book II: The Ego in Freud's Theory and in the Technique of Psychoanalysis 1954–1955, NYC.

Langebucher, W.R. (Ed.) (2008). *Paul Felix Lazarsfeld: Leben und Werk*, Vienna: Wilhelm Braunmüller.

Lazarsfeld, P. F. (2008). *Zwei neue Welten, Eine Episode in der Geschichte der empirischen Sozialforschung: Erinnerungen.* In: Langebucher, W.R. (Ed.).

Leibniz, G. W. (1720). *Lehr-Sätze über die Monadologie, ingleichen von Gott und seiner Existentz, seinen Eigenschafften und von der Seele des Menschen etc. wie auch Dessen letzte Vertheidigung seines Systematis Harmoniae praestabilitae wider die Einwürffe des Herrn Bayle.* (trans. Heinrich Köhler) Jena, Frankfurt und Leipzig.

Lenin, V. I. (1905). *The Two Tactics of Social-Democracy in the Democratic Revolution.* In: Lenin's Collected Works, 1962, Volume 9, 15-140, Moscow: Progress Publishers.

Levinas, E. (2010). *Otherwise than Being or Beyond Essence.* Springer Netherlands.

Lind, G. (2016). How to Teach Morality: Promoting Deliberation and Discussion, Reducing Violence and Deceit, Berlin.

López Bórbon, L. (1987). *Un Nuevo Mapa Cultura: en Construir ciudadanía desde la cultura*, retrieved from: https://de.scribd.com/document/64475110/PDF-Construir-Ciudadania

Lubich, C. (2007). *Essential Writings. Spirituality, Dialogue, Culture*, London: New City.

Lubich, C. (2008). *No Thorn Without a Rose: 99 Sayings by Chiara Lubich*, London: New City.

Lubich, C.; Povilus, J. M.; Falmi, D. (2019). *Gesù in mezzo.* Roma: Città nuova editrice.

Luft, J., Ingham, H. (1955). *The Johari Window. A graphic model for interpersonal relations*, Western Training Laboratory in Group Development, University of California.

Luhmann, N. (1984). *Soziale Systeme. Grundriss einer allgemeinen Theorie*, Ffm.

Luhmann, N., Schorr, Karl.-Eberhard. (Eds.) (1986). *Zwischen Intransparenz und Verstehen. Fragen an die Pädagogik*, Ffm.

Luhmann, N. (2012a). *Macht im System*, Berlin.

Luhmann, N. (2012b). *Introduction to Systems Theory*, Cambridge.

Madörin M. (2010). *Care Economy – eine Herausforderung für die Wirtschaftswissenschaften.* In: Bauhardt, C. and Çağlar, G. (Eds). Gender and Economics: Feministische Kritik der politischen Ökonomie, Wiesbaden: Verlag für Sozialwissenschaften.

Maritain, J. (1943). *Christianisme et démocratie*, New York: Éditions de la Maison Française.

Marx, K. (1844-1932). *Economic and Philosophical Manuscripts,* Moscow: Progress Publisher.

Marx, K. (1953). *Die Frühschriften,* Unter Mitarbeit von Siegfried Landshut. Stuttgart: Alfred Kröner.

Marx K. (1975). *A Contribution to the Critique of Hegel's Philosophy of Law*, 'Introduction' Karl Marx and Frederick Engels, *Collected Works*, vol. 3, New York: International Publishers.

Marx, K. (1975). *Contribution to the Critique of Hegel's Philosophy of Law. Introduction (1844)*. In: MECW, Volume 3. London: Lawrence & Wishart, 175–187.

Marx, K. (1976). *Theses on Feuerbach (1845)*. In: MECW, Volume 5, London: Lawrence & Wishart, 3–6.

Marx, K. (1987a). *Outlines of the Critique of Political Economy* [*Grundrisse*, 1857-58], Karl Marx and Frederick Engels, *Collected Works*, vol. 29, New York: International.

Marx, K. (1987b). *Outlines of the Critique of Political Economy* (Rough Draft of 1857-58) [Second Instalment]. In: MECW, Volume *28*. London: Lawrence & Wishart, 5–417.

Marx, K. (1988). *General Rules of the International Working Men's Association*, Karl Marx and Frederick Engels, Collected Works, New York: International Publishers.

Marx, K. (1989a). *Theories of Surplus Value*, Karl Marx and Frederick Engels, Collected Works, vol. 32, New York: International.

Marx, K. (1989b). *Critique of the Gotha Programme*. In: MECW, Volume 24. London: Lawrence & Wishart, 75–99.

Marx, K. (1996). *Capital. Volume I*. In: MECW, Volume 35. London: Lawrence & Wishart.

Marx, K. (1998). *Capital. Volume III*. In: MECW, Volume 37. London: Lawrence & Wishart.

Marx, K. and Engels, F. (1959). *Briefe Januar 1856 – Dezember 1859*, Werke Bd 29 (MEW, Band 29).

Marx, K. and Engels, F. (1976) *Manifesto of the Communist Party (1848)*. In: MECW, Volume 6. London: Lawrence & Wishart, 477–519.

Marx, K. and Engels, F. (1976). *Collected Works*, vol. 5, New York: International Publishers

Marx, K. and Engels, F. (1977). *Collected Works*, vol. 3, New York: International Publishers, retrieved from: https://archive.org/details/economicphilosophicmanuscripts1844/page/n63/mode/2up>.

Masala, C. (2018). Weltunordnung: Die globalen Krisen und das Versagen des Westens, Munich: Beck.

Masters, T., Uelmen, A. (2011). *Focolare. Living a Spirituality of Unity in the United States*, Hyde Park: New City Press.

McCloskey, D.N. (2016). *Bourgeois Equality. How Ideas, not Capital or Institutions, Enriched the World*, Chicago and London: University of Chicago Press.

Merton, T. (1992). *Thomas Merton: Spiritual Master: The essential writings*, (Edited by Lawrence S. Cunningham), New York: Paulist Press.

Mogherini, F. (2016). *The new Global Strategy for the EU's Foreign and Security Policy: Shared Vision, Common Action: A Stronger Europe*, retrieved from: ht tps://europa.eu/globalstrategy/en/global-strategy-promote-citizens-interests.

Morgenthau, H. J. (1948). *Politics Among Nations: the Struggle for Power and Peace*, New York: Alfred Knopf.

Morelly, É.G. (1964). *Gesetzbuch der natürlichen Gesellschaft oder der wahre Geist ihrer Gesetze zu jeder Zeit übersehen oder verkannt*, Berlin: Akademie.

Morin, E. (2002). *Introducción a una política del hombre*, Barcelona: Editorial Gedisa.

Olmstead, T. (1948). *History of the Persian Empire,* University of Chicago [here utilized the translation in Greek by E. Πέππα, Ιστορία της Περσικής Αυτοκρατορίας, εκδ. Οδυσσέας, Αθήνα 2002].

Ostrom, E. (1990). *Governing the Commons. The Evolution of Institutions for Collective Action*, Cambridge/New York: Cambridge University Press.

Ostrom, E. (2005). *Understanding Institutional Diversity*, Princeton/Oxford: Princeton University Press.

Ostrom, E. (2009). *Beyond Markets and States: Polycentric Governance of Complex Economic Systems,* Prize Lecture. (Accessed August 22, 2019), retrieved from: https://www.nobelprize.org/uploads/2018/06/ostrom_lecture.pdf

Ostrom, E., Helfrich, S. (2011). *Was mehr wird, wenn wir teilen: Vom gesellschaftlichen Wert der Gemeingüter*, München: Oekom.

Pariser, E. (2011). *The Filter Bubble. What the Internet Is Hiding from You,* New York.

Parson, W. (1995). *Public policy: An introduction to the Theory and Practice of Policy Analysis*, Edward Elgar Publishing Limited.

Pepe, E. (2018). *Un'avventura nell'unità*, Roma: Città NuovaX.

Perani, C. (1980). *Libertação e espiritualidade*, Cadernos do CEAS, 66.

Pirozzi, N., Tortola, P.D. and Vai, L. (2017). *Differentiated Integration: A-way forward for Europe.* In: EU60, Re-founding Europe. The Responsibility to propose, Rome: Istituto Affari Internazionali.

Polanyi, K. (1934). *Fascism and Marxian Terminology*, vol. 3, no. 57, New Britain.

Polanyi, K. (1944a). *Chronik der großen Transformation*, loc.cit.

Polanyi, K. (1944b). *The Great Transformation: The Political and Economic Origins of Our Time*, Boston: Beacon, 2001.

Polanyi, K. (2018). *On Freedom* (transl. Eric Canepa). In: Brie, M. and Thomasberger, C. (Eds): Karl Polanyi's Vision of a Socialist Transformation, Montreal: Black Rose Books.

Papa Francesco, Scalfari, E. (2013). *Dialogo tra credenti e non credenti*, Torino: Einaudi – La Repubblica.

Pope Benedict XVI, (2009). Encyclical Letter *Caritas in veritate*, Vatican: Libreria Editrice Vaticana.

Pope Francis, (2013a). Apostolic Exhortation *Evangelii Gaudium.* Vatican: Libreria Editrice Vaticana.

Pope Francis, (2013b). Encyclical letter *Lumen fidei*, Vatican: Libreria Editrice Vaticana.

Pope Francis, (2014a). *Address to the Council of Europe*, (accessed August 22, 2019), retrieved from: http://m.vatican.va/content/francesco/en/speeches/2014/november/documents/papa-francesco_20141125_strasburgo-consiglio-europa.pdf

Pope Francis, (2014b). *Address to the European Parliament*, November 25th, http://w2.vatican.va/content/francesco/it/speeches/2014/november/documents/papa-francesco_20141125_strasburgo-parlamento-europeo.html

Pope Francis, (2015). Encyclical Letter *Laudato Si'* – on Care for Our Common Home. Vatican: Libreria Editrice Vaticana.

Pope Francis, (2016). *Message of His Holiness Pope Francis to the popular Movements*, http://w2.vatican.va/content/francesco/en/speeches/2016/november/documents/papa-francesco_20161105_movimenti-popolari.html

Pope Francis, (2017a). *Message of His Holiness Pope Francis for the Celebration of the Fiftieth World Day of Peace.*

Pope Francis, (2017b). Apostolic Constitution *Veritatis Gaudium,* Vatican: Libreria Editrice Vaticana.

Pope Francis, (2018). Apostolic Exhortation *Gaudete et Exsultate* – on the call to holiness in today's world, Vatican: Libreria Editrice Vaticana.

Pope John XXIII, (1961). Encyclical Letter *Mater et magistra*, Vatican: Libreria Editrice Vaticana.

Pope John XXIII, (1963). Encyclical Letter *Pacem in terris*, Vatican: Libreria Editrice Vaticana.

Pope John Paul II, (1987). Encyclical Letter *Sollicitudo rei socialis*, Vatican: Libreria Editrice Vaticana.

Pope John Paul II, (1991). Encyclical Letter *Centesimus annus*, Vatican: Libreria Editrice Vaticana.

Pope John Paul II, (1995). Encyclical Letter *Evangelium vitae*, Vatican: Libreria Editrice Vaticana.

Pope Leon XIII, (1891). Encyclical Letter *Rerum novarum*, http: //www.vatican.va/content/leo-xiii/en/encyclicals/documents/hf_l-xiii_enc_15051891_rerum-novarum.html

Pope Paul VI, (1964). Encyclical Letter *Ecclesiam Suam,* Vatican: Libreria Editrice Vaticana.

Pope Paul VI, (1965). Pastoral Constitution *Gaudium et spes*, Vatican: Libreria Editrice Vaticana.

Prats, J. (2004). *De la burocracia al Management y del management a la gobernanza*. In: Instituciones y desarrollo, núm 3.

Ramminger, M. und Segbers F. (2018). *Alle Verhältnisse umzuwerfen. … und die Mächtigen vom Thron zu stürzen,* Berlin: Rosa-Luxemburg-Stiftung und ITP Kompass

Ratzinger, J. – Benedikt XVI. (2011). Jesus von Nazareth. Zweiter Teil Vom Einzug in Jerusalem bis zur Auferstehung, Freiburg Basel Wien: Herder Verlag.

Rawls, J. (1993). *Political Liberalism*, New York: Columbia University Press.

Reich, W. (1946). *The Mass Psychology of Fascism (*transl. Theodore P. Wolfe), New York: Orgone Institute Press.

Robinson Jr., C. A. (1957). *The extraordinary ideas of Alexander the Great.* In: The American Historical Review, Vol. 62, No. 2.

Rohr, R. (2018). *Awakening to our True Self*, (accessed August 22, 2019) retrieved from: https://cac.org/awakening-to-our-true-self-2018-07-31/

Ropelato, D. (2006). *Notas sobre participación y fraternidad, en el Principio olvidado: la fraternidad*, Buenos Aires: Ciudad Nueva.

Ruppel, J., Stratmann, R. (2018). Schulz von Thun, F.: *Miteinander reden: Kommunikationspsychologie für Führungskräfte,* Hamburg.

Russell, J. (2003). *The Tai Chi Two-person Dance: Tai Chi with a Partner*, Berkeley.

Russell B. et al. (1955). *The Russell-Einstein Manifesto*, signed by Max Born, Percy W. Bridgman, Albert Einstein, Leopold Infeld, Frédéric Joliot-Curie, Herman J. Muller, Linus Pauling, Cecil F. Powell, Joseph Rotblat, Bertrand Russell, and Hideki Yukawa, retrieved from: https://pugwash.org/1955/07/09/statement-manifesto/

Schattschneider, EE. (1960). *The semisovereign people, Holt.* New York: Rinehart y Winston.

Schein, E.H. (2013). *The process of dialogue: creating effective communication,* retrieved from: https://thesystemsthinker.com/the-process-of-dialogue-creating-effective-communication/

Schulz von Thun, F. (1998). *Miteinander reden*, Band 3: Das Innere Team und situationsgerechte Kommunikation, Hamburg.

Schulz von Thun, F. (2002). *Ways Towards Mutual Understanding. A Conversation.* In: The End of Tolerance?, London.

Schulz von Thun, F. (2004). *Seven Tools for Clear Communication*, The Hamburg Approach in English Language, Hamburg.

Searle, J. R. (1969). *Speech Acts. An Essay in the Philosophy of Language*, Cambridge.

Searle, J. R. (1979). *Expression and Meaning. Studies in the Theory of Speech Acts*, Cambridge.

Selchow, S. (2014). *Die Apokalypse duldet keinen Sachzwang: Ein Gespräch mit Ulrich Beck und Bruno Latour*. In: faz, May 15, 2014. (accessed August 22, 2019), retrieved from: http://www.faz.net/-gsf-7pc6j

Sen, A. (2004). *La democrazia degli altri. Perché la libertà non è un'invenzione dell'Occidente*, Milano: Mondadori.

Senge, P. M. (1990). *The Fifth Discipline: The Art and Practice of the Learning Organization*, New York.

Senge, P., Cambron-McCabe, N., Lucas, T., Smith, B., Dutton, J., Kleiner, A. (2000). *Schools that learn. A Fifth Discipline Fieldbook for Educators, Parents, and Everyone Who Cares About Education*, London.

Shaffer, D.R. (2008). *Social and personality development,* CA: Belmont.

Sloterdijk, P. (1998). *Sphären I – Blasen*. Ffm.

Sloterdijk, P. (2002). *Erwachen im Reich der Eifersucht. Notiz zu René Girards anthropologischer Sendung*. In: Girard, R., Ich sah den Satan vom Himmel fallen wie einen Blitz. Eine kritische Apologie des Christentums. München: Carl Hanser.

Sperber, M. (1988). *Like a Tear in the Ocean: A Trilogy*, New York: Holmes & Meier.

Spivak, G.C. (1990). *The Postcolonial Critic. Interviews, Strategies, Dialogues*, New York: Harasym.

Staab, P. (2019). *Digitaler Kapitalismus. Markt und Herrschaft in der Ökonomie der Unknappheit*, Berlin: Suhrkamp.

Steinmair-Pösel, P. (2019). *Im Gravitationsfeld von Mystik und Politik. Christliche Sozialethik im Gespräch mit Maria Skobtsova, Dorothee Sölle und Chiara Lubich*, Paderborn.

Stieglitz, J.E. (2019). *Sechs, setzen ipg-journal,* Friedrich-Ebert-Stiftung, retrieved from: https://www.ipg-journal.de/regionen/global/artikel/detail/sechs-setzen-3867/?utm_campaign=_40_20191115&utm_medium=email&utm_source=newsletter>, 13

Stuke, T. (2015). *Mit Werten führen? Weiterbildungsmanagement zwischen externen Ansprüchen und individuellen Vorstellungen*, Bad Heilbrunn.

Συρόπουλος, Σ. Δ. (2004). Δαρείος ο Α' ο Μέγας. Ο εμπνευσμένος διαμορφωτής της Περσικής αυτοκρατορίας, Ιστορικά Θέματα 27.

Tillich, P. (1964). *Das Christentum und die Begegnung der Weltreligionen, Schriften zur Religionsphilosophie, Gesammelte Werke*, vol. 5, Stuttgart: Evangelisches Verlagswerk.

Torno, A. (2012). *Chiara Lubich. A Biography*, New York.

Toro, J. (2014). *El Ethos Que cuida,* retreived from: http://hdl.handle.net/11520/23420

Traynor, I. (2012). *Eurozone crisis: United States of Europe may be the only way to save euro*, In: The Guardian, Monday 4 June 2012 http://www.guardian.co.uk/business/2012/jun/04/eurozone-crisis-united-states-europe

Tuckman, B. (2001). *Developmental Sequence in Small Groups.* In: Group Facilitation: A Research and Applications Journal, Number 3, 66–81 (Reprinted from Psychological Bulletin, Volume 63, Number 6 (1965), 384-399.

Tuckman, B., et al. (1977). *Stages of small-group development revisited*. In: Group and Organization Studies, 2, 4, 419–426.

Van den Brande, L. (2017). *Reaching Out to EU citizens: A New opportunity 'About Us, with Us, for Us'*, Brussels: Publications Office of the EU: Luxembourg

Vogt, M. (2015). *Auf einen anderen Lebensstil setzen! Was will die Umweltenzyklika von Papst Franziskus erreichen,* (accessed August 22, 2019), retreived from: https://www.paulusakademie.ch/wp-content/uploads/2015/09/Referat-Dr.-Markus-Vogt-Universita%CC%88t-Mu%CC%88nchen.pdf

Wandinger, N. (2003). *Die Sündenlehre als Schlüssel zum Menschen: Impulse K. Rahners und R. Schwagers zu einer Heuristik theologischer Anthropologie,* Beiträge zur Mimetischen Theorie 16. Münster: LIT.

Watson, A. (2006). *The Evolution of International Society. A comparative historical analysis*, Taylor and Francis Book Ltd., [Here utilized the translation in Greek: Η εξέλιξη της διεθνούς κοινωνίας. Μια συγκριτική ιστορική ανάλυση, μτφ. Λ. Στροίκου, επιμ. Χ. Παπασωτηρίου – Π. 'Ηφαιστος, εκδ. Ποιότητα, Αθήνα 2006].

Watzlawick, P. (1993). *The language of change. Elements of therapeutic communication*, New York, London.

Watzlawick, P. (2014). *Pragmatics of human communication: A study of interactional patterns, pathologies and paradoxes*, New York, London.

Weber, M. (1906), *Zur Lage der bürgerlichen Demokratie in Russland*, Archiv für Sozialwissenschaft und Sozialpolitik, Band 22, Beiheft, 353

Welles, C. B. (1962). *The Discovery of Sarapis and the Foundation of Alexandria*. In: Historia 11.

Wight, M. (1977). *Systems of States* for essays on the Graec-Persian and the European system of administration, Leicester: Leicester University Press.

Wilde, M. J. (2007). *Vatican II. A Sociological Analysis of Religious Change,* Princeton University Press, Princeton and Oxford.

Wilkinson, R. H. (2003). *Complete Gods and Goddesses of Ancient Egypt*, Thames & Hudson LTD.

Wolter, M.I. et al. (2016). *Industrie 4.0 und die Folgen für Arbeitsmarkt und Wirtschaft*, IAB Forschungsbericht 8/2015, retrieved from: hdoku.iab.de/forschungsbericht/2015/fb0815.pdf

Wright, E.O. (2010). *Envisioning Real Utopias*. London; New York: Verso, 2010.

Ziegler, J. (2009). *Ein Kind, das jetzt aus Hunger stirbt, wird ermordet,* https://www.deutschlandfunkkultur.de/ein-kind-das-jetzt-am-hunger-stirbt-wird-ermordet.1008.de.html?dram:article_id=162385

Zimmerman, K. D. (2012). *Neither Social Revolution Nor Utopian Ideal: A Fresh Look at Luke's Community of Goods Practice for Christian Economic Reflection*. In: Acts 4:32–35. _Heythrop Journal_ 53 (5):777-786.

Zuboff, S. (2016). *The Secrets of Surveillance Capitalism.* In: Frankfurter Allgemeine Zeitung, updated 5 March 2016, retreived from: https://www.faz.net/aktuell/feuilleton/debatten/the-digital-debate/shoshana-zuboff-secrets-of-surveillance-capitalism-14103616.html

Zeitdiagnosen

Claudio Giulio Anta
Albert Einstein – Wege zum Pazifismus
Albert Einstein ist als Vater der Relativitätstheorie bekannt, er war jedoch auch einer der bedeutendsten Pazifisten der ersten Hälfte des zwanzigsten Jahrhunderts. Mithilfe seines pragmatischen Pazifismus versuchte er, den Dilemmata und Problemen die Stirn zu bieten, die aus den politischen Verhältnissen seiner Zeit herrührten: der Beginn des Großen Kriegs, die Schaffung und das Versagen des Völkerbunds, das Aufkommen totalitärer Regimes, der Ausbruch des Zweiten Weltkriegs, die Eskalation des Kalten Kriegs, die Einrichtung der Vereinten Nationen mit ihren institutionellen Schwächen.
Bd. 45, 2020, 270 S., 34,90 €, br., ISBN 978-3-643-91253-4

Hayrettin Ökçesiz
Das Wesen des Rechts ist das Widerstandsrecht
Essays und Vorträge. Aus dem Türkischen von Johannes Neuner
Nach den „Denkträumen" ist dies das zweite Buch des Autors in deutscher Sprache. Die hier abgedruckten Texte erschienen ursprünglich, über einen längeren Zeitraum hinweg, in verschiedenen türkischen Zeitungen und Zeitschriften wie auch Festschriften. Diese Essays und Vorträge sind direkt oder indirekt ein Plädoyer für den Mut auf eine bessere Welt und auch Wegweisungen zu ihr. Widerstand ist hier als Grundrecht des Menschen das Hauptinstrument dieser Urhoffnung. Denn nur durch das Anerkennen dieses Rechts auf Widerstand können die Würde und die Freiheit des Individuums Wirklichkeit und Wahrheit werden.
Bd. 44, 2020, 188 S., 44,90 €, br., ISBN 978-3-643-14551-2

Michael Wolf
Tempo
Die Dynamik von Moderne, Zivilisation und Kapital
Die Krise der modernen Welt ist nichts Neues. Sie begleitet sie von Anbeginn der Moderne und ist überall dort der Fall, wo Modernisierung stattfindet. Die Veränderungen und Umwälzungen, die damit einhergehen, sind stets ambivalent. Sie zerstören Altes, um Raum für Neues zu schaffen. Aber die Veränderungen lassen sich schlecht vorhersehen oder gar planen. Die Märkte sagen eher die Wahrheit als die Planer oder die Propheten. Das muss man aber ertragen können oder, besser noch, man muss mitmachen und sich der Evaluation der Märkte aussetzen. Wer dies nicht mag oder nicht wagt, beschwört gerne überholte Utopien wie Sozialismus oder Kommunismus, die längst gescheitert sind und dabei ihre brutale Inhumanität unter Beweis gestellt haben. Die Leistungen der Zivilisation, der Moderne und des Kapitalismus sind nicht hintergehbar. Wirkliche Verbesserungen kann es nur von dem erreichten Stand der Zivilisierung, der Modernisierung und der Kapitalisierung aus geben.
Bd. 43, 2020, 134 S., 19,90 €, br., ISBN 978-3-643-14587-1

Gunnar Skirbekk
Epistemic Challenges in a Modern World
From "fake news" and "post truth" to underlying epistemic challenges in science-based risk-societies
Bd. 42, 2019, 88 S., 24,90 €, br., ISBN 978-3-643-91171-1

Francesca Ferré
Discours à la Nation catalane
Bd. 41, 2019, 174 S., 19,90 €, br., ISBN 978-3-643-91167-4

Andreas Heuer
Carl Schmitt und die Krise des gegenwärtigen Liberalismus
Bd. 40, 2019, 128 S., 24,90 €, br., ISBN 978-3-643-14469-0

Nicole Grochowina; Herbert Lauenroth; Lothar Penners (Hg.)
Prophetie im Prekären
Reflexionen zum „Miteinander in Europa"
Bd. 39, 2019, 116 S., 24,90 €, br., ISBN 978-3-643-14467-6

Friedensgutachten

der Hessischen Stiftung Friedens- und Konfliktforschung (HSFK), des Bonn International Center for Conversion (BICC) und des Instituts für Friedensforschung und Sicherheitspolitik an der Universität Hamburg (IFSH)

Bonn International Center for Conversion BICC, Leibniz-Institut Hessische Stiftung Friedens- und Konfliktforschung HSFK, Institut für Friedensforschung und Sicherheitspolitik an der Uni Hamburg IFSH, Institut für Entwicklung und Frieden INEF
Friedensgutachten 2019
Das Friedensgutachten 2019 analysiert aktuelle Gewaltkonflikte. Mit friedenswissenschaftlichem Zugang zeigt es Trends der internationalen Außen-, Sicherheits- und Entwicklungspolitik auf und gibt Empfehlungen für Bundesregierung und Bundestag. Die deutschen Friedensforschungsinstitute (BICC / HSFK / IFSH / INEF) geben das Gutachten seit 1987 jährlich heraus, seit 2018 in neuem Format.
Bd. 27, 2019, 146 S., 12,90 €, br., ISBN 978-3-643-14351-8

Bonn International Center for Conversion BICC; Leibniz-Institut Hessische Stiftung Friedens- und Konfliktforschung HSFK, Institut für Friedensforschung und Sicherheitspolitik an der Uni Hamburg IFSH, Institut für Entwicklung und Frieden INEF
Friedensgutachten 2018
Bd. 26, 2018, 112 S., 12,90 €, br., ISBN 978-3-643-14023-4

Friedensgutachten 2017
herausgegeben von Bruno Schoch, Andreas Heinemann-Grüder, Corinna Hauswedell, Jochen Hippler, Margret Johannsen
Bd. , 2017, 310 S., 12,90 €, br., ISBN 978-3-643-13758-6

Friedensgutachten 2016
herausgegeben von Margret Johannsen, Bruno Schoch, Max M. Mutschler, Corinna Hauswedell, Jochen Hippler
290 S., 12,90 EUR, br., ISBN 978-3-643-13370-0

Friedensgutachten 2015
herausgegeben von Janet Kursawe, Margret Johannsen, Claudia Baumgart-Ochse, Marc von Boemcken, Ines-Jacqueline Werkner
258 S., 12,90 EUR, br., ISBN 978-3-643-13038-9

Friedensgutachten 2014
herausgegeben von Ines-Jacqueline Werkner, Janet Kursawe, Margret Johannsen, Bruno Schoch, Marc von Boemcken
368 S., 12,90 EUR, br., ISBN 978-3-643-12556-9

Friedensgutachten 2013
herausgegeben von Marc von Boemcken, Ines-Jacqueline Werkner, Margret Johannsen, Bruno Schoch
336 S., 12,90 EUR, br., ISBN 978-3-643-12151-6

Friedensgutachten 2012
herausgegeben von Bruno Schoch, Corinna Hauswedell, Janet Kursawe, Margret Johannsen
352 S., 12,90 EUR, br., ISBN 978-3-643-11598-0

Friedensgutachten 2011
herausgegeben von Margret Johannsen, Bruno Schoch, Corinna Hauswedell, Tobias Debiel, Christiane Fröhlich
404 S., 12,90 EUR, br., ISBN 978-3-643-11136-4

LIT Verlag Berlin – Münster – Wien – Zürich – London
Auslieferung Deutschland / Österreich / Schweiz: siehe Impressumsseite

Studies on South East Europe

edited by Univ.-Prof. Dr. Karl Kaser (Graz)

Nikol Dziub; Greta Komur-Thilloy (Éd.)

Penser le multiculturalisme dans les marges de l'Europe

Ce sont les fragments à la fois d'une histoire des pratiques du multiculturalisme et d'une généalogie de la notion de multiculturalisme que se propose de réunir ce volume lui-même multiculturel et interdisciplinaire (littérature, ethnologie, sociologie, histoire, sciences politiques, sciences du langage, sciences de l'éducation), et ce à partir de l'étude de quelques productions politico-culturelles propres à un territoire complexe où la « rencontre multiculturelle » a pris alternativement la forme de l'affrontement et celle de la communion : le Caucase.

Andra-Octavia Cioltan-Drăghiciu

„Gut gekämmt ist halb gestutzt"

Jugendliche im sozialistischen Rumänien

Rumänien ist ein Land, das nach 30 Jahren Demokratie immer noch durch Nepotismus und Korruption auffällt. Warum der Weg zu einem modernen Staat mühsam verläuft, ist eine zentrale Frage in der rumänischen Öffentlichkeit. Dieses Buch verfolgt die Ursachen des schwierigen Transformationsprozesses zurück in die 70er und 80er Jahre, indem es erklärt, unter welchen Bedingungen die TrägerInnen der postsozialistischen rumänischen Gesellschaft sozialisiert und welchen Diskursen sie ausgesetzt wurden. Es handelt sich dabei um eine Analyse, die zur Vergangenheitsbewältigung in der rumänischen Gesellschaft beitragen soll, denn nur wer seine Vergangenheit versteht und annimmt, kann die Gegenwart neugestalten.

Bd. 24, 2019, 228 S., 34,90 €, br., ISBN 978-3-643-50907-9

Nikol Dziub

« Son arme était la harpe »

Pouvoirs de la femme et du barde chez Nizami et dans *Le Livre de Dede Korkut*

Bd. 23, 2018, 264 S., 39,90 €, br., ISBN 978-3-643-91053-0

Dominik Gutmeyr; Karl Kaser (eds.)

Europe and the Black Sea Region

A History of Early Knowledge Exchange (1750 – 1850)

Bd. 22, 2018, 416 S., 34,90 €, br., ISBN 978-3-643-80286-6

Lena Mirošević; Gregory Zaro; Mario Katić; Danijela Birt (eds.)

Landscape in Southeastern Europe

Bd. 21, 2018, 176 S., 29,90 €, br., ISBN 3-643-80283-5

Enriketa Pandelejmoni

Shkodra

Family and Urban Life (1918 – 1939)

Bd. 20, 2019, 298 S., 34,90 €, br., ISBN 978-3-643-91017-2

Dominik Gutmeyr

Borderlands Orientalism or How the Savage Lost his Nobility

The Russian Perception of the Caucasus between 1817 and 1878

Bd. 19, 2017, 316 S., 34,90 €, br., ISBN 3-643-50788-4

Basilius J. Groen

Aufstieg, Kampf und Freiheit

Nikos Kazantzakis, seine *Asketik: Die Retter Gottes* und die griechisch-orthodoxe spirituelle und liturgische Tradition

Bd. 18, 2015, 162 S., 29,90 €, br., ISBN 978-3-643-50697-9

LIT Verlag Berlin – Münster – Wien – Zürich – London

Auslieferung Deutschland / Österreich / Schweiz: siehe Impressumsseite

Theologie Ost – West

Europäische Perspektiven

hrsg. von Prof. Dr. Janez Juhant (Universität Ljubljana) und Prof. Dr. Albert Franz (Universität Dresden)

Milos Lichner (Ed.)
Hope
Where does our Hope lie? International Congress of the European Society for Catholic Theology (August 2019 – Bratislava, Slovakia)
vol. 28, 2020, ca. 600 pp., ca. 49,90 €, br., ISBN-CH 978-3-643-91330-2

Robert Petkovšek; Bojan Žalecc (Eds.)
Transhumanism as a Challenge for Ethics and Religion
vol. 27, 2020, ca. 232 pp., ca. 34,90 €, br., ISBN-CH 978-3-643-91297-8

Robert Petkovšek; Bojan Žalecc (Eds.)
Ethical Implications of One God
The Significance of Monotheism
The issue of the ethical implications of monotheism is a very relevant topic from the point of view of contemporary humanities and social science, and from the perspective of the cultural and political condition in Europe and at the global scale. Therefore a scientific book devoted to this subject makes a lot of sense. Throughout the history and in present times, monotheism has been subjected to several sharp criticisms. On the other hand, we find also very different evaluations of it. They stress its positive and even crucial contribution to peace, forming of rational, non-violent, tolerant culture and society, to the scientific, political and cultural development, to democracy etc. The book offers fresh interdisciplinary perspectives - mainly from the point of view of humanities - on the ethical aspects of monotheism, broadens the scientific understanding of it, and establishes a basis for resolving conflicts to which the understanding of monotheism is relevant or even decisive.
Bd. 26, 2020, 208 S., 29,90 €, br., ISBN 978-3-643-91126-1

Tonči Matulić
Metamorphoses of Culture
A Theological Discernment of the Signs of the Times against the Backdrop of Scientific-Technical Civilisation
The book *Metamorphoses of Culture* was originally published in Croatian language in 2008. It is worth noting that this book was awarded the *Grand Prix – Croatian Book of the Year 2008* in April 2009. The author in the book seriously takes the stimulus of the Second Vatican Council that says: "With the help of the Holy Spirit, it is the task of the entire People of God, especially pastors and theologians, to hear, distinguish and interpret the many voices of our age, and to judge them in the light of the divine word, so that revealed truth can always be more deeply penetrated, better understood and set forth to greater advantage" (*Gaudium et spes*, no. 44). This book brings author's hearing, distinguishing and interpreting some of today's burning signs of the times in the light of the Gospel against the backdrop of scientific-technical civilisation.
Bd. 25, 2018, 684 S., 69,90 €, br., ISBN 978-3-643-91049-3

Stanko Gerjolj
Dramatik der biblischen Familienbeziehungen
Eine Herausforderung für die Erziehung heute
vol. 24, 2020, ca. 240 pp., ca. 34,90 €, br., ISBN-CH 978-3-643-91038-2

Marie-Jo Thiel; Marc Feix (éds.)
Le défi de la fraternité
The Challenge of fraternity. Die Herausforderung der Geschwisterlichkeit
Bd. 23, 2018, 640 S., 39,90 €, br., ISBN 978-3-643-91018-9

LIT Verlag Berlin – Münster – Wien – Zürich – London

Auslieferung Deutschland / Österreich / Schweiz: siehe Impressumsseite